The Home We Build Together

The Home We Build Together

Recreating Society

JONATHAN SACKS

continuum

Continuum UK
The Tower Building
11 York Road
London SE1 7NX

Continuum US
80 Maiden Lane
Suite 704
New York, NY 10038

www.continuumbooks.com

First published 2007

British Library Cataloguing-in-Publication Data
A catalogue record for this book is available from the British Library.

ISBN 9780826480705

Typeset by YHT Ltd, London
Printed and bound by
Cromwell Press Ltd, Trowbridge, Wiltshire

Contents

For Syma and Henry Weinberg
In thanks for all you have given our community

Acknowledgements

My thanks to Professor Leslie Wagner, David Frei and the dayanim of the London Beth Din, and to Justin McLaren for reading the manuscript and making many helpful suggestions. As always I am indebted to my office staff for their wonderful support. No one could have asked for a finer agent than Louise Greenberg or publisher than Robin Baird-Smith: it is an honour and pleasure to work with them. My thanks go to the whole team at Continuum. Yet again my deepest debt of gratitude is to Elaine for sustaining me throughout.

Part 1

How Did We Get Here?

Chapter 1

Introduction

For there is no longer a general understanding among civilized men: they cannot fall upon a common allegiance to assuage their partisanship; they have no consensus of accepted ideas. Yet these things they must have if they are to restore the civilized order. There are no end of fashionable opinions. But as against the convictions of those who are ready to kill or be killed to achieve their ends, the civilized arguments are subtle, complicated and effete. In the epochal crisis of our time the cause of civilization is being defended by men who possess a great tradition that has become softened by easy living, by men who have forgotten the necessities in which their principles were wrought.[1]

Walter Lippman

Multiculturalism has run its course, and it is time to move on. It was a fine, even noble idea in its time. It was designed to make ethnic and religious minorities feel more at home in society, more appreciated and respected, better equipped with self-esteem and therefore better able to mesh with the larger society as a whole. It affirmed their culture. It gave dignity to difference. And in many ways it achieved its aims. Britain, for example, is a more open, diverse, multicoloured, energizing, cosmopolitan environment than it was when I was growing up. It is less insular, homogeneous, grey – more a microcosm of our global, interconnected world.

But there has been a price to pay, and it grows year by year. Multiculturalism has led not to integration but to segregation. It has allowed groups to live separately, with no incentive to integrate and every incentive not to. It was intended to promote tolerance. Instead the result has been, in countries where it has been tried, societies more abrasive, fractured and intolerant than they once were. Britain, Spain, Denmark, France and the United States have all suffered tensions that have led thoughtful politicians to ask whether a new approach might be necessary. The most chilling example has been Holland. There, sociology professor and politician Pym Fortuyn said, shortly before he was killed (by an animal rights activist), 'If you try to discuss multi-culturalism in the UK, you're labelled a racist. But here we're still free to talk, and I say multicultural society doesn't work. We're not living closer, we're living apart.'[2]

Dutch multiculturalism has exacerbated the very problem it was intended to solve: so Paul Sniderman and Louk Hagendoorn, authors of a recent book on the subject, conclude.[3] The outcome has been 'to encourage exclusion rather than inclusion. The policy put in place to achieve conciliation has created division'. The fact that this happened in Holland sent a shiver down my spine. The Netherlands were the birthplace of liberty in the modern world, at least in northern Europe. It was from there that, in 1655, Rabbi Manasseh ben Israel came to London to argue for the readmission of Jews to England. It was there that Spinoza, a thinker who challenged the views of Jews and Christians alike, constructed the most powerful of all early arguments for a free society. If Holland is riven by internal tensions, then the situation is serious.

It is striking that the argument against multiculturalism in Britain has been led, not exclusively but noticeably, by people who would naturally be thought of as its beneficiaries. One has been the African Archbishop of York, John Sentamu. Another is the former chairman of the Commission for Racial Equality, Trevor Philips, educated in Guyana. A third has been myself, a Jew. Each of us in our different ways has strong reason to seek a society that values difference. Perhaps it is easier for those not quite at the heart of society to see the wider ripples pebbles make. Perhaps we have reason to sense more rapidly when things are going wrong. But they are going wrong.

Losing Society

Multiculturalism is only one aspect of the wider problem to which this book is addressed: social breakdown in liberal democracies. Is there such a thing as society any more? Should there be? And if there should, how can we rebuild the structures of our life together in pursuit of the common good?

The argument I will be making is emphatically not for a return to the way things were in the 1950s. It is the opposite. Western liberal democratic societies *are* diverse: that is a fact and also a value. This was, after all, Aristotle's argument against Plato who conceived of the Republic as a tightly-bonded unit guarded against change.[4] Diversity is essential to political life, argued Aristotle. It is also, today, inevitable. The desire to go back to the past – reactionary politics – is always misconceived and often deeply dangerous.

The case outlined in these pages is resolutely future-oriented. We are a diverse society. But we are also a fragmenting one. We are no longer sure what British or Dutch identity is. Politicians, commentators and moralists urge minorities to integrate. But into what? To integrate, there must be something to integrate into. To become socialized, there must be such a thing as society, a proposition some politicians have famously denied. Nations are constituted by, among other things, a shared moral code. But liberalism in its modern guises, and still more in its postmodern ones, denies that there is such a thing as a shared moral code. It argues, instead, that we should be maximally free to do our own thing, live our own lifestyle, refuse to conform. What then becomes of the idea of *belonging*?

We tend to think that the problems of multiculturalism have to do with minorities. In fact they have to do with everyone. Sir Keith Ajegbo, in his 2007 report on the teaching of citizenship in British schools, discovered that white pupils in areas of high ethnic mix 'can feel beleaguered and marginalised, finding their own identities under threat as much as minority ethnic children might not have theirs recognised'.[5] One white pupil in her teens, after hearing in a lesson that other members of her class came from the Congo, Portugal, Trinidad and Poland, said that she 'came from nowhere'. When the concept of national identity dissolves, we can all feel unhoused, deracinated, strangers in a strange land.

My argument will be that we need to engage in something rarely consciously undertaken in Britain before because it was taken for granted, namely *society-building*. We need to reinvigorate the concept of the common good. Society is where we come together to achieve collectively what none of us can do alone. It is our common property. We inhabit it, make it, breathe it. It is the realm in which *all* of us is more important than *any* of us. It is our shared project, and it exists to the extent that we work for it and contribute to it.

At times of no change, or slow change, society-building happens subliminally. We become, in a significant word, 'socialized'. We learn the unspoken rules. When I first went to university I discovered that you must never look as if you studied. 'I didn't do any work', people would say coming back from a vacation. 'Did you?' The correct answer, I discovered, was 'No'. Clearly all the students worked hard. There was intense competition for a place, all the more so for a high grade in the final exams. The convention was, though, that you had to act as if the acquisition of knowledge happened mysteriously without any conscious effort on your part. If you worked, you were 'grey'. This was a carry-over from the age of amateurism, the curious British class-code that held that work was something other people did for you. Already by the late 1960s it was a complete anachronism, but it survived. There was a British way of doing things, and you – or as they said in those days, 'one' – conformed. Belonging meant internalizing the rules. When there are no rules any more, when traditions die and codes of conduct disappear, when respect for institutions is minimal and national pride has become national self-laceration, then we deceive ourselves if we think we have the prerequisites for social cohesion. It is not that this minority or that does not play by the rules. It is that there are no rules to play by any more. Such a situation is unsustainable.

One of the most remarkable people I ever met, the late Lena Rustin, was a speech therapist specializing in stammering children. Many therapists who deal with this problem teach children 'techniques'. Lena believed that techniques alone were not enough. The child's stammer is not just a speech dysfunction: it is part of the dynamic of the family as a whole. If the child was to change, then every relationship in the family had to be renegotiated.

So it is with social cohesion. Often the blame is laid at the door of ethnic or religious minorities as if it were their fault alone. If they would only learn 'techniques' – the British way of doing things – the problem would disappear. That, I believe, is not so. The problem is not of this minority or that, but of the entire network of relationships that together constitute a culture. To cure it, we will all have to change. And we will only change if we understand how the pieces of the problem fit together.

For several decades we have adopted a set of cultural habits predicated on the idea that the individual is all that matters. By this I do not mean that ours is a selfish society. Far from it. The collective grief we felt for the victims of the tsunami, the vast numbers who enlisted to Make Poverty History, the widespread concern about global warming, the high proportion of people who volunteer for some form of service to others – all these tell us that Britain is still a place of high altruism. But we also need to turn that altruism inward, to our own society. Problems look easier from a distance. Close to, they reveal themselves in all their complexity. And our problems are complex.

Technologies of Culture

Social integration has been on the agenda at least since the 1960s, when the spectre of racism in its post-war forms first became acute. What no one could foresee then was the revolution about to take place in communications technology. I recall reading in 1990 a book called

Megatrends 2000.[6] One word was conspicuous by its absence: internet. It did not yet exist. As Bill Clinton noted, when he took up office as President of the United States in 1993, there were only 50 sites on the World Wide Web. By the time he left office eight years later there were 350 million.[7] Equally, many of us were unaware of the potential impact of satellite television. That did not enter public consciousness until the first Gulf War in January 1991, when many rushed to have it installed so that they could watch the progress of the war on CNN. Even the word 'globalization' had not yet fully entered public consciousness. It is, however, precisely these things that have given dramatic impetus to much that has happened in recent years.

The revolution in information technology and instantaneous global communication has had two major effects: one well known, the other less so. The first has been its impact on the global economy. This has not only involved the transfer of manufacturing industry from the West to the East. It has also, unpredictably, seen the outsourcing of service industries – accounting, secretarial work, even the booking of hotel places by phone – to countries like India. What this will mean for the economies of the West a half-century from now is hard to predict, harder still to internalize.

The second, though, is still not fully appreciated, namely its destructive impact on everything once known as a national culture. The birth of the nation state in the late eighteenth and early nineteenth centuries was a political event. But it was also, and no less significantly, a cultural event. The Industrial Revolution needed, and made possible, a standardization of national cultures: their language, and above all their education. Partly this was achieved through an earlier communications revolution, printing and the spread of books and newspapers, and partly through schools. It was, we recall, only in 1870 that universal compulsory education made its appearance, even in Britain, the world's leader in industry.

The nation state grew out of the need to have an urban workforce capable of operating standard procedures. It meant the end of the corporate state, and of an educational system in which schools were largely built by religious bodies. It was important that everyone could read and write, speak a standard English and share a set of habits and values. Culture in the broadest sense was conveyed not only by schools and newspapers but also by neighbourhoods and associations: churches, friendly societies, community groups, the entire range of trust-creating bodies that promoted what Alexis de Tocqueville called 'the art of association'.[8] If you were an immigrant, as my late father and both sets of grandparents were, you adapted fast. Otherwise you could not survive.

Today with the click of a mouse you can read newspapers, listen to radio or watch television in real time anywhere in the world. My satellite television offers over 900 channels. I can watch the news (usually bad) in Albania and Azerbaijan, Latvia and Lebanon, Sweden and Slovakia. Through the internet I can listen to not only national but also local radio anywhere. I can read the *Washington Post*, the *Pakistan Times*, *Le Monde*, *La Stampa* and *The Australian*. In the eleventh century, speaking about the Jewish love for Jerusalem, the Spanish-Jewish poet Judah Halevi wrote, 'I am in the West but my heart is in the East.' Today that is no longer a literary conceit but a daily reality. What happens to a national culture then?

My father came to Britain from Poland in the first decade of the twentieth century. What might he have done had he come a century later? In those days he had to learn English to make contact with the world outside. He acquired British culture; he admired it; he made sure we, his four sons, made ourselves at home in it. He had no choice; neither did we. Had he come today he could watch Polish television, listen to Polish radio, read the Polish press. Through internet technologies he could be in spoken and visual contact with friends and family thousands of miles distant as if they were living next door. His 'hello' would imply no 'goodbye'. Physically he might be here, but mentally he might still be there.

Global communications, especially the internet, have in effect abolished space, or at least our experience of space. Yet the nation state was predicated on space. It was a political-social-economic-cultural phenomenon that brought together a group of people, however heterogeneous, because they lived in the same region. They might be quite different, but they were neighbours. They occupied the same territory. They shared the same language. They lived under the same political system. They were part of the same economy. When my family came to Britain, they were opting to share its fate. They were sacrificing their past for the sake of what they saw as a better future. They were moving home.

Today, thanks to globalization and the ease and low real cost of travel, no one has to make that choice any more. What then becomes of identity? Britain is *where* we are, but in what sense is it *who* we are? Citizens of the world, we no longer have a sense of the local, which is where identity begins. The nation state is fragmenting before our eyes. What, in such a world, is the meaning of the word 'home'?

The one thing that kept nation states together was the fact that their citizens shared a language, a culture, a sense of history and collective destiny. Multiculturalism, far from counteracting the centrifugal forces of our time, accelerates and amplifies them. It has become hard for any of us to say what national identity is any more. The last time a serious attempt was made to do so – the famous 'Cool Britannia' slogan of the late 1990s – it was in the form of a marketing slogan or a corporate logo rather than any deeply rooted set of characteristics or experiences. The famous so-called Tebbitt test – which team would you support? – was almost equally superficial. From 'land of hope and glory' to a cricket team in one generation.

The result is highly destabilizing, especially in terms of the management of conflict. Almost any clash anywhere in the world now has the potential to go global. What might, twenty years ago, have been a local problem, dealt with locally, by people who understood the issue and the people involved, can now be transmitted internationally through email and the internet and set off a series of protests with a ferocity beyond anyone's power to control. We should be exporting a message of coexistence from Britain to conflict zones elsewhere. Instead, we are importing messages of conflict from lands far away to Britain. The result is serious, and the danger may get worse.

One reason is that ethnic identities are rapidly becoming religious identities, and unlike ethnicities, religions are global. They were the first-ever effective global cultures, more powerful and far longer lasting than the empire of Alexander the Great or that of pre-Christian Rome. That is a fact of great consequence, not only for Europe but even for what was once thought of as the world's greatest melting pot, the United States. For what America found is that though ethnicity – language, culture, cuisine – tends to fade, religious identity does not fade.

Putting all this together we have all the ingredients for an ever more unstable world, one in which conflicts in Iraq, Afghanistan, Kashmir and Israel are no longer far away. They are, as they say, coming to a cinema near you. They can wreck friendships in Luton or Leicester, cause violence on the streets of Manchester or Birmingham, and poison relationships on one university campus after another. A world in which a minor incident somewhere can become a cause célèbre everywhere is not one in which it is pleasant or safe to live. There is no need whatsoever to add weapons of mass destruction to the equation to see how dangerous the environment is.

Defending Liberal Democracy

The good news is that Britain is well poised to address these problems. The leaders of its faith communities – Christian, Jewish, Muslim, Hindu, Sikh, Buddhist, Jain, Zoroastrian and Bahai – know one another. They work well together. The day after the 7/7 London terror attack, the then Home Secretary Charles Clarke called us together, fearing there might be inter-ethnic violence. He did not know, until we explained it to him, that we were all friends. We had worked at good community relations. So have civic and interfaith groups throughout the country.

Besides which, Britain has long been a pioneer in tolerance, civility and respect for difference. The late J. L. Talmon pointed out the difference between two kinds of liberalism.[9] There was the British kind, which 'assumes politics to be a matter of trial and error' and which 'recognizes a variety of levels of personal and collective endeavour, which are altogether outside the sphere of politics'. And there was the continental kind 'based upon the assumption of a sole and exclusive truth in politics'. One is pragmatic, easy-going, based on friendship, respect for traditions, and occasional 'dining with the opposition'. The other is abstract, theoretical, prepared to sacrifice people for principle, and institutions for ideology. In a world of clashing civilizations, the British tradition is still worth saving.

I write as one who believes in the dignity of difference. If we were all the same, we would have nothing unique to contribute, nor anything to learn from others. The more diverse we are, the richer our culture becomes, and the more expansive our horizons of possibility. But that depends on our willingness to bring our differences as gifts to the common good. It requires integration rather than segregation, and that in turn means that we must have a rich and compelling sense of the common good. Without it, we will find that difference spells discord and creates, not music, but noise.

Thinking about liberal democracy is ultimately to think about freedom and what it takes to defend it. By 'freedom' I mean collective freedom, the freedom we share. I do not mean individual freedom, the freedom to buy what you want, and be what you buy. At its highest, collective freedom honours the human person and gives each of society's members maximal respect. It allows people to live out their deepest commitments without oppression and fear, valuing difference while binding us together in shared pursuit of the things we can only achieve together. Such freedom has little to do with power, and nothing to do with imperialism. It has to do with a certain conception of the human person as a choosing, responsible moral agent.

The debate about multiculturalism, if it is to be serious and not a call to a series of quick fixes, deserves to take place in this larger context. What is at stake is a moral order – liberal democracy – that took three centuries to achieve and two world wars to defend. It was born against the backdrop of a series of wars of religion in the sixteenth and seventeenth centuries. It engaged some of the West's finest minds: Milton, Hobbes, Locke, Spinoza, Thomas Jefferson, Alexis de Tocqueville, John Stuart Mill. One of the most dangerous aspects of our present condition is that we have largely forgotten this battle of ideas. In fact we are ill-equipped for any battle of ideas. A nation that remembers its failures and forgets its successes, that has lost self-respect while conferring self-esteem on everyone else, does not inspire confidence, least of all in those living in its midst who have other sources of identity.

Liberal democracy is in danger. Britain and the other nation states of the West are becoming places where free speech is increasingly at risk, non-political institutions are becoming politicized, university campuses are turning into ideological arenas, and a combination of political correctness and ethnic-religious separatism are eroding the graciousness of civil society. Religious groups are becoming pressure groups, focusing on sectarian interests rather than the common good. Boycotts and political campaigns are infecting professional bodies. Culture is fragmenting into non-communicating systems of belief in which civil discourse ends and reasoned argument becomes impossible. The political process is in danger of being abandoned in favour of the media-attention-grabbing gesture, with the threat of violence never far from the surface. The politics of freedom risks descending into the politics of fear. This has already begun to happen, and if we do not take countermeasures collectively, and soon, it will happen increasingly in the future.

To sustain a free society we are going to have to reinvigorate the environments in which it was born, lives and has its being. We will have to strengthen culture-creating institutions and renew the much-worn, almost threadbare, concept of the common good. We will have to work together on this with men and women of goodwill in every faith and none. Freedom is lost when it is taken for granted. We have taken ours for granted for too long. What worries me most of all is the systemic inability of a morally relativistic culture to say what we all share. When you declare all cultures equally valid, and say that to judge one better than another is judgemental and condescending, you destroy the possibility, the very language, of shared belonging. That cannot be right. There are universals. We all need food and shelter; we all need to communicate with others; we all need to make space for difference if others are to make space for us. Liberal democracy is about togetherness-in-difference, and we begin to lose it when we notice the difference but forget the togetherness.

The loss of national identity and the fragmentation of society are part of larger structural shifts that have taken place in the postmodern, late-capitalist world. These include the loss of confidence in morality and the fear that any strong belief whatsoever may lead to the 'authoritarian personality' and a potentially genocidal state. They involve the breakdown of the family and the consequent loss of a belief in parenthood as the responsibility of one generation to the next. They include the sheer pace and reach of the global economy and the

11

sometimes brutal impact of the free market on values like locality and loyalty. We live in a world of global elites who may be closer to their corporate partners thousands of miles away than to their next-door neighbours. All of these things have had an impact, reducing our sense of being bound in a common fate with those around us and those who will come after us.

This means that we are going to have to think again about what binds us together in a single fate with a shared identity. It is precisely the diverse nature of Western societies today that is our protection against narrow nationalisms of the kind that have produced dictatorships and genocides. We have to learn to live together, valuing equally our differences and our commonalities. The perennial problem of civilization, given new depth and pathos in our time, is how to manage our separateness and togetherness, our differences and interdependencies. Both are equally important. *If we were completely different we could not communicate. If we were exactly alike we would have nothing to say.* Politics is the art of living with difference, and how we deal with it shapes much else in our world.

The structure of the book is simple. In the first part, I look at the processes that have brought us to where we are: the loss of moral consensus, the impact of technology on culture, the failure of national self-confidence, the breakdown of the family, and the inward turn from society to community. In the second, I sketch the rudiments of a theory of society-building. This is a neglected area in the history of political thought. In the third, I outline some of the ways we might strengthen civic nationalism, the identity that comes not from colour or creed, but from the fact that, with all our differences, we come together to build something larger than any of our groups could achieve alone.

Society, I argue, is *the home we build together.* Christians, Jews, Hindus, Sikhs, Muslims, atheists, agnostics and secular humanists. To do this we need a shared language. The democratic conversation must include all of us. We must be prepared to explain ourselves to one another, and to listen to one another. Because we are different, each of us has something unique to contribute. What matters is that we contribute – to society as a whole, not just to our particular subsection of it.

I begin by telling three stories, parables, metaphors of the different ways minorities and the majority can relate. On this, all else will depend.

Chapter 2

Society as Country House, Hotel or Home

Fellowship, community, shared patriotism – these essential values of our civilization do not come from just buying and consuming goods together. They come from a shared sense of individual independence and personal effort ... We need jobs, dignified employment at decent pay; the kind of employment that lets a person say to his community, to his family, to his country, and most important, to himself, 'I helped to build this country. I am a participant in its great public ventures. I am somebody.'[1]

Robert F. Kennedy

Three parables. In the first, a hundred strangers have been wandering around the countryside in search of a place to stay. Eventually they arrive at the gate of a large country house. The owner comes to the gate, sees the strangers and asks them who they are. They tell him their story. He gives them a warm smile. 'How good to see you,' he says. 'As you can see, I have an enormous home. Far too big for me, actually. There are hundreds of empty rooms. Please feel free to stay here as long as you like. I look forward to your company. From now on consider yourself my guests.'

A lovely story. But not entirely so for the strangers in the long run. They have a place to live, and yes, their host is exactly as he seemed at first, welcoming, hospitable, capable of apparently endless generosity. There is only one thing wrong as far as they are concerned. However generous their host, he remains the host, and they are guests. It is his home, not theirs. The place belongs to someone else. That is *society as country house.*

The second: A hundred strangers in search of a home find themselves in the middle of a big city. There they find a hotel. It is large, comfortable, and has every amenity. The visitors have money enough to pay the hotel bills. They book their rooms, unpack, and stay.

13

The rules are simple. They are free to do what they like, so long as they don't disturb the other guests. Their relationship with the hotel is purely contractual. They pay money in return for certain services. They may look at other hotels to see whether they charge less or offer more amenities, but by and large they are satisfied where they are.

The hotel offers the newcomers a freedom and equality they did not have on the first model. They are guests, but so is everyone else. There is only one problem. A hotel is where you stay, not where you belong. You feel no loyalty to a hotel. You don't put down roots there. It doesn't become part of your identity. A hotel is a gathering of strangers who have no reason to become anything other than strangers. Yes, after a while you recognize your fellow guests. You bid them good morning. You discuss the weather and the football. But it remains a place where everyone is, in the biblical phrase, 'a stranger and sojourner'. That is *society as hotel.*

The third: A hundred strangers arrive at a town. There they are met by the mayor, councillors and local residents. The mayor says: 'Friends, we welcome you. It is good to have you among us. Sadly, as you can see, there is no country house where we might accommodate you. Nor do we have a hotel. There is, though, something we can offer you.

'We have a patch of empty land: large enough to accommodate homes for all of you. We have bricks and building materials. We have experts here who can help you design your homes, and we will help you build them. Meanwhile we will offer you hospitality while the homes are being built. Let us do this together.'

So it happens. Unlike the country house, the newcomers have to build their own long-term accommodation. Unlike the hotel, they do not merely pay. They invest their energies in what they build. Their relationship with the place is not purely contractual. They helped build it; it is their achievement; it is of their making. That means they can never be entirely detached from it. What we build embodies something of us. At the same time, the people of the town have made it clear that the houses they build must be, in some broad sense, congruent with the architectural character of the town as it is. So the homes they build are recognizably of the place where they are, not the place they have come from. Not only have they made a home; they have made themselves *at* home, in this landscape, this setting, this place.

This is a more demanding model than the previous two. But it also yields more. The newcomers feel – as they did not on the country-house model – that they have earned their place in this, their new home. They have a self-respect that was not available to them as guests. And unlike the hotel model, they have a real relationship with the people of the town. They have worked together on the plans. They have laboured together in the act of building. They have the sense of being part of a team that comes when any group, friends or strangers, work together for an extended period on a constructive project. In fact, when the houses are finished, the new arrivals and the people of the town celebrate together. That too is a symbolic act, a ceremony of bonding, a ritual of belonging.

By working together, the locals and the newcomers have meshed as part of what is now an enlarged community. The erstwhile strangers have achieved something their counterparts in the other two narratives did not. They have given as well as received. They have created something for themselves. We are what we build. The best way of feeling at home is to be able to point to some feature of the landscape and say to your child or grandchild: 'I helped build that.' They have added something to the town, and the townspeople know it.

The newcomers still occasionally seem strange. They speak and act and dress differently from the locals. But those long sessions of working together have had their effect. The locals know the newcomers are serious, committed, dedicated. They have their own ways, but they have also learned the ways of the people of the town, and they have worked out a modus vivendi, a rough and ready friendship. The two groups respect one another with that unspoken regard that comes when you work with others on a shared project to which each brings his or her own special gifts. Making something together breaks down walls of suspicion and misunderstanding, even though that is not the aim of the project at all. That is society as *the home we build together.*

Society as Country House

The strangers in these stories could be anyone: immigrants, refugees, asylum-seekers, ethnic minorities, or members of a religious community other than the Church of England: Catholics, Jews or people from the Free Churches. The parables could be about class, or regional cultures seeking a place at the centre, or Scotland, Wales and Northern Ireland before devolution. The three parables represent three ways of thinking about society and identity.

The first, the country house, speaks about host and guests. There are insiders and outsiders, the majority and minorities. There is one dominant culture, and if you don't belong to it, you don't really belong at all. You are not 'one of us'. This is the *assimilationist* model, known in early-twentieth-century America as 'the melting pot'. It says, minorities must lose their identity in order to belong.

The second, the hotel, says the opposite. Minorities don't have to give up their identities in order to belong, because there is no such thing as belonging at all. There is no one dominant culture; there is no national identity. There are no outsiders because there are no insiders either. This is the multiculturalism model. The danger is that it turns society into a series of non-intercommunicating rooms. It can lead to *segregation*.

The third model, the home we build together, values the identities of both the majority and minorities. It says: we are different, but that does not mean there is nothing to bind us in shared belonging. What makes us different is what we *are*, what unites us is what we *do*. We create the common good. Society is not static but dynamic. It is not just something we inherit and inhabit: it is something we make. The more different we are, the richer the possibilities of what we make together. That means seeing difference not as separation but as contribution. Yes, we have our private rooms, but we also have our public spaces, and those public spaces matter to all of us, which is why we work together to make them as expansive and gracious as we can. That act of making creates belonging. This is society as *integration without assimilation*.

The country-house model prevailed in Britain until the 1950s. There was a mainstream, 'the establishment' – white, Anglo-Saxon, Christian, represented by the Royal family, the Church of England, Oxbridge, the civil service, and the myriad institutions, customs, conventions, class distinctions, buildings, sights and sounds that were 'forever England'. And then there were the folks who arrived from time to time, such as French Huguenots, Irish Catholics and Jews. There was a received way of doing things, and the English could spot an outsider, a not-one-of-us, with unerring accuracy.

In England such divisions and distinctions were relatively mild compared to what they were on the Continent. The French had, since the Revolution, a strong Republican tradition that recognized no intermediary institutions between the individual and the state. Jews might be Jews, Protestants could be Protestants, but such identities were invisible and never allowed to intrude into public space. Germany had a strong ethnic identity. To be German meant being part of the *Volk*, the Race (with a capital R). Herder had taught that there were no cultural universals, that each nation had its distinctive characteristics. The pseudo-science of race proved it. You could tell a person's race by the shape of their skull. No acculturation could turn a non-Aryan into an Aryan. These were, therefore, monocultures in a way Britain never quite was.

So Britain, though it has had its share of racist and xenophobic attitudes, even race riots and violence, rarely admitted them into the mainstream of political debate. There were always contra-voices: Thomas Babington Macaulay arguing for Jewish emancipation in 1831, Beatrice Webb in 1889 writing favourably about the East End Jews, Winston Churchill arguing in 1904 against any retreat from 'the old, tolerant and generous practice of free entry and asylum to which this country has so long adhered and from which it has so greatly gained'. As early as 1701, Daniel Defoe was reminding his fellow-countrymen:

> Thus from a mixture of all kinds began,
> That het'rogeneous thing, an Englishman:
> In eager rapes, and furious lust begot,
> Betwixt a painted Britain and a Scot.
> Whose gend'ring off-spring quickly learn'd to bow,
> And yoke their heifers to the Roman plough:
> From whence a mongrel half-bred race there came,
> With neither name, nor nation, speech nor fame.
> In whose hot veins new mixtures quickly ran,
> Infus'd betwixt a Saxon and a Dane ...
> A true-born Englishman's a contradiction,
> In speech an irony, in fact a fiction.[2]

Britain had been for so long a mix of races and cultural influences that it never developed a narrow ethnic nationalism. In 1904, at the height of widespread public fears that Britain was being overrun by immigrants, Ford Maddox Ford could hark back to that long-standing self-awareness: 'In the case of a people descended from Romans, from Britons, from Anglo-Saxons, from Danes, from Normans, from Poitevins, from Huguenots, from Irish, from Gaels, from modern Germans and from Jews, a people so mixed that there is in it hardly a man who can point to seven generations of purely English blood, it is almost absurd to use the almost obsolescent word "race". These fellows are ourselves.'[3]

Britain's country house had more to do with class than race. As Voltaire, an Anglophile, put it, England is a nation 'where the arts are all honoured and rewarded, where there is a difference between the stations in life, but none other between men except that of merit'.[4] The nation of shopkeepers recognized that diversity was good for business. Newcomers brought contacts and expertise that were potentially useful to a maritime power already engaged in global trade. Together with the Venetians and the Dutch they had learned the truth that Montesquieu, another Anglophile, articulated: 'The natural effect of commerce is to lead to peace. Two nations that trade together become mutually dependent: if one has an interest in buying, the other one has in selling; and all unions are based on mutual needs.'[5] Voltaire saw this at work in the City of London: 'The Jew, the Mohametan and the Christian transact together as if they all profess'd the same religion, and give the name of infidel to none but bankrupts.'[6]

So, the British country house was spacious, but there were still hosts and guests. Catholics lacked the right to attend university, get a degree, enter government service or enter Parliament until 1829. Jews and members of the Free Churches had to wait longer. Britons' sense of superiority tended to be extended to the world at large, especially those over whom it ruled as an imperial power, rather than to minorities within its midst. But it was still capable of outbursts of xenophobia, especially when immigration began to rise at the end of the nineteenth century. Foreigners, said *Truth* magazine in 1893, 'are in fact deceitful, effeminate, irreligious, immoral, unclean and unwholesome'.[7] Two world wars, though, brought the nation together, as wars always do. It was not until the 1960s that another model began to emerge.

The Procedural State: Society as Hotel

By then immigrants had arrived in unprecedented numbers from the former colonies: 210,000 by 1958. In 1961, 130,000 came in a single year.[8] They came from the Caribbean, India, Pakistan, West Africa and Cyprus. There were sizeable communities of Hindus, Sikhs and Muslims. New waves followed in the wake of political crises: Kenya under Kenyatta, Uganda under the regime of Idi Amin. There were refugees from communist countries: Hungary in 1956, Czechoslovakia in 1968. Half-hearted legislative attempts were made to stem the flow. In 1968 Enoch Powell made his notorious speech warning of impending violence: 'Like the Roman, I see the Tiber flowing with much blood.' The far right, in the form of the National Front, began to make an impact. In the early 1980s there were street fights in Bristol, Deptford and Southall, and riots in Brixton, London, and Toxteth, Liverpool. Racism was in the air.

It was against this background that the idea of multiculturalism began to coalesce. Initially it was a response to racism. Local government officials were trained in anti-racist awareness. Schools were encouraged to drop assimilationist policies. Instead, the children of immigrants were to be encouraged to preserve their own cultures and languages. When the headteacher of a school in Bradford, Ray Honeyford, warned that this would be divisive, he was sacked.[9]

Then in 1989 a controversy arose over Salman Rushdie's novel *The Satanic Verses*, regarded by many Muslims as an assault on their faith. It was a provocative book, and if it was intended to widen the boundaries of free speech, it failed. In January, copies of the book were burned in Bradford. In February, in Iran, Ayatollah Khomeini issued a fatwa urging that Rushdie be killed. Six people died in riots in Islamabad. In Belgium two Muslims who defended Rushdie were killed. So was Rushdie's Norwegian translator. Attempts were made on the lives of his translators in Italy and Japan. Rushdie himself was forced to live under police protection for a decade. It was the first of many battles between liberalism and multiculturalism. Which takes priority: free speech or the protection of people's religious convictions? Does tolerance mean respecting cultures you regard as intolerant? These were and are genuine dilemmas, reminding us how easy it is to fracture the fragile strands that weave difference together. Cohesion needs self-restraint on all sides. Yet self-restraint has ceased to be a value in the contemporary West. Authenticity, 'letting it all hang out', and aggressive self-assertion have taken the place of civility, and we all lose thereby.

The real clash is between liberalism and multiculturalism. Liberalism is about the rights of individuals, multiculturalism about the rights of groups, and they are incompatible. Common to both is that they see the relationship between citizens and the state as purely contractual. By the late 1980s the idea that a nation had a dominant culture, reflected in its laws and institutions, had quietly died. Political parties no longer represented different visions of the good. Daniel Bell called this 'the end of ideology'.[10] In the new dispensation, parties compete in showing that each gives a better deal: more services for less taxation. This is politics as management. It marks the birth of the *procedural state*,[11] distinguished by its principled neutrality on matters of identity and morality. Society becomes a hotel. You pay the price; you get a room; and you are free to do what you like so long as you do not interfere with the other guests.

The trouble is that a hotel is a place where no one is at home. You cannot feel loyalty to a society that claims to have no identity whatsoever. Loyalty means particularity: this place not that, this language not that, these buildings, this landscape, this history, this culture. Liberalism and multiculturalism privatize identity: one by attributing it to the individual; the other to the ethnic or religious community. But there is, intentionally, no overarching structure of meaning to hold it all together.

The strains began to show in the summer of 2001 when there were civil disturbances in three northern towns: Bradford, Oldham and Burnley. The Home Secretary, David Blunkett, commissioned what became known as the Cantle Report.[12] The authors were alarmed by 'the depth of polarisation of our towns and cities'. They spoke of the various groups living 'parallel lives' that 'often do not seem to touch at any point'. Ethnic groups were not evenly distributed, geographically or economically. They tended to cluster together in enclaves. For minorities bent on preserving their identity, this is always the option of choice: to live among people like you rather than among strangers.

This means that schools are often dominated by one group or another rather than by a cultural mix. Even where school populations are diverse, when pupils go home, they and their families tend to socialize with people who share their background and beliefs. The authors of the Cantle report were surprised by this. They should not have been. Residential clustering is almost universal among newly arrived immigrant groups. People need the support of friends if they are to survive the challenges of adjusting to a new home. That is what happened in Spitalfields in London's East End.[13] First came the Huguenots. Then, in the late nineteenth century, the Jews. Now they are Bangladeshis. In fifty years' time they will be something else. The great house of worship on the corner of Fournier Street and Brick Lane began life as a Huguenot chapel, then became Methodist; in 1898 it became a synagogue and in 1976 a mosque. Immigrants huddle together to keep warm in a new climate. They always will.

But by 2001 it was clear that multiculturalism was not working. It was keeping groups apart. It was hindering their integration into British life. It was failing to prevent divisive attitudes, and sometimes violent conflict. In 2004, David Goodhart, editor of *Prospect* magazine, published an essay, 'The Discomfort of Strangers', in which he argued that ethnic divisions were endangering the sense of national solidarity on which the welfare state is based: we 'not only live among stranger citizens but we must share with them'.[14] We spend a large part of our income on taxes to support public services because we feel part of the 'us' held together by a common culture. But 'as Britain becomes more diverse that common culture is being eroded'. There is a conflict between solidarity and diversity. So long as liberalism prevailed we could think in terms of the individual as such, the universal human condition. But multiculturalism is the opposite of universalism. It is, as it were, a new form of tribalism. The fragmentation of Britain, warned Goodhart, may lead to ever greater reluctance to fund public services, as people ask, 'Why should I pay for the people not like me?'

The debate intensified after the 7 July 2005 terror attacks in London and the traumatic discovery that the perpetrators were British citizens, born and educated in Britain, yet violently hostile to it. The then chairman of the Commission for Racial Equality, Trevor Phillips, warned that 'we are sleepwalking our way to segregation'.[15] The nation was becoming 'more divided by race and religion' and 'more unequal by ethnicity'. Universities 'have started to become colour coded, with virtual "whites keep out" signs in some urban institutions'. The Archbishop of York, John Sentamu, a Ugandan and the first member of an ethnic minority to become an archbishop, also attacked multiculturalism, which to him seemed to say, 'let other cultures be allowed to express themselves but do not let the majority culture at all tell us its glories, its struggles, its joys, its pains'.[16] A failure of England to rediscover its culture anew would lead only to greater extremism.

These themes were taken up by Prime Minister Tony Blair in a speech on 8 December 2006 entitled, 'The Duty to Integrate: Shared British Values'.[17] There were, he said, limits to multiculturalism. It was supposed to be not a 'celebration of division but of diversity'. The right to be in a multicultural society 'was always implicitly balanced by a duty to integrate, to be part of Britain'. Those who shun integration 'contradict the fundamental values that define Britain today: tolerance, solidarity across the racial and religious divide, equality for all and between all'. Tolerance, he said, is non-negotiable, 'So conform to it or don't come here'. It was the strongest speech ever given by a prime minister on social integration.

Post-Multiculturalism

Where next? If multiculturalism has failed, what should take its place? One of the most interesting analyses was given by the figure who had brought the phrase 'clash of civilizations' to widespread public attention: Samuel Huntington.[18] In the wake of 9/11, Huntington had often been read as endorsing the clash between the West and Islam. In fact, those who read the book through to the end discovered in the last chapter that his view was diametrically opposite. He did *not* believe that the West should seek to impose democratic freedoms on other nations: 'Western belief in the universality of Western culture suffers three problems: it is false; it is immoral; and it is dangerous.' America should not try to impose American values on the world. It should try to impose American values on America.

America was in trouble. The West was in disarray. It was undergoing 'moral decline, cultural suicide, and political disunity'. Among the symptoms were a rise in crime and other antisocial behaviour, the disintegration of the family, a loss of social capital, a weakening of the work ethic in favour of 'a cult of personal indulgence', and 'decreasing commitment to learning and intellectual activity'. These became the subject of his next book, *Who Are We?* published in 2004.[19]

America, having embraced multiculturalism, was in danger of losing its identity. It now had to decide what its relationship should be with the rest of the world. There are, Huntington said, three choices: 'Americans can embrace the world, that is, open their country to other peoples or cultures, or they can try to reshape those other peoples and cultures in terms of American values, or they can maintain their society and culture distinct from those of other peoples.' He called these, respectively, the options of cosmopolitanism, imperialism or nationalism. Imperialism he ruled out for the reasons he had given in the earlier book. Cosmopolitanism he also saw as inadequate, because a country cannot be held together by political principles alone. They lack 'the deep emotional content and meaning provided by kith and kin, blood and belonging, culture and nationality'. The remaining option was nationalism: the return to America's past as a Christian country. 'America cannot become the world and still be America. Other peoples cannot become American and still be themselves. America is different, and that difference is defined in large part by its Anglo-Protestant culture and its religiosity.'

This analysis might work for America, which G. K. Chesterton once described as 'a nation with the soul of a church'. It will not work for Britain or most other European nations. They are far more secularized than America. Their non-Christian minorities are proportionally larger. They lack the tradition of presidential religious rhetoric that, as we will see in chapter 10, is a convention of American public discourse. And they have, as America does not, negative memories of ecclesiastical power. Huntington's suggestion was, in fact, an invitation to return to the pre-multicultural past. In politics as in life, walking backward is hazardous. We are where we are and we cannot go back. Multiculturalism, despite its shortcomings, was a genuine advance over the politics of exclusion and narrow nationalism.

That is why I suggest a new model. Society is the home we build together. This moves us forward not back. Unlike the country-house model, it is about collective belonging. In a diverse society, there should be no distinction between host and guest, majority and minorities, insiders and outsiders. Unlike the multicultural model, it sees diversity not in terms of self-enclosed communities but as an enrichment of the culture we all share. It is about bringing our several gifts as contributions to the common good. Because we are different we each have something unique to give – not to ourselves and our communities alone but to all of us and the life we share. This means *integration without assimilation.* There are, and will continue to be, Christians, Jews, Muslims, Hindus, Sikhs and all the other shades of the rainbow. But what we make, we make together.

Like multiculturalism, integrated diversity values the dignity of difference. But it relates it less to what we are than to what we give. Our multiplicity makes possible a highly differentiated set of contributions to the common good. We speak a common language, though we do so with a variety of accents and dialects. We are committed to a common project, society. We are engaged in building something together. We are part of a team. *What* we build should be the central topic of the democratic conversation, a conversation scored for many voices, covering many subjects, but unified around the question: What kind of society do we seek to create for the sake of our children and grandchildren not yet born? Because the team contains so many different talents, it will achieve what could not be achieved by any single group alone.

Each of the three key words in the phrase carries a specific charge. 'Home' means that we care about belonging. Britain is not just *where* we are but also *who* we are. 'Build' means that we focus on responsibilities, not just rights; contributions, not claims. This means an activist politics, in which we do more than vote. We get involved, especially at a local level. We volunteer. We see community service as an essential part of citizenship. 'Together' means integration, not segregation. Inter-religious harmony is promoted less by dialogue than by working together on community-based projects. As I explain in chapter 15, I call this a side-by-side rather than a face-to-face approach to difference.

Before moving on to the implications of the third model, I want in the following chapters to explore in more detail how we came to be where we are. Politics, culture and society do not just happen. They are as they are because people think in terms of certain ideas – and ideas have a history. Unless we understand that history we will fail in our efforts to redirect it. How did the country house (in America, the melting pot), and then the hotel come to be metaphors of society? In the next chapter I tell the story from the point of view of one minority: the Jewish community.

Chapter 3

A Brief History of Multiculturalism

I ponder all these things, how men fight and lose the battle and the thing they fought for comes about in spite of their defeat and when it comes turns out not to be what they meant and other men have to fight for what they meant under another name.[1]

William Morris

In 1908 a play opened to great acclaim in Washington DC. Its author was an English Jew, Israel Zangwill.[2] Among the audience that night was Theodore Roosevelt who praised the play and agreed to have a revised edition dedicated to him in 1914. It had successful runs in several cities throughout America, and clearly touched a chord. Its title came to sum up an entire generation's approach to identity in the New World. It was called *The Melting Pot*.

Zangwill's hero is a Russian Jew, David Quixano, who had come to America in the wake of the 1903 Kishinev pogrom in which his family had been killed. He is a composer, and has written a symphony called *The Crucible* into which he pours all his hopes for a new social order. He meets and falls in love with a Russian Christian, Vera Revendal, who had been imprisoned by the Czarist government for revolutionary activities. The dramatic climax comes when David meets Vera's father, Baron Revendal, and recognizes him as the Russian officer who had led the troops during the pogrom: the man responsible for his parents' death.

The point about Zangwill's rewriting of *Romeo and Juliet* is that this time the ending is non-tragic. Revendal admits his guilt, David's symphony is performed, and David and Vera kiss. It is a period melodrama almost unreadable today, but the passion of Zangwill's dream is palpable. This is how David describes the faith that has led him to America:

25

America is God's crucible, the great Melting-Pot where all the races of Europe are melting and re-forming. Here you stand, good folk, think I, when I see them at Ellis Island, here you stand in your fifty groups, with your fifty languages and histories and your fifty blood hatreds and rivalries. But you won't be long like that, brothers, for these are the fires of God you've come to ... A fig for your feuds and vendettas! Germans and Frenchmen, Irishmen and Englishmen, Jews and Russians – into the Crucible with all of you. God is making the American.

The melting pot was the American counterpart of the English country-house ideal. What made America different was that there was no long-established culture: no house, no host, no guest, no royal family, no landed aristocracy, no established church. It was an immigrant society. But out of this, people hoped, something unprecedented would emerge. The old world – Russia, pogroms, ethnic and religious conflict, bloodshed – is what David, and by implication Zangwill's contemporaries, had come to America to escape from. Something composite, amalgamating the best of Europe's past while bidding farewell to Europe's worst, was being born. Here in the modern version of the Promised Land, 'the great Alchemist melts and fuses' the different faiths and ethnicities 'to build the Republic of Man and the Kingdom of God'.

Zangwill's play popularized a sentiment expressed more than a century before by the French writer J. Hector St. John Crèvecoeur who had settled in New York and written *Letters from an American Farmer* (1782).[3] What, he asked, is 'the American, this new man?' He is the child of parents born in Europe, but he becomes an American by 'leaving behind him all his ancient prejudices and manners ... Here individuals of all nations are melted into a new race of men, whose labours and prosperity will one day cause great changes in the world.'

What made Zangwill's play so compelling in 1908 was that this was the time when mass immigration to the United States from Eastern Europe was at its height. Americans were torn between shock at the Kishinev pogrom and fears that the new arrivals, less Westernized than the earlier immigrants, would be unassimilable. From this perspective Zangwill's drama offered reassurance.

Yet the real pathos of the plot lies in the fact that Zangwill was writing as a Jew who no longer wanted to be a Jew. His real hope was for a world in which the entire lexicon of racial and religious differences is thrown away. Behind this lies the tragedy of European Enlightenment and emancipation. It had promised a new era in which reason would replace religion, and tolerance take the place of prejudice; where all would be equal and none discriminated against.

The English Country House

In Britain, things took a somewhat different course. Jews had been here since the eleventh century. Edward I expelled them in 1290, but in 1656 under Cromwell they returned. More precisely – since there was already a small community of *conversos*, Jews forcibly converted to Christianity who retained their identity in secret – they were given permission to practise their religion in public. The community stayed small until the nineteenth century and suffered little persecution. Many of them were merchants in the City of London.

It was only with the outbreak of pogroms in Eastern Europe in the 1880s that mass immigration began. The new arrivals were clustered in the East End of London. They were destitute, unskilled and lived in cramped tenements. Many of them worked in sweatshops under conditions that shocked Victorian social reformers such as Charles Booth and Beatrice Webb who came to observe them.

For the first time there was real hostility. The locals, themselves poor and in search of work, felt that they were being overrun and their livelihoods threatened. In 1887 a letter writer to *The Times* complained of 'foreign paupers replacing English workers and driving to despair men, women and children of our blood.'[4] The *East London Advertiser* identified the culprits: 'The swarms of foreign Jews who have invaded the East End labour market are chiefly responsible ...'[5] Joseph Chamberlain, the Liberal Unionist politician, said that England was fast becoming 'the dumping ground of Europe'.[6] In 1903 the MP for Stepney, Major Evans Gordon, said at a constituency meeting, 'There is hardly an Englishman in this room who does not live under the constant danger of being driven from his home, pushed out into the streets, not by the natural increase of our own population, but by the off-scum of Europe.'[7]

The off-scum eventually integrated, creating businesses such as Marks and Spencer, Tesco and Shell Petroleum, clothing stores such as Moss Bros and Burtons, writers such as Harold Pinter and Peter Schaffer, theatre and film producers, politicians, academics, soldiers, judges, boxers, poets, philosophers and Nobel Prize winners. There is a story of hope here. The same abuse directed at Jews a hundred years ago has been turned successively on the Irish, West Indians, Pakistanis, Bangladeshis and the rest. Yet each has gone on to enrich our culture.

One thing, though, is striking about the way the Jewish community responded to the anti-alien mood of the late nineteenth and early twentieth centuries. They adapted. They made the most strenuous efforts to belong and look as if they belonged, and if they did not, the more established Jewish community did not mince words in telling them to do so. 'If they intend to remain in England,' wrote the *Jewish*

Chronicle in 1881 about the East European Jews, 'if they wish to become members of our community, we have a right to demand that they will show signs of an earnest wish for a complete amalgamation with the aims and feelings of their hosts.'[8] Their motives were mixed. Undoubtedly they felt that integration was important in its own right. But they also feared that they would be caught up in the backlash if the new arrivals failed to anglicize. The *Jewish Chronicle* made this clear in 1883:

> Our most pressing task is to civilize this mass of wronged and tortured creatures, and we may depend upon it, that unless we perform this duty and perform it speedily, an outcry will arise against the newly come Hebrews which will react terribly upon the comfort and reputation of the older settlers. We owe it to our religion and to our brotherly feeling, we owe it to an enlightened view of self-interest, to deal promptly and mercifully with the inflowing current from the torbid sea of Russian despair and degradation.[9]

Morris Joseph, minister of the (Reform) West London Synagogue, told the new arrivals that they had a 'duty to leave behind them the ideas and habits that were tolerated in Russia'. The Jewish Lads' Brigade was formed to anglicize its charges, iron out 'the ghetto bend', and 'instil into the rising generation all that is best in the English character, manly independence, honour, truth, cleanliness, love of active health-giving pursuits'. Educational establishments like the Jews' Free School trained its pupils to be model Englishmen and women. Louis Abrahams urged parents to reinforce the message of the school:

> Strengthen the efforts of the teachers to wipe away all evidence of foreign birth and foreign proclivities, so that your children shall be so identified with everything that is English, in thought and deed, that no shadow of anti-Semitism might exist, that your boys and girls may grow up devoted to the flag which they are learning within these walls to love and honour, that they may take a worthy part in the growth of this great Empire, whose shelter and protection I hope will never be denied them.

Acculturation, the acquisition of the language and manners of England, and patriotism took a higher priority than specifically Jewish instruction, though the pupils were certainly taught to take pride in their people and their faith. The truth is that the Anglo-Jews of those days saw no conflict between these aims. They were English men and women 'of the Jewish persuasion'. Victorian values were, for the most part, Jewish values as well.

They had three immense advantages: twenty-six centuries of history as a religious and ethnic minority in countries throughout the world; an established community that could help the newcomers to adjust; and living role models of successful integration. The key figure was Sir Moses Montefiore, an observant Jew, a communal lay leader and President of the Board of Deputies of British Jews, and a well-known figure among the general public, Sheriff of the City of London and a close personal friend of Queen Victoria.

On his 99th, and again on his hundredth birthday, *The Times* published leaders in his honour.[10] The latter, on 24 October 1884, is a particularly fascinating document. It speaks of Montefiore's philanthropy to Christians and Jews alike. It pays tribute to the synthesis he had created between the two identities: 'He has been the victorious defender of persecuted Jews because he was the perfect English gentleman.' In his own person he had 'solved once for all the problem of the competence of the most faithful of Jews to be not the less a complete Englishman.' The article ended with a stern admonition to the rest of the Jewish community to follow his example: 'the determination to show, by his life, that fervent Judaism and patriotic citizenship are absolutely consistent with one another'.

That is society as country house. Jews embraced it in Britain as eagerly as Zangwill did the American melting pot. It brought good news and bad. It encouraged newcomers to integrate. Jews heard this, and did it. By 1895 a reporter from the *Daily Graphic* who had visited the Jews Free School to see how the immigrant children were doing, reported: 'When they leave, they all speak English with a regard for grammar and a purity of accent far above the average of the neighbourhood.'[11] They developed a love of England that was deep and genuine.

The downside was that however much they integrated, they were still guests. Others knew it. They knew it. Isabel Colegate captures the mood precisely in her novel, set just before the outbreak of the First World War, *The Shooting Party*.[12] A group of guests is spending the weekend in the country house of Sir Randolf Nettleby. One of the guests is a highly assimilated Jew of the Disraeli kind. As he arrives, the host asks a guest, 'Is the Israelite not among us?' At one point, the Jewish visitor makes a gesture that, to the other guests, calls to mind, 'something ancient, Levantine, subtle and insinuating'.

When the host is as gracious as the English, being an outsider may be no more than a minor discomfort. But in France and Germany it was more serious. There too, Jews absorbed the culture of their hosts, only to find themselves confronted with a hostility that gave rise to a new word, anti-Semitism, coined in 1879, by the German journalist Wilhelm Marr. Anti-Semitism was different from its Christian precursor, anti-Judaism. Europe, in the wake of the French Revolution, was now in principle secular and egalitarian. Religiously-based prejudice was no longer respectable. Instead, hatred had to find a new source of authority. For the children of the Enlightenment, that meant science. It came in the form of 'social Darwinism' (the strong survive; the weak die) and the pseudo-science of race. Thus racial anti-Semitism was born. The more insightful of Europe's Jews immediately recognized that the new hate was far more dangerous than the old. People can change their religion. They cannot change their race.

Few summed up more eloquently than Theodor Herzl, in 1897, the failure of the nineteenth century to grant equality to the Jew:

We have sincerely tried everywhere to merge with the national communities in which we live, seeking only to preserve the faith of our fathers. It is not permitted us. In vain are we loyal patriots, sometimes superloyal; in vain do we make the same sacrifices of life and property as our fellow citizens; in vain do we strive to enhance the fame of our native lands in the arts and sciences, or her wealth by trade and commerce. In our native lands where we have lived for centuries we are still decried as aliens, often by men whose ancestors had not yet come at a time when Jewish sighs had long been heard in the country ... If we were left in peace ... But I think we shall not be left in peace.[13]

What led Herzl to this conclusion was the scene he witnessed in Paris after the verdict of the Dreyfus trial in 1895. Dreyfus, a highly assimilated Jewish officer in the French army, had been accused (wrongly, as many suspected) of being a spy. Crowds gathered outside the courtroom, shouting 'Death to the Jews!' That was when Herzl decided, as had Zangwill, that there was no future for Jews in Europe. A half-century later Herzl's fears came true in a way he could not have imagined in his worst nightmare. By 1945, more than half of Europe's Jews had been murdered, turned to ash in Auschwitz, Treblinka and Bergen-Belsen.

Cultural Pluralism

Meanwhile, at the same time that *The Melting Pot* was being shown, another young secular Jew, Horace Kallen, was testing his ideas out on the classes he taught at Harvard. Eventually, in 1915, he published them in *The Nation*, in the form of an article entitled 'Democracy Versus the Melting Pot'.[14]

Kallen did not believe that the melting-pot idea was workable or even desirable. People cannot abandon their identities: 'Men may change their clothes, their politics, their wives, their religions, their philosophies, to a greater or lesser extent: they cannot change their grandfathers.' Ethnicity is indelible. 'Jews or Poles or Anglo-Saxons, in order to cease being Jews or Poles or Anglo-Saxons, would have to cease to be.'

What then? The very newness and openness of America offered another possibility: that the different groups might preserve their differences while at the same time forming a new kind of nation. After all, the United States was, as its name implied, a federation of states. Why not apply that idea culturally as well as territorially?

America might then become 'a democracy of nationalities, co-operating voluntarily and autonomously through common institutions'. It would be a place where Germans, Poles, Swedes, Irish and Italians all retained their customs and traditions, coexisting under a single political umbrella. 'The common language of the commonwealth, the language of its great tradition, would be English, but each nationality would have for its emotional and involuntary life its own particular dialect or speech, its own individual and inevitable aesthetic and intellectual forms.'

Where Zangwill foresaw the disappearance of difference into a new hybrid or cosmopolitan identity, Kallen argued for its continuation. This for him was both a fact and a value. It was a fact because we are who we are through our family and its history. But it was also a value because, as Kallen put it, 'creation comes from the impact of diversities'. Mix Italians and Irish and Jews, and new and exotic flowers will bloom. Kallen himself preferred a musical metaphor: 'As in an orchestra, the different instruments, each with its own characteristic timbre and theme, contribute distinct and recognisable parts to the composition, so in the life and culture of a nation, the different regional, ethnic, occupational, religious and other communities compound their different activities to make up the national spirit. The national spirit is constituted by this union of the different.'

Kallen called this vision *cultural pluralism*, and it was the first articulation of what became, more than half a century later, multiculturalism. It was not without its difficulties. On the one hand, Kallen was opposed to residential or cultural ghettoes. He wanted the various 'nationalities' to meet and mix and contribute to society as a whole. At the same time, he wanted them to preserve their identity against assimilation and diffusion. That is a very narrow line to tread.

Nor was the idea without its critics. The great American philosopher and educationalist John Dewey, in a lecture given a year after the appearance of Kallen's argument, gave a different account of the way an ethnic mix might be finessed with a shared identity: 'The American is himself Pole-German-English-French-Spanish-Italian-Greek-Irish-Scandinavian-Bohemian-Jew-and so on. The point is to see to it that the hyphen connects instead of separates. And this means at least that our public schools shall teach each factor to respect every other, and shall take pains to enlighten all as to the great past contributions of every strain in our composite makeup.'[15] Where Kallen wanted a fruit bowl, Dewey preferred a fruit salad.

The times, though, were hardly ideal for either of these reflections. The First World War led Americans to be disenchanted with Europe. Differences were hard to see as a blessing when they led to millions of deaths for no very clear cause. Then there were racist reactions against new immigrant communities. There was the 'Red Scare' and rising activity on the part of the Ku Klux Klan. There was pressure to end mass immigration, on which severe limits were placed by the 1924 Immigration Act. Then came the Great Depression, turning people's thoughts to survival, not the higher reaches of culture.

Above all, the Second World War put an end to thoughts of creative diversity. The need of the hour was national unity. Franklin D. Roosevelt was blunt and unequivocal: 'The principle on which this country was founded and by which it has always been governed is that Americanism is a matter of the mind and heart; Americanism is not, and never was, a matter of race and ancestry. A good American is one who is loyal to this country and to our creed of liberty and democracy.'[16] For the time being, cultural pluralism was put on hold.

The Birth of Multiculturalism

Why then did it re-emerge in the 1970s, in America, Britain and other parts of Europe, as a compelling doctrine and as government policy? Writing about Holland, Paul Sniderman and Louk Hagendoorn make a surprising statement.[17] They say, in effect, that multiculturalism was not initially a policy designed to make immigrants feel at home, but the opposite. It was 'adopted out of convenience'. The 1970s witnessed mass immigration into Holland: refugees from Sri Lanka, Iran, Iraq, Somalia and other African countries, and workers from Morocco, North Africa and Turkey, to meet a shortage of unskilled labour.

The assumption at that time was that they would stay briefly and then return home. Government policy was therefore to sustain their ties to their places of origin rather than to Holland. 'Hence the government programmes to sustain the culture of minority immigrants – to ensure for example that they continued to speak the language of the country they came from, even if they did not master the one they were in. The objective was to equip them to leave – which is to say, to discourage them from staying.' On this account, Holland acquired multiculturalism the way the British acquired an empire: in a fit of absentmindedness.

True or not, it is striking how, at a particular point in time, Europe and America gave up on what had been a guiding principle ever since the seventeenth century, whether it was called integration, acculturation or assimilation. The principle of *Cuius regio, eius religio* – the religion of the ruler is the religion of the people – might no longer be in force, but the idea of one nation, one culture, was. Minorities were expected to conform, learn the rules, speak the language, know the history: to belong. That was not regarded as oppressive. After all, those who came had chosen to come. They knew what they were joining as well as what they were leaving. Any society has its rules. In free societies, they tend to be unwritten, informal, sustained by social expectation rather than law. But every society has a character of its own, and will usually choose not to lose it. The more self-confident a society is, the more inclusive will that character be.

Somehow, with little public debate, this principle disappeared, not just in one country but several. Now it began to be assumed – differently in different countries, to be sure – that immigrant groups should not be expected to acculturate. They were, within limits, to sustain their own languages and cultures. In some places they were resourced to build their own schools and social and welfare institutions; in others, state schools provided instruction in the newcomers' traditions, with teachers drawn from the relevant ethnic or religious group. For the first time, it was the wider society, not the newcomers, who were expected to adjust. As a member of a religious minority myself, I welcomed these changes but I was also puzzled by them. What happened? What changed?

Behind this development I sense three intellectual influences. The first was a school of thought whose most famous exponent was Isaiah Berlin, about whom Noel Annan wrote that 'He seems to me to have written the truest and most moving of all interpretations of life that my own generation made.'[18] Berlin, like Karl Popper and Friedrich Hayek, came to Britain to escape Nazi Germany or Soviet Communism. Each was haunted by the fear of tyranny and totalitarianism, and more generally of ideology, religious or secular. They knew that the attempt to create heaven on earth usually achieves the opposite result.

Like Kallen, Berlin believed in pluralism. There is, he argued, no Platonic heaven in which all ideals coexist in harmony. The very idea is misconceived. There is no conceivable universe in which all good things coexist. You cannot combine Greek military courage, Roman civic pride, Christian humility, Taoist wisdom and Buddhist other-worldliness into a single system. You cannot cast characters from a Greek tragedy, a Shakespearean comedy, a D. H. Lawrence novel and a Henry James short story in the same narrative. Even within a culture, ideals collide. You can have equality at the cost of freedom, or freedom at the cost of equality, but not both at the same time.

Values, cultures, civilizations are *incommensurable*, meaning, they are not part of a single spectrum; they are not measurable against one another by a single scale. Liberal democracy happens to be the way we live, but there are other ways, and no particular reason to choose this rather than that. Although Berlin did not say so, and might well not have agreed, it might be in the spirit of his beliefs to say that a decent society is one that mirrors the pluralism of human values. Hence, a multicultural society.

A second factor was the pervasive feeling that nationalism – the great idea of the nineteenth century – had failed. It had given rise to two world wars and tens of millions of deaths. Far from being inclusive it had led to the new phenomenon of anti-Semitism, and more generally, to racism. It took a long time for the feeling to set in. Primo Levi wrote his memoir of life in Auschwitz, *If This is a Man*, in 1946, but at that time almost no one wanted to read it. Not until the 1960s did the Holocaust seriously enter public consciousness. The 1960s were also the time of Martin Luther King and the battle of African-Americans for civil equality. These were momentous events, and they pointed to serious failings: one within European culture; the other within America. The idea of one nation, one culture, began to be seen as the root of all evil, for in Europe it was a culture that excluded Jews, and in America it excluded blacks.

A third idea, also influential at this time, was the one associated with Abraham Maslow, Erich Fromm and Theodore Adorno: the 'author-itarian personality'.[19] Many Nazis claimed at the Nuremberg Trials that 'they were only obeying orders'. Adorno and others argued that it was the very culture (part Lutheran, part Kantian) of strict duties and obedience that made the Holocaust possible in the first place. Accep-tance of social conventions and submission to authority were the soil in which anti-democratic movements were able to grow. They gave rise to a wish for strong leaders: Hitler, Mussolini, Lenin, Stalin. They stunted personal and psychological growth and thus the capacity to resist tyr-ants and tyrannies. Hence: authority bad; personal autonomy good.

For the first time in several centuries, an entire adult generation lost confidence in its ideas and institutions. In America this was com-pounded by Vietnam; in France by the youth protests of 1968; in Britain by rock, pop, eastern mysticism and drugs. It was the greatest explosion of romanticism since Rousseau, in the sense given by T. E. Hulme.[20] Romanticism, he said, is the belief that people are basically good, and the best you can do is to minimize the limits placed on them by society. Classicism is the idea that the human being is 'an extraordinarily fixed and limited animal whose nature is absolutely constant. It is only by tradition and organization that anything decent can be got out of him.' For classicism, social order is essential to civilization. For romanticism, it is oppressive. The 1960s marked a new dawn of romanticism.

So monoculturalism came to be seen as trebly discredited. It reflected a false view of human ideals. It belonged to nationalism and its tainted offspring, war. And it was needlessly repressive of individuality and authenticity. For a while, almost any non-Western culture seemed to be a better option than the homegrown product. The Enlightenment had failed. The West had lost moral credibility. Let other cultures flourish; let a thousand flowers bloom. When the multiculturalists came to storm the citadel of Western civilization, they found the fort deserted, the soldiers fled.

So Britain was the country house; America the 'melting pot'. These were different phenomena but both were assimilationist. Minorities would have to lose their identity or remain at the margins. In England they would progressively resemble the old; in America they would dissolve into something new. But society had a single identity. Nations were communities of character. Each had its own culture, which newcomers were expected to adopt.

This is the background against which Horace Kallen mounted his theory of pluralism. He believed that ethnic and religious minorities would and should preserve their identity while sharing a common language and an overarching political system. It was an idea ahead of its time. In the tough world of the 1920s to 1940s, there were more pressing issues: depression, unemployment, then war. These called for national unity, not diversity.

Multiculturalism emerged, more as a fact than a value, in the 1970s in the wake of mass migration from non-Western to Western nations. It was not produced by, but found a supportive environment in, the intellectual mood of the time. The idea of one nation, one culture, had come to seem dangerous and wrong. But there was something else happening at the same time, of great consequence: the slow demise of morality itself, conceived as the moral bond linking individuals in the shared project of society. To this I now turn.

Chapter 4

The Defeat of Freedom in the Name of Freedom

It is indeed a truth, which all the great apostles of freedom ... have never tired of emphasizing, that freedom has never worked without deeply ingrained moral beliefs and that coercion can be reduced to a minimum only where individuals can be expected as a rule to conform voluntarily to certain principles.[1]

Friedrich Hayek

Man is a moral being only because he lives within established societies. There are no morals without discipline and authority, and the sole rational authority is the one that a society is endowed with in relation to its members. Morals do not look like obligations to us – and therefore can have no sense of duty – unless there exist about us and above us a power which gives them sanction.[2]

Emile Durkheim

One scene stays with me from my teenage years. It was the early 1960s. A new television programme had taken the public by storm. It was called *That Was The Week That Was*, or TW3 for short. It was one of the first of the satirical reviews of a new generation. The team of David Frost, Millicent Martin, Ned Sherrin and the rest took the news of the week and turned it into an often brilliantly funny series of sketches. It was to post-war British solemnity what *The Importance of Being Earnest* was to Victorian England. It was a nation unbending to laugh at itself. Subjects that had hitherto been sacrosanct – royalty, religion, authority figures – were all grist to its mill. The programme went out live, to allow it to comment on the latest news.

One of its most provocative features was a waspish weekly monologue by the journalist Bernard Levin. Levin was intelligent, combative, acerbic and deliberately provocative. On one occasion in 1963, as he was about to begin, a tall, upper-class Englishman walked onto the stage and said, with studied politeness, 'One minute, Mr Levin, before you begin; it won't take a minute. Would you stand up a second?' Levin, nonplussed, stood up. The man then hit him. He was angered, apparently, by a negative review Levin had written about a play in which the man's wife had acted. It was, for me at any rate, a defining moment. People didn't do that kind of thing, at least not on television, and certainly not with that kind of accent.

I forgot about it. But that image came back to me as one European country after another witnessed scenes of violence: by pickets during the miners' strike of 1983–84, rampaging football fans, drivers succumbing to 'road rage', single-issue lobbyists like the anti-poll tax protestors, environmentalists and animal rights activists, then by people angered by Danish cartoons or the Pope. Recall that in the 1940s, George Orwell, not a man given to misty-eyed sentimentalism, could write: 'The gentleness of the English civilization is perhaps its most marked characteristic.'[3] In 1946 the Hungarian humorist George Mikes observed that 'An Englishman, even if he is alone, forms an orderly queue of one.'[4] Where did the violence come from? Or rather, since violence is something to which all human groups are prone, how was it once kept in check, and why is it no longer? Something fundamental happened between the 1940s and 1960s, and I want in this chapter to track one dimension of that change.

The Enforcement of Morals

In the late 1950s and early 1960s a debate took place that established the parameters of much that has happened since. It was between a distinguished English judge, Lord Devlin, and the Professor of Jurisprudence at Oxford, H. L. A. Hart. Its theme was law, morality and society. How much of what we regard as moral should be translated into law? Ultimately the question was about society itself. Do we need a shared morality? Does society have a moral base?

These questions were occasioned by the 1957 Wolfenden Committee Report on Homosexual Offences and Prostitution. At that time, homosexual activity was illegal; it had been criminalized in 1885. The law led to some notorious cases, most famously that of Oscar Wilde who was found guilty of 'gross indecency' and served a prison sentence in Reading jail. The question now was: Should homosexual behaviour be decriminalized?

The Wolfenden Committee thought it should. In doing so it formulated a far-reaching principle. There is, it argued, a clear distinction between morality and law. 'It is not, in our view, the function of the law to intervene in the private lives of citizens.' Not everything that is immoral is, or should be, illegal: 'there must remain a realm of private morality and immorality which is, in brief and crude terms, not the law's business.' An act can be a sin but not a crime. Society may believe homosexual behaviour to be wrong, but to forbid it by force of law is inappropriate and over-intrusive. It should be decriminalized. It eventually was, ten years later.

The Report evoked a thoughtful response by Lord Devlin, who argued that the committee had overlooked a fundamental fact. There is such a thing as society and it has a moral foundation. Society is not just an agglomeration of individuals doing what they like so long as they do not harm others. It has a moral code into which citizens are socialized, and without which there cannot be a society:

> Society means a community of ideas; without shared ideas on politics, morals, and ethics no society can exist ... If men and women try to create a society in which there is no fundamental agreement about good and evil they will fail; if, having based it on common agreement, the agreement goes, the society will disintegrate. For society is not something that is kept together physically; it is held by the invisible bonds of common thought. If the bonds were too far relaxed the members would drift apart. A common morality is part of the bondage. The bondage is part of the price of society; and mankind, which needs society, must pay its price.[5]

Devlin's argument led in turn to the formulation of a counterargument by Professor Hart.[6] In his *Law, Liberty and Morality* (1963) he argued that the moral consensus presupposed by a society need not be as extensive and tightly fitting as Lord Devlin believed. There were, and are, areas within a given society that are left to individual conscience, and there is no universal rule telling us which belongs to personal choice and which to enforced consensus. In any case, such matters change over time. There was enough holding Britain together without that having to include a law forbidding homosexual behaviour. The committee in his view was right.

As Hart himself pointed out, his view was merely a restatement of a principle set out a century before by John Stuart Mill.[7] In his *On Liberty* (1859), Mill had maintained that 'the only purpose for which power can be rightfully exercised over any member of a civilised community, against his will, is to prevent harm to others. His own good, either physical or moral, is not a sufficient warrant.'

In Victorian England, Mill lost the battle. A century later, his successors won. The 1960s saw the enactment of a series of liberalizing laws. In 1961, suicide ceased to be a crime. This might seem a minor and obviously humane measure, but Hart spelled out its significance: it was 'the first act of Parliament for at least a century to remove altogether the penalties of the criminal law from a practice both clearly condemned by conventional morality and punishable by law'.[8] It was the beginning of the end of England as a Christian country; that is, one in which Christian ethics was reflected in law. It was a prelude to other and more significant reforms. In 1967 abortion was legalized, as was homosexual behaviour.

Collectively these changes represented a decisive move away from the idea that society had, or was entitled to have, a moral code at its base, a 'thick' or substantive morality covering many areas of life that might otherwise be regarded as private. Society was no longer conceived of in terms of a moral consensus. The law would intervene only to prevent individuals from harming one another. So long as that was avoided, individuals were free to live as they chose. It was the beginning of *society as a hotel.*

The liberal revolution took place against the backdrop of the heady days of the 1960s: the Beatles, the youth culture, Woodstock, hallucinogenic drugs, transcendental meditation and Eastern gurus such as the Maharishi Mahesh Yogi. It was a decade of what Mill called 'experiments in living'. It was also a time of theological controversy. The then Bishop of Woolwich had written a short theological text, *Honest to God*, which created a firestorm of debate around the phrase 'the death of God'. Could the traditional beliefs of the church still be maintained? Here was an Anglican bishop arguing otherwise, and the debate spread beyond the confines of Britain.

The liberal revolution of the 1960s was the culmination of a whole series of ideas that had been long in the making and involved thinkers such as David Hume and Immanuel Kant. The end result was the belief that morality could no longer be thought of as the code of a society. It was the choice of individuals. Only Nietzsche understood how momentous this revolution would be. In 1882 he wrote this in *The Gay Science*:

The madman jumped into their midst and pierced them with his eyes. 'Where is God?' he cried; 'I will tell you. We have killed him – you and I. All of us are his murderers. But how did we do this? How could we drink up the sea? Who gave us the sponge to wipe away the entire horizon? What were we doing when we unchained this earth from its sun? Where is it moving now? Where are we moving? Away from all suns? Are we not plunging continually? Backward, sideward, forward, in all directions? Is there still any up or down? Are we not straying, as through an infinite nothing? Do we not feel the breath of empty space? Has it not become colder?'[9]

Seven years later, Nietzsche went mad and spent the last eleven years of his life in care. Society without God, morality or meaning, was like being cast adrift in space. Yet when it happened, in the 1960s, it did so without drama. That was the effect of a century of intellectual deconstruction.

After Virtue

The first person to sound a warning that these developments might be fateful and dangerous was Alasdair MacIntyre in his 1981 book, *After Virtue*.[10] Moral language, he said, had broken down. All we have left is fragments of earlier beliefs. The words survive; the beliefs that gave them meaning do not. We are unable to have genuine moral arguments any more. We think we can, but we no longer have a shared language. Words merely provide our moral desolation with a front. Behind the scenery, all is emptiness.

What happens when we lose moral consensus? All that is left are sentences stripped of meaning. We think we are stating facts when, actually, all we are doing is expressing our feelings. Morality is reduced to taste. 'Good' and 'bad' become like *yum* and *yugh*: I like this; I don't like that. Imagine two people, one of whom says, 'I like ice cream,'; the other, 'I don't.' They are not arguing. Each is simply declaring his or her taste. Now imagine two people, one saying, 'I approve of abortion,' the other, 'Abortion is evil.' This does not sound like a mere matter of taste. For one, abortion represents a woman's right to choose, for the other, it destroys the foetus' right to life. We *do* argue about morality – or so we think.

That, said MacIntyre, is because we are left with fragments of earlier ages, when there were moral codes. Society has changed faster than our thought-patterns have. We have lost the basis of morality as a shared set of values holding society together. We are living 'after virtue'; that is to say, in an age in which people no longer have roles and duties within a stable social structure. When that happens, morality becomes a mere façade. Arguments become interminable and intolerable. The only adequate answer to an opposing viewpoint is: 'Says who?' In a debate in which there are no shared standards, the loudest voice wins. The only way to defeat your opponents is to ridicule them, make them look absurd, weak, reactionary, prejudiced. Hence MacIntyre's famous judgement that 'Modern politics is civil war carried out by other means.'[11] When words fail, violence is waiting in the wings. Violence, said Alan Brien, is the repartee of the inarticulate.

41

Political Correctness: From Thoughtfulness to Thought-Control

After Virtue appeared before the full flowering of a phenomenon that proved MacIntyre's point: political correctness. Political correctness began as a form of verbal etiquette.[12] The old became senior citizens. Racial minorities became people of colour. The handicapped became people with disabilities. That was appropriate and sensitive. We should avoid language that offends, stigmatizes, ridicules, diminishes or demeans. The Talmud has such a code.[13] It is called *lashon sagi nahor*, the language that calls the blind 'clear-sighted'. It takes people's feelings seriously and believes that concern for human dignity should be reflected in the way we speak.

Political correctness, however, did not end there. It moved on to stigmatize one Western convention after another as racist, sexist, heterosexist, ageist, and so on. Much has been written about political correctness. All that concerns me is why it appeared when and where it did. In the past, sensitivity-of-speech was good manners, civility, politeness. It was not *political.* How it became so is of the utmost importance.

If there is no agreed moral truth, we cannot reason together. All truth becomes subjective or relative, no more than a construction, a narrative, one way among many of telling the story. Each represents a point of view, and each point of view is the expression of a group. On this account, Western civilization is not truth but the hegemony of the ruling elite. Therefore, it must be exposed and opposed. Western civilization becomes the rule of dead white males. There are other truths: Marxist, feminist, homosexual, African-American, Hispanic-American, and so on. Which prevails will depend not on reason but on power. Force must be met by force.

Lacking a shared language, we must attack the arguer, not the argument. This is done by ruling certain opinions out of order, not because they are untrue – there is no moral truth – but because they represent an assault on the dignity of those who believe otherwise. So: Christians are homophobic. People on the political right are fascist. Those who believe in the right of Jews to a state are racist. Those who believe in traditional marriage are heterosexist. Political correctness, created to avoid stigmatizing speech, becomes the supreme example of stigmatizing speech.

One example: recall that in 1957 the Wolfenden Committee, then the cutting-edge of liberalism, declared that homosexual behaviour was a sin, but should not be a crime. In 2004, Rocco Buttiglioni, Minister for European Affairs in the Italian Government and in private life a Catholic, was chosen by the president of the European Commission, Jose Manuel Barrosso, to be its commissioner of justice. He was subjected to questioning by the Commission, during which he acknowledged that, as a Catholic, he believed that homosexual behaviour is a sin but should not be a crime. He was then disqualified from taking up office on the grounds that his *private moral convictions* were 'in direct contradiction of European law'. He described this as the 'new totalitarianism'. Right or wrong, one thing is clear: the new tolerance is far less permissive than the old intolerance.

It is also a complete reversal of the views of John Stuart Mill. According to Alan Ryan, Mill's argument in *On Liberty* had more to do with public opinion than legislation.[14] It is not only law that can take away our freedom, but also public ridicule and scorn. Mill wrote:

> The worst offence of this kind which can be committed by a polemic is to stigmatise those who hold the contrary opinion as bad and immoral men. To calumny of this sort, those who hold any unpopular opinion are peculiarly exposed ... [U]nmeasured vituperation employed on the side of the prevailing opinion really does deter people from professing contrary opinions, and from listening to those who profess them.[15]

Mill spoke bitterly about 'the peculiar evil of silencing an opinion'. How then did a movement that began by accepting Mill's views on liberty, eventually produce an outcome directly opposed to his views?

It happened because Mill believed in truth, and his postmodernist successors do not. They believe in power. When truth dies, its place is initially taken by personal choice. That is what happened in the 1960s. But the process does not stop there. The ruthless – those who seek to impose their views on others – sense the vacuum and exploit it. They mobilize opinion, using whatever is left of the once rich, now impoverished, public consensus.

What is left in the West are two concepts: rights and authenticity, the freedom to 'be yourself'. No traditional morality is translatable into this language, because traditional moralities speak about duties not rights, and about obligations not freedoms. So any traditional morality can be defeated using the new language. A Christian society on campus can be banned because it is 'homophobic': by holding to their beliefs, Christians are assaulting the rights of individuals freely to choose their sexual orientation. Any group defined by a moral code can be held to be prejudiced against those who do not share that moral code, and thus guilty of denying people's right to be otherwise. This is not fantasy. As we saw, it cost Rocco Buttiglioni his job. It has also turned every university into a potential battleground.

Nor does it stop there. If it did, the result would be a triumph for libertarianism, the idea that everyone is free to choose his or her own morality. But if 'authenticity' applies to individuals, it also applies to groups, among them religious groups. To understand the implications, perform the following thought experiment. A small group of radical Christians decide that Western society, having abandoned Christianity, is now hastening to its doom. They want to reverse that decline. They can no longer argue for the truth of Christianity. But they can mobilize political support for it.

They link up with radical Christians elsewhere. They document the persecution of Christians in many parts of the world: Nigeria, Lebanon, Saudi Arabia, Pakistan. They produce videos; they distribute them through the internet. They tell horrifying stories; they generate a discourse; they invent a word, 'Christophobia'. They study revolutionary methods. They create cells of activists, linked by email. They generate sympathy. Even those not otherwise inclined to be radical Christians are none the less shocked by what they see and hear. Meetings are held at campuses throughout the country. There is a groundswell of support.

Next, confrontations are staged. The radicals do something calculated to offend the authorities. They decide, for example, to interrupt every lecture on one campus with a prayer. The university authorities take action to ban the behaviour. That is what the radicals intended, and they are ready. They gather a large crowd carrying banners accusing the university of Christophobia. There are scuffles. Television crews, pre-warned, are there to record the scene. It is shown, that night, on the news.

Up and down the country, Christian groups stage protests. The university, fearing for its reputation, backs down. The radicals, having won a victory, plan further confrontations. They spread the news to groups in other countries. The protests become global. Every university now knows that it can no longer oppose the radicals. The university is local; the radicals are global. The radicals now have, in effect, a free hand on every campus.

The radicals are deeply opposed to homosexuality. The gay rights activists, having won the battle in the short term, lose it in the long. Their opponents have studied their methods and used them – more extensively and more ruthlessly. The radicals do not confront the gay rights activists directly. They merely ensure that they will feel deeply uncomfortable holding meetings on campus. The radicals have, in fact, undone the liberal revolution without once mentioning the word 'sin' or 'vice' or 'wrong'. All they have needed, in fact, is evidence that some Christians are being persecuted somewhere in the world; the technologies of video, internet and email; the words 'rights' and 'authenticity'; and the methods of revolutionary and totalitarian politics. This thought experiment is no mere hypothesis. Something very like it has already happened in Britain, according to the account given by Ed Husain in his recent *The Islamist.*[16]

What has happened in this scenario? Morality has mutated into politics. Morality is about virtue; politics is about power. Once virtue no longer makes sense to society as a whole – this is what MacIntyre meant by the phrase 'after virtue' – then power is all that is left. Of course that is not what John Stuart Mill or the Wolfenden Committee intended: quite the opposite. They sought a society in which people were free to act as they chose without the interference of others. And that is what happened at first. But there is a phenomenon whose significance in human affairs cannot be sufficiently emphasized: the law of unintended consequences. Processes, once begun, develop in unanticipated ways. Movements designed to maximize liberty are taken over by those opposed to liberty. It happened in the French Revolution, it happened in the Russian Revolution, and it is happening today. No one has better described what happens when the pursuit of truth becomes the will to power than Shakespeare in *Troilus and Cressida*:

> Force should be right; or rather, right and wrong,
> Between whose endless jar justice resides,
> Should lose their names, and so should justice too.
> Then every thing includes itself in power,
> Power into will, will into appetite;
> And appetite, an universal wolf,
> So doubly seconded with will and power,
> Must make perforce an universal prey,
> And last eat up himself.[17]

Intellectual Betrayal

Something else happens when morality dies. Some resort to power but others, who in another age might have offered resistance, become passive, even enthusiastic, bystanders. Ethics can mutate into aesthetics of a particularly violent, barbaric kind. Nietzsche associated this with the Greek god Dionysus. Freud called it *thanatos*, the death-instinct. One of the most shocking aftermaths of 9/11 was the response of two icons of European postmodernism, the composer Karlheinz Stockhausen and the social theorist Jean Baudrillard. Stockhausen waxed ecstatic about the destruction of the Twin Towers, calling it 'the greatest work of art imaginable for the whole cosmos ... Minds achieving something in an act that we couldn't even dream of in music, people rehearsing like mad for ten years, preparing fanatically for a concert, and then dying ... You have people that focused on a performance and then 5,000 people are dispatched to the afterlife, in a single moment. I couldn't do that. By comparison, we composers are nothing.'[18]

Asked by a reporter whether he was suggesting that art justified crime, he explained: 'It is a crime because the people were not agreed. They didn't go to the "concert". That is clear. And no one gave them notice that they might fly apart [*draufgehen*]. What happened there spiritually, this jump out of security, out of the everyday, out of life, that happens sometimes *poco a poco* in art. Otherwise it is nothing.' In Stockhhausen's aestheticisation of violence I heard an echo of the culture that allowed civilized and educated men to listen to Beethoven string quartets in Auschwitz-Birkenau while a million and a quarter Jews, and others, were being gassed, burned and turned to ash: mass murder as performance art.

In a lecture given shortly after 9/11, subsequently published as *The Spirit of Terrorism*, Baudrillard said:

> The moral condemnation and the holy alliance against terrorism are on the same scale as the prodigious jubilation at seeing this global superpower destroyed – better, at seeing it, in a sense, destroying itself, committing suicide in a blaze of glory. For it is that superpower which, by its unbearable power, has fomented all this violence which is endemic throughout the world, and hence that (unwittingly) terroristic imagination which dwells in all of us.
>
> The fact that we have dreamt of this event ... is unacceptable to the Western moral conscience. Yet it is a fact ... At a pinch we can say that they *did* it, but we *wished for* it ... When the two towers collapsed, you had the impression that they were responding to the suicide of the suicide-planes with their own suicide.[19]

Doubtless these are men of integrity and intelligence; doubtless there is an inscrutable logic to these intellectual impostures. But if I thought they represented a larger tendency in European thought, I would advise my children to leave Europe now and bring up their children as far away as possible.

In 1927, Julien Benda published a book called *Le Trahison des Clercs*, 'the betrayal of the intellectuals'. Benda's argument was that once intellectuals pursued truth and kept themselves above the political fray. Now, however, intellectuals had become politicized. 'Our age', said Benda, 'is indeed the age of the *intellectual organization of political hatreds.*'[20]

That seems to me an accurate description of what has begun to happen on university campuses worldwide. When boycotts, bans and excommunications begin to shape the environment inhabited by academics, journalists, unions and professional bodies, when contrary views are delegitimated and those who hold them excluded from arenas that were once regarded as citadels of free speech and the pursuit of truth, then we live in dangerous times. All it takes for evil to happen is for intelligent men to anaesthetize the moral sense of a generation. This may become the *trahison des clercs* of our age.

Where Conversation Ends, Violence Begins

So a series of events that began in the 1960s fundamentally changed the terms of society and moral debate. Until recently, serious thinkers argued that society depends on moral consensus. Without that, there is no such thing as society, merely the clamour of competing voices and the clash of conflicting wills. This view began to crumble with the rise of individualism. People began to see morality in terms of personal autonomy, existential choice, or the will to power. If morality is private, there is no logic in imposing it on society by legislation.

But if there is no moral truth, there is only victory. The pursuit of truth mutates into the will to power. Instead of being refuted by rational argument, dissenting views are stigmatized as guilty of postmodernism's cardinal sin: racism in any of its myriad, multiplying variants. Thus John Stuart Mill's greatest fear, the 'tyranny of the majority', or what has recently been called 'the dictatorship of virtue', has come to pass. Institutions once dedicated to intellectual freedom have become politicized.

So moral consensus disappears and moral conversation dies. Opponents are demonized. Ever-new 'isms' are invented to exclude ever more opinions. New forms of intimidation begin to appear: protests, threats of violence, sometimes actual violence. For when there are no shared standards, there can be no conversation, and where conversation ends, violence begins.

That is what, in retrospect, I saw in the assault on Bernard Levin in 1963. It was the first sign that structures of civility, restraint and the moral mediation of conflict, undermined by satire, are our only barriers against barbarism and the will to power. Mill foresaw this as well:

[W]henever and in proportion as the strictness of the restraining discipline was relaxed, the natural tendency of mankind to anarchy reasserted itself; the State became disorganized from within; mutual conflict for selfish ends neutralized the energies which were required to keep up the contest against natural causes of evil; and the nation, after a longer or briefer interval of

47

progressive decline, became either the slave of a despotism, or the prey of a foreign invader.[21]

Thus is freedom betrayed in the name of freedom, and tolerance destroyed in the name of tolerance. To a society that continues along this road, there is no happy ending.

Chapter 5

Victims

In multicultural politics it is an advantage to be injured. Every injury, every act of discrimination or disrespect, every heedless, invidious, or malicious word is a kind of political entitlement, if not to reparation then at least to recognition. So one has to cultivate, as it were, a thin skin; it is important to be sensitive, irritable, touchy.[1]

Michael Walzer

When people believe that their rights and their group pride have been injured by someone from another group, they are all too often ready to respond in a violent fashion that goes beyond any practical or instrumental use. Groups are a vital part of human social life and are necessary for survival, but they also reflect a built-in predisposition toward a certain pattern of antagonism.[2]

Roy Baumeister

On Monday 16 April 2007, Cho Seung Hu, a Korean student at Virginia Tech, went on a shooting rampage and killed 32 people. It was the worst massacre of its kind in American history, the latest in a sequence of horrors including Columbine, Colorado, in 1999. It was a shocking atrocity, and one must be very careful indeed in drawing any general conclusions from the acts of a disturbed and pathological individual.

Nonetheless, there were features of the case that made it a peculiarly modern crime. The pathology of evil is beyond the scope of this book; the story we tell ourselves about ourselves is not. 'Every age', wrote Christopher Lasch, 'develops its own peculiar forms of pathology, which express in exaggerated form its underlying character structure.'[3] The way we think and act, the imaginative resources we have for understanding ourselves, are given by the prevailing culture. Culture

49

does not determine how we act, but it shapes the account we give of why we act.

The killings took place in two phases. Between them Cho paused and took time to post a package of materials to an American broadcasting station. It included photographs, a long written statement and a video. They had been prepared beforehand and had taken weeks to assemble. Cho knew what he was doing. He gambled on the probability that if he sent these materials to a television network, they would be shown, however sickening they were. Like video-making suicide bombers, he counted on the media to give him a blaze of publicity, his 'fifteen minutes of fame'. They did.

This is something new and troubling. A world without strong networks of family and community is a world of strangers. It fails to answer to our need for recognition, emotional intimacy, the 'listening other'. In such a world people do strange things. They proclaim their principles on tee-shirts. They wear their designer labels on the outside. They confess not in the privacy of the confessional but in the publicity of Oprah Winfrey-style television programmes. They compete to be on *Big Brother* and other forms of Reality TV. The distinction between public and private becomes blurred. Lacking the supportive bonds of friendship, people communicate their needs and aspirations to strangers. Having lost the infrastructure of community, life takes on the character of Ancient Greece and Rome: the culture of public spectacle.

The new media democratize attention. Anyone can become a celebrity overnight by way of YouTube or MySpace. If we can do something eye-catching enough it will bring us to public notice in a way never before possible. To be sure, there is a positive side to this. It makes us aware of crimes against humanity far away. The Holocaust depended on secrecy; the internet strips secrecy of its veils. The downside is that it gives a new dimension to terror. This influenced the 9/11 attacks, subsequent suicide bombings and many other horrors of contemporary life. The age of global media has given birth to the new phenomenon of violence as photo-opportunity. Those who commit such atrocities calculate that an act that is sufficiently brutal or grotesque will prove irresistible to television networks and users of the internet. If attention is a reward, then ours is an age that rewards spectacular violence.

Cho's testimony was described in the press as 'rambling'. It was not. It was lucid and focused. It was a tirade of envy, resentment and rage. I want to focus on just one aspect of his statement: its self-righteousness. These are some of the things he said:

> You had a hundred billion chances and ways to have avoided today. But you decided to spill my blood. You forced me into a

corner and gave me only one option. The decision was yours. Now you have blood on your hands that will never wash off ... Thanks to you, I die like Jesus Christ, to inspire generations of the weak and the defenceless people ... Do you know what it feels like to be spit on your face and have trash shoved down your throat? Do you know what it feels like to dig your own grave? Do you know what it feels like to have your throat slashed from ear to ear? Do you know what it feels like to be torched alive? Do you know what it feels like to be humiliated and be impaled upon a cross and left to bleed to death for your amusement?[4]

These are, of course, the rantings of a madman. As it turned out, Cho had already been judged by a psychiatric hospital and a Virginia court to be mentally ill, a potential danger to himself and others. But there is something significant here. Cho had defined himself as a victim. He was the innocent party. In murdering more than thirty people, he was, in his own mind, defending and avenging himself. Never do people commit evil so brutally as when they believe they are doing so in the name of justice. They are innocent. It is the victims who are guilty. It was Cho's fellow students who, in his mind, were the instigators, the perpetrators, the danger, the threat. They had humiliated him. They had damaged his self-esteem. They had failed to hear his pain. There is much in this that is insane. But there is also something that is a commentary on our times: the psychology and politics of victimhood.

The Perpetrator as Victim

Roy Baumeister has shown in his majestic study, *Evil*, that people rarely do wrong believing it is wrong.[5] One of the marks of the pathological personality is that the person concerned believes himself justified in what he did. He was protecting himself from a threat. Someone had humiliated him, abused him, 'disrespected' him. Abusive husbands say that they have been abused by their wives. Many violent criminals believe that it is they who have been unjustly treated. They expect others to sympathize with what they have done. They see themselves as victims. And victims take revenge.

The same can apply to societies as a whole. Stuart Kaufman has shown how, in the former Yugoslavia, Slobodan Milosevic and Franjo Tudjman manipulated the stories Serbs and Croats told about themselves, playing on their fears and painting an image of themselves as heroic victims.[6] The history of the various groups in the Balkans is labyrinthine and complex, and there are many ways, as there always are, of constructing the narrative. Both leaders used ancient history to portray their respective groups' noble past and centuries-old grievances. They manipulated fear of others to make people feel threatened by the very existence of their neighbours.

Milosevic, in particular, played on the theme of the Battle of Kosovo in 1389 when the Serbs were defeated by the Ottomans, ushering in five centuries of Muslim rule. Contemporary fears can be greatly amplified when set in historic context, when people can be made to feel not only that they are acting in self-defence when carrying out a brutal assault, but that they are also avenging their ancestors and righting a remembered wrong. Once the emotional context has been set, people can come to believe quite extraordinary things. This is what one woman told the Reuters journalist Andrej Gustincic at the start of the Bosnian war:

> 'Do you see that field?' asks a Serbian woman, pointing to a sloping meadow by the Drina river. 'The jihad (Muslim Holy War) was supposed to begin there. Foca was going to be the new Mecca. There were lists of Serbs who were marked down for death,' the woman says, repeating a belief held by townspeople and gunmen. 'My two sons were down on the list to be slaughtered like pigs. I was listed under rape.' None of them have seen the lists but this does not prevent anyone from believing in them unquestioningly.[7]

Kaufman's study of this and other ethnic conflicts leads him to the conclusion that 'In mass-led conflicts such as these – clashes of self-proclaimed victims – the widespread acceptance of historical myths justifying hostility and the reality of long-standing popular hostility essentially is the explanation for ethnic war. The rest is details.'[8] The politics of victimhood is the most dangerous politics there is.

Hate is a virus. The human body has a defence against viruses: the immune system. So has the body politic. It is called the moral sense, the collective conscience. But just as a virus can neutralize the immune system by posing as part of the body's own defences, so hate can enlist the moral sense by the way it tells the story: we are victims just as our ancestors were. In so doing, it mobilizes a range of emotions: fear, revenge, honour, self-protection, self-righteousness, and above all a sense of justice.

One of the glaring weaknesses of philosophy through the centuries has been its failure to explain radical evil. We act rightly because of knowledge, said Plato; sympathy, said Hume; impartiality, said Adam Smith; rationality, said Kant. None of these explain how otherwise normal human beings come to commit truly horrendous crimes, especially when done in the name of a larger cause: God, ideology or the defence of a nation.

The people who murdered Jews and Muslims during the Crusades or burned witches in the sixteenth century were, as far as we can tell, normal human beings: loyal husbands, decent fathers, good neighbours. There was nothing different, 'evil', about them. Writing about Adolf Eichmann, one of the architects of the Holocaust, Hannah Arendt spoke about 'the banality of evil'. The Hutus who murdered 800,000 Tutsis and their sympathizers in a hundred days in Rwanda had lived among them for decades. The common factors in all these cases are change, fear, a sense of threat, the projection of that threat onto a scapegoat, and from there to murder as self-defence.

The book of Genesis, in its account of the first sin, highlights the fact that Adam and Eve defined themselves as victims. Confronted by God, Adam blames Eve: 'The woman you put here with me—she gave me some fruit from the tree, and I ate it.'[9] Eve blames the serpent: 'The serpent deceived me, and I ate.' It wasn't me. It was someone else. I was a victim. Someone else was the guilty party. The biblical verdict is unequivocal. Once we deny responsibility and define ourselves as victims, paradise is lost.

The Politics of Victimhood

There is a vast difference between pathological and non-pathological victimhood, and I intend no comparison whatsoever. There *are* real victims. There is injustice and oppression, inequality and exclusion, and in the past whole groups – Jews, blacks, gypsies, women, homosexuals – found themselves subjugated, marginalized, ill-treated and ignored. Those injustices must be fought and ended. That surely is a given. Sympathy and compassion, the emotions we feel toward victims, are among the constitutive elements of the moral sense. They define what is best in the great ethical and religious traditions. Nothing I say in this chapter should be taken as qualifying these emotions and the acts they evoke.

What is profoundly dangerous is the *politicization* of victimhood: its transfer from individuals to groups, and from there to the public square. In every age there are victims and we must help them. 'Do not stand idly by the blood of your neighbour,' says the Bible.[10] 'Learn to do right,' says Isaiah. 'Seek justice. Relieve the oppressed. Defend orphans. Plead for the widow.'[11] What is new and dangerous is the culture of victimhood. It involves the blurring of the boundaries between the personal and the political. It has to do with what Philip Rieff called 'the triumph of the therapeutic'.[12] It also involves a fateful shift in politics: from the individual to the group.

Recall that the liberal revolution of the 1960s was undertaken in the name of the individual. It was the individual who had rights; the individual who should be free to live as he or she chooses so long as there is no harm to others. The 2007 Berlin Declaration of the European Union makes this explicit: 'For us, the individual is paramount. His dignity is inviolable. His rights are inalienable.' The American Declaration of Independence used similar language: 'all men are created equal' and are 'endowed by their Creator with certain unalienable Rights ...' This is classical liberalism, with its roots in the biblical idea that each individual is created in the image of God. Liberal politics at its best is, or aspires to be, class-, colour-, gender-, race- and religion-blind.

There were excluded groups. Eventually, after a struggle, they were accorded equal rights. In many cases the process is not yet complete. Yet the ultimate victory was not in doubt. Western civilization is predicated on the dignity and integrity of the individual. That is not to say that the Bible cannot be quoted to justify oppression. It can. Abraham Lincoln said about the defenders and opponents of slavery alike: 'Both read the same Bible and pray to the same God, and each invokes His aid against the other.'[13] But, in the end, the dominant strand in Western thought is that our ultimate focus is on the individual as such, prior to any attributes: male, female, black, white, rich, poor, Jew, Christian, believer, non-believer. It is the individual who has rights, freedom, a claim to dignity and access to justice.

A series of changes took place, as we have already noted, after the 1960s. The divides that had driven politics hitherto, especially class and wealth, became less salient. Other, more 'lifestyle' issues took their place. At first these were construed in terms of the individual, but eventually they came to be framed in terms of groups: first Jews, then African-Americans, then women, then gays. It was not merely that these groups sought equal rights, though they did. The real change was that they defined themselves as oppressed. This was a fundamental shift: from classical liberalism to neo-Marxism spliced with postmodernism. Far from seeking recognition as individuals, they sought it as groups, defined not in terms of socio-economic class, but in terms of race, gender, sexual orientation and eventually religion.

This was a seismic shift. Liberal politics does not deny the significance of groups. We are who we are because of the various groups to which we belong. What liberal politics did, however, was to create space for such groups *outside the political domain* in that crucial third region between the individual and the state known as civil society. We belong to this neighbourhood, that church, this professional body, these charitable organizations. They give us our sense of identity, our ideals, our opportunity to be bound to others in bonds of altruism. But in the political domain we enter on equal terms with everyone else, as individuals possessed of inalienable dignity. The shift from individuals to groups, far from being an advance, was a regression to a pre-modern political dispensation: from the nation state to the corporate state, the state as a composite of different classes and confessions.

To this was added something quite new. In the medieval corporate state, groups negotiated for political and economic advantage. In the liberal state, individuals negotiated for the right to live as they chose so long as they did no harm to others. In the postmodern state, groups negotiate for something never before held to be the business of politics: recognition, regard, self-esteem. Culture became political. So did self-image. The traditional curriculum of canonical texts – the Bible, Shakespeare and the rest – was held to represent the hegemony of dead white males, and must therefore be changed. For it leads excluded groups to have a negative self-image, and this impacts on their life-chances. Marx had spoken about economic oppression. His latter-day successors speak about psychological oppression: our group under-achieves because it is discriminated against, if not explicitly then implicitly. This is an offence against the right of each group to self-esteem. We are the victims, not of a crime, but of a culture. We are the new oppressed.

This leads to the politics of competitive victimhood. We have been wronged. We are looked down on. We have a claim to what Bertrand Russell once called 'the superior virtue of the oppressed'. All this is true. But it cannot become political without destroying the very basis of liberal democracy, which is built on the threefold separation between nation, group and individual: between state, civil society and private life. When individual feelings (negative self-image) become part of the self-definition of the group, and when groups call for remedial action by the state, then *identity politics* or *the politics of recognition* is born. This is at the heart of contemporary multiculturalism and constitutes its greatest danger. As Michael Walzer has written:

> The members of oppressed groups have been encouraged – mistakenly, I think – to believe themselves injured above all by the disrespect of the dominant others and to seek the signs of proper regard. But a permanent state of suspicion about the demeaning or malicious things that are about to be said or done is self-defeating. It leads too often to a dead-end politics of anger and resentment.[14]

A decent society is one in which people work to redress disadvantage and deprivation. There are marginalized groups; there are groups that have suffered greatly in the past. There is everything to be said for a politics that strives for equal opportunity and human dignity. But there is a great difference between a future-oriented politics and one that focuses on grievances of the past; between a culture that emphasizes responsibility and one constructed around a greatly expanded notion of rights; between one that defines people as victims and one that helps genuine victims to recover their capacity for action and self-determination. Politics is about power and the distribution of resources. It is not about the psychology of self-esteem or the allocation of blame. When these boundaries are blurred, the result is deeply damaging to the good group-relations on which an ethnically and religiously diverse society depends.

From Agent to Victim

The culture of victimhood negates the moral basis of the Judaeo-Christian tradition. What makes that tradition distinctive is its emphasis on personal moral responsibility, the beliefs that we are free to choose, that we are made by our choices, and that we are morally accountable for the way we act.

This is set out early in the Bible in God's words to Cain before he murders Abel. 'If you do what is right, will you not be accepted? But if you do not do what is right, sin is crouching at your door; it desires to have you, but you must master it.'[15] We have a disposition to do wrong, for we are driven by our desires. Other people also have desires. Sometimes both cannot be satisfied. The other stands in my way. So I am faced with a choice. Do I regard the other as an obstacle to be overridden or removed? Or do I recognize his or her integrity as another person with the same desires and rights as mine? Cain chose the first, and killed Abel. Challenged by God he replied, 'Am I my brother's keeper?' meaning: Am I responsible for his fate? The road from denial of responsibility to violence and murder is slippery and short.

What Judaism and Christianity share, though they describe it in different ways, is a sharp sense of the power of evil and the struggle the moral life represents. Judaism calls it the evil inclination; Christianity, original sin. But we can overcome it: in Judaism, by the good inclination; in Christianity, through divine grace. So we are not the victims of powers beyond our control. Those powers meet in the mind, the heart, and the soul, and we must choose. That choice, between good and evil, the blessing and the curse, life and death, is endlessly reiterated in Moses' speeches in the book of Deuteronomy. Fate is in our hands. We are what we choose to be.

That is perhaps the single greatest difference between Judaism and Christianity on the one hand, and on the other the culture of Ancient

Greece. The Greeks believed in *moira* or *ananke*, the inexorable decree
of fate, often foretold by an oracle. Hence the story of Oedipus. Laius,
Oedipus' father, is told by the oracle that he will be killed, and his place
usurped, by his son. To avoid this fate, the infant Oedipus is left
chained to a rock to die. He is found, rescued and brought up by a
humble family, not knowing who his true father is. He is told by an
oracle that he will kill his father and marry his mother. To avoid this, he
leaves home. He meets a stranger. They argue, fight, and the stranger
dies. The stranger is, of course, Laius. The power of the drama lies in
the fact that everything the characters do to circumnavigate fate brings
them closer to its realization. That is the essence of Greek tragedy.
Human freedom is an illusion destined to be shattered on the
unyielding rock of inevitability.

Towards the end of his *God, a Biography*, Jack Miles makes a fascinating distinction between Greek and Shakespearean tragedy.[16] In
Greek tragedy the determinants of fate are external to the agent. They
are outside his or her control. In Shakespearean tragedy they are
internal. They form a struggle in the mind of the hero. That is what
makes Hamlet unlike Oedipus. In the case of Hamlet, the conflict lies
within: between 'the native hue of resolution' and 'the pale cast of
thought'. As Miles puts it: 'It is precisely the profound effect of the
Bible on European society that explains why Shakespearean tragedy is
as unlike Greek tragedy as it is.'

The difference lies between a culture of *tragedy* and one of *hope*. If we
have freewill then we are not slaves to fate. If at the heart of reality
there is a forgiving presence then we are not condemned by guilt.
'Penitence, prayer and charity avert the evil decree', goes one of the
most famous Jewish prayers. There is no fate that is inevitable, no
future predetermined, no outcome we cannot avert. Near the beginning of his *Antigone*, the French dramatist Jean Anouilh makes the
same distinction from precisely the opposite point of view:

> Tragedy is clean, it is restful, it is flawless ... In tragedy nothing is
> in doubt and everyone's destiny is known. That makes for tran-
> quility. There is a sort of fellow-feeling among characters in a
> tragedy: he who kills is as innocent as he who gets killed: it's all a
> matter of what part you are playing. Tragedy is restful; and the
> reason is that hope, that foul, deceitful thing, has no part in it.[17]

There are tragic cultures and there are hope cultures and, though
some combine elements of both, they are ultimately incompatible. In
hope cultures we are agents. We choose. Therefore the outcome is
unpredictable. It depends on what we decide, and that cannot be
known in advance. In tragic cultures we are victims. We are acted on by

forces beyond our control. They will eventually defeat even the strongest. The question is: why did the West move from a hope culture to a tragic one, from moral agency to victimhood?

Science and the Death of Freedom

What makes human action free is that it is future-oriented. It is action directed to a purpose. We seek to create a state of affairs that has not yet happened. The language of freedom is written in the future tense. We are not imprisoned in our past, nor are we condemned endlessly to repeat it. That we acted a certain way before does not mean that we will act in the same way again.

There is an asymmetry between past and future. The past is unchangeable; the future is not. The past is closed; the future open. That is the deep meaning of the verse in which Moses at the burning bush asks God who he is. God's reply, *Ehyeh asher ehyeh*, is often translated as 'I am who I am.'[18] This entirely misses the point of the original which literally means 'I will be what I will be.' God exists in the future tense, because he is the God of freedom. God is not part of nature. He created nature. Therefore he stands outside it. He is not bound by it. He is free. And to the extent that we are in God's image, we too are free. The gift God gives us is freedom itself. We too will be what we choose to be.

This sense of freedom was deeply undermined by the Enlightenment. One of its driving ideas was the search for explanation independent of religion. The paradigm was science. In science, knowledge is based on no prior conviction or creed but simply on observation and inference. Regular coincidences of two phenomena, X and Y, lead to the formulation of laws of the form, 'If X happens then, all other things being equal, so will Y', or in short, 'X causes Y.' Scientific explanation is the search for causal relationships.

But a cause always precedes its effect. A stone thrown at the window causes the glass to shatter. The shattered glass does not retroactively cause the stone to be thrown. Scientific explanation is thus, by definition, backward-looking. The past causes the present. This may be fine for natural phenomena. It is anything but fine for human action. It would mean that if our acts have causes, they lie in the past. All talk of the future – intention, motive, aspiration, aim – is essentially meaningless. We may have the thought that by doing X we were seeking to bring about Y, a not-yet-realized future. But this is an illusion. We *think* we are free. In fact our acts are causally determined. It follows that if science can fully explain human behaviour and everything we do is causally determined, then we are not free agents. We are victims of forces beyond our control. To be sure, practitioners of the social sciences are fully aware of the difference between physical events and human acts. The problem lies not in the social sciences themselves but in a popular culture (sometimes aided and abetted by popular scientists) that fails to recognize the limits of causal explanation. A 'scientific' culture is a tragic culture in the Greek sense. We are Laius or Oedipus, driven against our will to an unavoidable fate.

The history of the past three centuries has been the story of the progressive dethronement of the idea of human freedom. For Auguste Comte, human action was determined by the same laws of matter that explained the orbits of the planets and stars. For Spinoza, all relationships were causal. The universe, including the human universe, is governed by immutable laws. For Karl Marx, human behaviour is determined by economic forces; for Freud, by unconscious and primal drives. For Durkheim, they are governed by society. Durkheim's most famous theory was that suicide – normally thought of as a supremely personal decision – is related to structural features of society, most significantly *anomie*, the breakdown of moral order. For neo-Darwinians and evolutionary psychologists behaviour is caused by our genes. They, in turn, are the result of chance and necessity, random genetic mutation and the pressures of natural selection.

Hence the paradox, the hidden contradiction, at the very heart of the Enlightenment project. On the one hand, we believe we are unprecedentedly free to do whatever we choose. On the other, the very idea of human freedom has come under unprecedented assault. We think we act because we choose. In fact, however, what we do has nothing to do with what we choose and everything to do with what our genes, our class, our parents, our society or our evolutionary origins have made us.

Nowhere can this be more clearly seen than in jurisprudence and the logic of punishment. For centuries (up to and including Kant), people believed that punishment was retribution for wrongdoing. Today, almost no one believes in retribution or the theory of justice on which it rests. Retribution presupposes guilt which presupposes freedom. Today, however, to a greater or lesser extent, we are all regarded as victims of our background, our genes, our social circumstance, our upbringing. Hence the strange phenomenon for which it would be hard to find a precedent, that often today courts evince more consideration for the criminal than for his or her victim (the Restorative Justice movement is an attempt to redress this imbalance).

Rights and Recognition

The second revolution has to do with rights, specifically the right to self-esteem. I will have more to say about rights in chapter 11, but suffice it to say that the concept was born in the seventeenth century as part of the theory of social contract. Rights belonged to the idea of limited government. They were a defence against excessive intrusion of the state into the lives of individuals.

The state was built on a social contract in which individuals transferred the free exercise of some of their powers to a central authority: the king, ruler or government. They did so to protect themselves from the twin dangers of lawlessness within and foreign conquest from without. If the cure was not to be worse than the disease, there had to be some powers individuals did *not* hand over. In the language of the American Declaration of Independence, they were 'inalienable'. For Hobbes this was the right to life; for Locke the right to property; for Jefferson, 'life, liberty and the pursuit of happiness'. Whatever the list, the meaning was clear. Rights were a limit on state power. They defined a territory in which the individual was free to exercise responsibility for his or her fate.

In the mid-twentieth century, rights became the opposite: an argument for more government intervention, not less. It was for the government to provide education, full employment, welfare benefits, medical treatment, pensions and so forth. What had been done previously mainly by voluntary or self-help groups – churches, charities and friendly societies – became, in the second half of the twentieth century, governmental functions. Rights ceased to be a defence of the individual *against* the state. They became claims by the individual *on* the state. That makes sense for material goods. It makes much less sense for psychological goods.

Self-esteem and rights come together in the politics of recognition. If self-esteem is part of human dignity, then we have a right to it. If our identity is bound up with our group, then our group has a right to it. If rights are a claim on the state, then the state has a responsibility to ensure it. Both movements, from agency to victimhood, and from rights-as-freedoms to rights-as-claims, are in the same direction: from a world in which our behaviour is the result of our choices to one in which it is the product of external forces. This, in the most profound sense, is the politics of unfreedom. It is intellectually confused and morally damaging.

It does not make sense to say that I have the right to demand that you think well of me or the group to which I belong. I do not have the right to insist that you have any opinions whatsoever, for it is your inalienable right to think as you choose. That freedom is fundamental to a free society, and in a free society I may not purchase my freedom at the expense of yours. Yes, I should have the right to be protected against incitements to violence against me or my group, but that is all. In a free and diverse society I must live with the fact that some people will think that the way I live is wrong. That is the price I pay for the freedom to think that the way other people live is wrong. Without that I do not have the freedom to think at all.

Identity politics is deeply and inexorably divisive. If the withholding of recognition is a form of oppression, then one way of achieving recognition is to show that I have been oppressed. The logic is as follows: the group to which I belong is a victim; it has been wronged; therefore we are entitled to special treatment. This gives rise to an endlessly proliferating list of the aggrieved. Each of their claims is surely true, but you cannot build a free society on the basis of these truths, just as you cannot heal trauma by endlessly attending to your wounds. A culture of victimhood sets group against group, each claiming that its pain, injury, oppression, humiliation, is greater than that of others. We have suffered; we are victims; therefore you must put it right.

A liberal society is one in which we respect the equal dignity of all. But that is not because we respect every way of life, every code or creed. It is because we respect something more fundamental than codes or creeds, namely the human person as such. We hold human life sacred, regardless of what people do with their lives. We honour people's freedom to choose even if we regard their choices as reprehensible and wrong. We have equal dignity; we have the freedom to 'be ourselves'; we have the freedom to belong to this or that group. But we do not have the right to be well-regarded, to be thought highly of. People do not win respect by insisting on the right to be respected. Respect is earned: that is what makes it respect.

The most surprising thing I learned from the many Holocaust survivors I have known is that they did not define themselves as victims. They concentrated on surviving. They focused on the future. Most did not speak about the past, even to their children. They knew that if they turned back to look on the destruction they would, like Lot's wife, be unable to go on. Some did look back: many survivors, sometimes decades later, committed suicide.

The best we can do for victims, individually and collectively, is to help them recover their power over their own lives, their self-confidence, their willpower, their capacity for action and self-determination. One of the great figures of the twentieth century, Viktor Frankl, discovered in the concentration camps that the greatest source of the will to live is the idea of a task not yet completed, a call to some work not yet done.[19] In the nightmare kingdom where everything was done to make the victims lose their sense of humanity – seizing their

61

possessions, shaving their hair, starving them, giving them numbers instead of names – he found that there was one freedom that could not be taken away: the freedom to decide how to respond. Even that one sliver of freedom was enough in many cases to restore the will to live. Those who have a 'why', he used to say in the name of Nietzsche, can withstand almost any 'how'.

Health, happiness, optimism, hope: these things are the products of a sense of control over one's life. That means taking responsibility. The flight from responsibility into victimhood is the oldest of all human temptations. As we saw, the Bible attributes it to the first human beings. But it is negative, destructive, it robs us of trust in the world, it leads us to see fate as a conspiracy directed against us. It leads us to the impotence of anger and the anger of impotence. The best way of curing a victim is to help him cease to think of himself as a victim.

The politics of victimhood is bad politics.[20] The psychology of victimhood is bad psychology. A victim is by definition an object not a subject, passive rather than active, a done-to rather than a doer. If you see yourself as a victim, then you locate the cause of your condition in something outside yourself. That means that you cannot change your situation. This is the condition Martin Seligman calls 'learned helplessness', and it leads to depression, fear and resentment.

The Voluntary Victim

That Monday in April 2007 at Virginia Tech, as Cho Seung Hu was murdering his victims, a 76-year-old engineering professor Liviu Librescu was about to begin his class. He was a Holocaust survivor born to Romanian Jewish parents. His father had been deported by the Nazis. He himself was sent as a child to a Soviet labour camp. Returning to Rumania after the war, he was forced out of academic life because of his Zionist sympathies. Eventually, after a long campaign, he was able to emigrate to Israel.

In 1986 he spent a sabbatical in America and decided to stay. He loved teaching, and refused to retire. Hearing gunshots nearby on that fateful morning, he rushed to the classroom door, holding it shut while his students escaped through a window. When the killer fired shots at the door, they hit him. He died; his students lived. One of the survivors wrote to Librescu's wife about that last moment: 'He was holding the door closed and looking over his shoulder to make sure everybody else was safe. It was the bravest thing I have ever seen.'[21] I find it moving that a man who survived two of the worst tyrannies of history, dedicated the rest of his life to learning and teaching, and ended it by choosing to die rather than let his students become victims.

Chapter 6

Technology and the Fragmentation of Culture

'Tis all in pieces, all coherence gone ...[1]

John Donne

On 12 September 2006 Pope Benedict XVI delivered an academic lecture at the University of Regensburg where he had previously taught as a professor of theology. His theme was religion and reason, his thesis that religion and reason belong together. In the course of the lecture he quoted a fourteenth-century Christian scholar who made a negative observation about Islam. It was, perhaps, a careless line. It may, some argued, have been distorted in translation; others suggested that the Pope had made it clear that he did not subscribe to the view he quoted. At first there was no reaction. Within days, however, a global protest had been organized. There were condemnations from political leaders in Egypt, Somalia, Iran, Iraq, India, Malaysia, Pakistan, Indonesia, Yemen and Turkey. There were angry protests throughout the world. In London, demonstrators carried placards calling for the Pope's execution. A fatwa was issued in Pakistan. Effigies were burned in Basra. Churches were set on fire in Gaza. In Somalia an Italian nun was murdered. In Iraq, churches were bombed. In Baghdad two Christians were stabbed and killed. The Vatican issued an apology. The Pope himself apologized twice. Eventually, passions cooled. But scars remained.

Because of the ease and speed of electronic communications, an argument can go global overnight. People email their friends at home and abroad. Messages are amplified and multiplied via long lists of e-addresses. Campaigns are orchestrated. People's passions are aroused. Because it is easy to present a case in your own words, with your own slant, the temptation is overwhelming to portray the issue in terms of black and white: they are the persecutors, we the persecuted. So not only is the message distributed throughout the world, it is also distorted. Passions are inflamed. Protests mount. The temperature rises. Tensions explode. Within days, the argument goes global. The facts of the case, the context, and the other side of the argument are completely lost. By now, the mood is out of control. There is little you can do but back down, keep quiet and wait for the moment to pass, hoping that no irreparable damage has been done. The new media have the power to defeat most forms of conflict resolution. They are themselves vehicles of conflict creation and conflict intensification.

Almost anything anywhere can now become a worldwide cause célèbre if a handful of individuals choose to make it one. And the decontextualization that is the trademark of the internet means that the facts become more or less irrelevant. What matters is that someone, somewhere, feels offended: whether rightly or wrongly makes little difference. Communities are split apart. Individuals are enlisted in causes they do not understand, for reasons that may be spurious, adding fuel to an argument in a place they have never been, between people they do not know, on a subject they do not understand. Suspicions are raised, fears heightened, and societies divided. Paranoia thrives in cyberspace. Conspiracy theories are legion. Complex events are broken down into conflicting narratives of victimhood. Technologies create climates. The new information technology generates the cultural equivalent of global warming.

Print and the Nation State

Information technology is of the essence when it comes to social and political structures. There is nothing given about the way people see their identities beyond the basic ties of the kinship group. At various periods humanity has been organized into bands, tribes and confederations. There have been nations for a long time: Jews trace their national history to thirty-three centuries ago. There have been states – bodies politic – for a long time as well. The Mesopotamian city states go back to the dawn of civilization. So why is the *nation state* a relatively recent phenomenon, going back no further than the eighteenth century?

The short answer is that until recently politics and culture did not have the same boundaries. There were empires: political structures that brought under a single rule cities, provinces and nations whose members spoke different languages, practised different religions and lived by different customs and traditions. If empires were wise, they did not interfere too greatly with local cultures. Other than ensuring political loyalty and guarding against rebellion, they tended to believe in live-and-let-live, not as a matter of tolerance but of practical wisdom.

Impose your own faith on a subjugated people and you could incite rebellion, as the Greeks and the Romans found in the case of Jews. Rulers of empires controlled the key instrumentalities of power. Beyond that, they tended not to interfere with local culture, at any rate at a grass-roots level.

Even within a single country there was often not a single culture. Different regions had different dialects, sometimes different languages. In medieval France, writes Achille Luchaire, 'the country had disintegrated into provinces, and the inhabitants of each province formed a kind of little nation that abhorred all the others'.[2] A trace of that remains. As de Gaulle said: how can you govern a country with 246 different kinds of cheese? Different classes had different codes of conduct. Those who were part of the court practised 'courtesy'; people in towns (*civis*) were civil; in cities (*urbs*) they were urbane; in the countryside (*rus*) they were rustic, i.e. unpolished, plain, unrefined. Until the Industrial Revolution most people lived in small local communities. The squire, the local church, the school, bound people together in a dense web of interconnections that constituted local custom and culture. Government was top-down and relatively light. Culture was communal, not national in the modern sense.

What changed? According to Benedict Anderson in his influential book *Imagined Communities* it was the spread of print-based technologies.[3] Until the sixteenth century, cultures were 'sacral'. They believed in sacred texts written in holy languages. Chinese ideograms, the Latin of the Christian Bible and the Arabic of the Koran were believed to be not just conventional signs but mirrors of reality. In pre-print societies only a minority is literate, societies are hierarchical, and the variegated ranks they represent are themselves seen as reflections of the structure of the universe: the sun, the moon, the stars, the 'great chain of being'. Time had a meaning quite unlike what it has for us. Look at the stained-glass windows of medieval churches or illustrations of manuscripts and you will see the scenes and figures anachronistically portrayed. The buildings and the clothes people wear are taken from the time of the artist, not from antiquity. People had no sense of the past as 'a foreign country, they do things differently there'.

The arrival of printing, the spread of books, the development of accurate timekeeping and affordable watches changed all this. Together they secularized time and space. By 1500, at least 20 million books had been printed; in the sixteenth century there were a further 150–200 million. The seventeenth century saw the development of newspapers. By the end of the eighteenth century, Britain was manufacturing some 200 thousand watches a year. Words were no longer seen as sacred. Scholarly languages such as Latin were replaced by books, especially Bibles, in the vernacular. There was a vast spread of literacy, as well as the diffusion of a single national language throughout towns and the countryside.

Newspapers, too, transformed consciousness. Hegel said that for modern man reading the papers had taken the place of morning prayers. No longer were people dependent on word-of-mouth communication to know what was happening throughout the world. The daily press meant that large numbers of people followed the same news, told in the same words, in the same language at the same time. Newspapers helped create a sense of national community. The growth of railways brought the need for standardized timekeeping across large geographical areas. Once time had been measured in terms of activities – church services, for example. It now became homogenous across a tract of territory. Time was neutral, abstract, empty, an arena within which people could co-ordinate their activities.

So for the first time national cultures began to emerge, defined by a common language, literacy, shared texts, newspapers, and shared time measured by clocks and watches. Local cultures and languages began to wane. So too did international languages such as Latin. Words were no longer seen as pictures of ultimate reality. Travellers now knew, as did their readers, that there were thousands of languages and hundreds of cultures. Language was simply a set of conventions that united those who lived within a given territory. Time ceased to be 'the moving image of eternity', a vertical link joining past, present and future. It became the horizontal plane, the empty stage, on which contemporaries co-ordinated their activities. So Anderson argued.

Not everyone agreed. Ernst Gellner in his *Nations and Nationalism*, for example, put the opposite case.[4] It was not culture that produced the nation, but the nation that generated the culture. The reason was industrialization. The Industrial Revolution transformed culture in two fundamental ways. The modern economy required bureaucratic consistency, the like treatment of like cases. It also needed efficiency: the selection of the best means to a given end. Together these constituted 'rationality' and spelled the end of traditional ways of doing things. No longer were decisions made because that is how they had been made in the past. Nor were jobs allocated because of birth, family or class. Industrial society created the need for an interchangeable workforce: people who could operate standard procedures and adapt to new techniques. This required, for the first time, a national system of education. No longer would knowledge be the privilege of an elite. It would be available, in standardized forms, to everyone. The key institutions would be schools:

> The employability, dignity, security and self-respect of individuals, typically, and for the majority of men now hinges on their

education; and the limits of the culture within which they were educated are also the limits of the world within which they can, morally and professionally, breathe. A man's education is by far his most precious investment, and in effect confers his identity on him. Modern man is not loyal to a monarch or a land or a faith, whatever he may say, but to a culture.[5]

Whether Anderson is right or Gellner, the nation state was constituted by the spread of a uniform culture made possible or necessary by new technology. Technology, culture and the nation state go hand-in-hand. It follows that if new forms of technology, especially information technology, fragment culture, they will threaten the very existence of the nation state. That is what is happening today. The new instantaneous global communication technologies are not marginal to how we live our lives. They affect the most fundamental ways in which we think, act and associate. Other technological advances change particular aspects of life. Information technology changes life systemically. It restructures consciousness; it transforms society.[6]

Such changes happen very rarely. There have been four major developments in the past. The first was the invention of writing, in ancient Mesopotamia. That gave birth to civilization. For the first time one generation could hand on what it knew to the next, beyond the capacity of human memory. Knowledge became cumulative. A specific 'knowledge class' emerged. Record keeping became possible. So did large bureaucracies. The result was a growth in trade and the division of labour. The first city states were born.

The second, the invention of the alphabet, led to the growth of monotheism and a quantum leap in the human capacity for abstract thought. The first society to integrate the alphabet was ancient Israel. The people of the Bible were the first to conceive of the possibility of a society of universal literacy and equal dignity. Over the next few centuries virtually all the great civilizations were born. This was what is widely known as the 'axial age'.

The third was the development of the codex, the book as a set of pages bound together, rather than as a continuous scroll. Shortly thereafter, Christianity appeared, as did the written forms of what had hitherto been Judaism's oral tradition. This too generated cultural change. Scrolls tend to be proclaimed, codices to be read. Scrolls encourage narrative continuity. The codex allows for multiple versions and interpretations. One vivid example is the difference between the unified narrative of the Pentateuch and the four versions of the Gospels.

The fourth, as we have seen, was the invention of printing in the mid-fifteenth century. Directly or indirectly this led to all the phenomena we recognize as modern: the Reformation, the growth of science, the birth of the individual, the interiorization of morality from public code to private conscience, and all the other developments that led to industrialization, urbanization and the nation state.

We are living through the fifth revolution. The growth of computing, the modem, the mobile phone, the internet, email and satellite television will change life as much as, possibly more than, any epoch-making development in the past. Ours is a transitional age, as revolutionary as the move from hunter-gatherer to agriculture, or from agriculture to industry. We are at the beginning of this process, and we have no idea where it will lead. Prediction depends on 'all other things being equal'. When change is of this order, all other things are not equal. This means that in principle they are unpredictable.

The nation state was the product of a specific technology: printing. This made possible the diffusion of a single culture throughout a territory roughly coextensive with a political unit, a sovereign state. The combined impact of global internet technology and multiculturalism may well fragment European nations beyond repair, yet we have no other political entity capable of holding societies together. The nation state *is* a phenomenon of culture. In the eighteenth and nineteenth centuries, the great age of European nation states, the idea of a 'multicultural society' would have sounded like a contradiction in terms. Perhaps it still is.

Global Media and the End of Autonomous Cultures

With the new technologies, what changes? First, the idea of an autonomous national culture disintegrates. I witnessed this myself on one memorable occasion. For the whole of the first Gulf War, January–March 1991, I was in Israel together with my family. Thirty-nine times we had to put on our gas masks and go to a hermetically sealed room as Iraqi SCUD missiles rained down. People wanted to know what was happening. To prevent a national scare and to avoid broadcasting information that might have been helpful to Iraq, state radio and television gave out limited information. In massive numbers, people began to install satellite television so that they could watch the progress of the war on CNN. At a stroke, Israel ceased to be an autonomous culture.

In the early days of Zionism, figures such as Achad Ha-am argued that Israel should become what he called a 'spiritual centre' for the Jewish people. This was known as cultural Zionism. Israel would become the birthplace of a renascent Hebrew culture, built around the revival of Hebrew as a spoken and written language – the first time in

2,000 years that Jews had the chance of creating an indigenous culture. This happened in the early years of the state. What I saw was the collapse of this whole edifice almost overnight. Thirty or more television channels were being beamed into Israeli homes, many of them American. Israelis began picking up English with an American accent. Irretrievably thereafter, their culture would become ever more cosmopolitan. John Donne said, no man is an island. After satellite television, no culture is an island either.

The nature of authority changes also. If power or influence is measured by the ability to command attention, multi-channel satellite television and the internet decentralize power and deconstruct the voice of authority. During the Second World War, Winston Churchill was able to address the nation by radio. So, in the United States, could Roosevelt. Today if a prime minister or head of state makes a statement, there are a myriad of other channels to watch or listen to. One voice, any voice, is lost in the noise. No one can monopolize attention any more.

Culture fragments. The sheer multiplicity of channels means that culture is no longer a garment woven of many threads. There are dedicated channels devoted to sport, or history, or film, or music. Music itself is segmented into classical, pop, rock, indie, dance, electronic, R&B, soul, hip-hop, rap, hard rock, metal, country, jazz, folk, reggae, blues and golden oldies, each with their own devotees. Newspapers cover a range of topics. Now, via websites, you can preselect the kind of news you are interested in and never encounter the rest. The idea of culture as a national landscape of the mind is gone. Instead we live in non-intercommunicating rooms.

Until recently, national cultures were predicated on the idea of a canon, a set of texts that everyone knew. In the case of Britain they included the Bible, Shakespeare, anthologies of poetry such as Palgrave's *Golden Treasury* or Quiller-Couch's *Oxford Book of English Verse*, and the great novels: Jane Austen, Dickens and some modern classics. The existence of a canon is essential to a culture. It means that people share a set of references and resonances, a public vocabulary of narratives and discourse. Until the early 1950s a politician could quote the Bible and expect people to know what he was alluding to. No longer. I was once sitting next to a former editor of *The Times*. We did an impromptu experiment. The Prime Minister was about to speak. We agreed to listen for quotations. What would he take to be a shared text? The answer was predictable. The only quote he used was a television advertising slogan. Without a canon, there is no culture, only a series of subcultures.

Attention span has been radically reduced. Episodes of television series that would have lasted an hour are today being edited down to five minutes to fit the format of YouTube. Every so often I do a radio

69

reflection, *Thought for the Day*, on the BBC's morning news programme. Some years ago, the slot was reduced from three minutes to two minutes 45 seconds on the grounds that no one can concentrate for three minutes any more. In Victorian Britain, Gladstone thought nothing of speaking uninterruptedly for three hours. On television news, major political addresses are cut to, on average, eight seconds or two sentences. Speechwriters know this and plan the key soundbite in advance. This spells the end of argument, nuance and context. To see this, try reading any speech from the Victorian era. You will find it hard to get to the end of a single sentence, with its labyrinthine structure and subordinate clauses. The age of subtlety is dead.

To survive and attract an audience in the almost unlimited competition of today's media, radio and television news tend to focus on the dramatic. The result is adversarial. It is exciting when extreme opinions clash; boring when speakers agree. What emerges is a picture of the world that emphasizes irreconcilable difference and understates vast areas of consensus. In January 2001 the then Archbishop of Canterbury convened a gathering in Alexandria, Egypt, of the leading Muslim, Jewish and Christian religious leaders in the Middle East. They signed an agreement, the Alexandria Declaration, committing themselves to non-violent conflict resolution. It was potentially one of the most important steps towards peace in decades. The coverage in the Western press was almost non-existent. This helped to confirm the suspicion in the minds of politicians in the region that there is no role for interfaith dialogue in any peace process – as Track 2 diplomacy, for example. This is a terrible mistake. What it means is that the image of religion in the media is one of conflict, hate, violence and terror. We should not then be surprised if that is what religion becomes. Perception shapes reality. The media give us role models, and if they are violent and angry that is what at least some young people will aspire to be.

Globalization Unites and Divides

The situation is in many ways worse. As long as there were newspapers and a small number of radio and television news networks, people were exposed to a variety of views. Today we attend to only those media we choose; we focus only on the stories that interest us; we watch the channels whose interpretations we find congenial. If we see the world one way we will watch Al Jazeera; if another, we will watch Fox. We can, in effect, filter out the voices with which we disagree. We are exposed to a selectively edited version of reality.

This is massively amplified by the phenomenon of blogs, which often present the news in highly tendentious ways. One of the most significant uses of email address lists is to spread particular articles or snatches of television around the world. So whatever your particular reading of reality, if it is expressed by someone in the media, someone else will email it to you. The result is that our prejudices are confirmed, and need never be disturbed.

The reverse is also true: you will be sent emails of articles and interviews that exemplify your worst fears. The result is that many people, especially those whose access to news is through one of the new digital media, have a dualistic experience of the universe: us and them, the children of light against the children of darkness. It is not accidental that many of the most popular films – *Star Wars, Lord of the Rings, Superman, Batman, Spiderman, et al.* – have the same narrative structure: the hero battling against apparently overwhelming forces of evil. This used to be known as Gnosticism or Manichaeism, and it was alive and well at the time of the Dead Sea Scrolls and the Nag Hammadi gospels.

Paranoia and conspiracy theories, as I have said, thrive on the internet. Within hours of 9/11, stories were already circulating that the attack was the work of the CIA, or Mossad, the Israeli secret service. A book with this theme became a best-seller in France. Similar fantasies abound, about AIDS, SARS, even the tsunami. Successive opinion polls throughout the world have shown that in some countries large numbers of people believe these myths. They are only the tip of a much larger iceberg of fear bred by the new media, which create virtual enclaves of people huddling together for mutual support in a confusing and dangerous world.

This effect is hugely multiplied by one of the historic shifts of culture from the written word to the electronic image. For two thousand years, civilizations, or at least their elites, acquired their knowledge through texts and the act of reading. Leonard Shlain in *The Alphabet versus the Goddess*[7] makes the fascinating suggestion that text cultures privilege the left, analytical, hemisphere of the brain. Now, through television and internet-based videos, we have become a culture of the visual image. A single image – the photograph of a naked Vietnamese girl in agony after a napalm bombing raid – is said to have cost America the Vietnam War.

The contemporary strategists of terror have studied the impact of visual media and have become virtuosi in manipulating them for their own purposes: 9/11 was devised on the model of a Hollywood disaster movie. The recent spate of hostage takings, beheadings and other gruesome brutalities were calculated to inspire fear and repulsion. Images have immense emotive power. They have near-zero informational content. Without context, they might mean anything. There is evidence that terrorist groups in the Middle East have devised scenes specifically for the world's television cameras to suggest massacres that have never taken place. Other groups have used videos – of suicide bombers for example – to amplify anxiety. Western media have proved highly vulnerable to such manipulation. Some journalists may, others may not, understand how they are being used by the enemies of freedom to undermine freedom, but no major exposé has taken place.

So the new media are more effective in communicating hate and fear than anything the West has known since the witch-hunts of the sixteenth century. Exploiters of the internet in particular know that it is easier to present a black-and-white, good-and-evil, believers-and-infidels view of events than a nuanced account of complex conflicts. They know how easy it is to generate sympathy and support by painting a picture of persecution. They also know that, at a distance, facts become blurred. The locals know what happened, but communication is now global, and how am I in England to check whether an account of events far away is true or false, accurate or overstated? Distance destroys nuance. The further away you are, the easier it is to magnify events and demonize the other side.

This is especially so if the conflict has, or can be portrayed as having, a religious dimension. Religion, as already stated, is global. That is why it has emerged as the most powerful form of allegiance in a global world. National identity has nowhere near this degree of salience. Even the larger national groupings – the Commonwealth, say, or the European Union – have nothing like this power. An event in France may not send shockwaves round England. A skirmish on a Sydney beach is unlikely to evoke strong emotions in Brighton. But an assault on Muslims, Jews, or Hindus somewhere *does* have that effect among Muslims, Jews and Hindus elsewhere. They constitute a worldwide 'us'. If our fellow believers have been assaulted, humiliated or insulted, we feel the injury, anger and pain. Global media reinforce global identities, and of these, religious identities are by far the strongest. So a slight provocation can create an avalanche. No longer is it sufficient for politicians or religious leaders to reckon with the impact of their words on their intended audience. They must factor into the equation the possible impact of those words, detached from their original context, on countries thousands of miles away, that they may never have visited and whose culture they do not understand.

The new technologies, by uniting people globally, divide people locally. They strengthen non-national affiliations. They can make people feel more Hindu or Muslim or Jewish than British. They turn ethnic minorities into 'diasporas', people whose home and heart is elsewhere.[8] They amplify fear and erode trust. They simplify issues and weaken the politics of nuance and compromise.

Those who seek to build bridges find it difficult to make their voice heard. Eventually they give up trying, for in the current climate, the risk is great. In a polarized atmosphere, peacemakers are seen by their own side as betrayers. Culture as a nationwide unifying force atrophies. So does politics as the arena of mediated resolution. If you want to attract media attention today, it helps to be either exceptionally aggressive or exceptionally violent. The aggressive and violent know this and take full advantage. In an environment of information-overload, 'noise', the loudest, angriest voice wins. And so we find ourselves back in Hobbes' state of nature, in which life is nasty, poor, solitary, brutish and short. This has not happened in the West yet, but it has done so in ever more areas of the world.

The nation state was brought into being by one form of communications technology. It is today endangered by another. Whether the media, or politicians, or we, will recognize the danger in time, no one can be sure. Without a national culture, there is no nation. There are merely people-in-proximity. Whether this is sufficient to generate loyalty, belonging and a sense of the common good is an open question. National cultures make nations. Global cultures may yet break them.

Chapter 7

The Inward Turn

But epochs sometimes occur in the life of a nation when the old customs of a people are changed, public morality is destroyed, religious beliefs shaken, and the spell of tradition broken ... The country then assumes a dim and dubious shape in the eyes of the citizens; they no longer behold it in the soil which they inhabit, for that soil is to them an inanimate clod; nor in the usages of their forefathers, which they have learned to regard as a debasing yoke; nor in religion, for of that they doubt; nor in the laws, which do not originate in their own authority; nor in the legislator, whom they fear and despise. The country is lost to their senses; they can discover it neither under its own nor under borrowed features, and they retire into a narrow and unenlightened selfishness.[1]

Alexis de Tocqueville

Nothing can save England, if she will not save herself. If we lose faith in ourselves, in our capacity to guide and govern, if we lose our will to live, then, indeed, our story is told.[2]

Winston Churchill

In my first year at primary school I was given a lesson in identity. The Queen was about to have her coronation. And we, five-year-old citizens of the world, were given a present. A coronation spoon. To this day I am not quite sure what we were supposed to do with it. We were too young to drink tea or coffee and the spoon was too small for cornflakes. But no matter. We were British, loyal subjects of Her Majesty, and I had a spoon to prove it.

It's hard to believe it now, but every visit to the cinema in those days ended with the playing of the national anthem. Everyone stood still. To a young child it was solemn, mysterious, impressive. Who does that nowadays? We in the Jewish community still regularly sing the National Anthem at major events (on the 350th anniversary of Anglo-Jewry in 2006 we even sang it in Hebrew). We pray for the royal family each week. We have in our prayer books a special blessing, two thousand years old, which we say whenever we see the Queen. We are British and proud of it, but we know in our heart of hearts that such sentiments have become quaint and are less widely shared than they used to be by the public as a whole.

Identities, ironically in a globalizing world, have become smaller, more localized, more sectional and segmented. Where once immigrant groups were known by their place of origin (Pakistani-British, Irish-American), today they are more likely to be known by their religion. So we become Christians, Jews, Hindus, Sikhs, Muslims, and not even with a hyphen connecting us to -British. Meanwhile other labels have emerged that in the past would not have been seen as identities at all: women, gays, lesbians, people of colour, the differently abled, senior citizens. Once these were *what* we were, not *who* we were. Almost anything, it seems, can nowadays become the basis of an identity, except what once united us: being British.

Why? Undoubtedly what I was picking up in my childhood was the after-effect of war. National identities are never as intense as they are then. That was especially the case during the Second World War when, during the Blitz, Britain's own cities were part of the battleground. Increasingly over the years, though, national identity has become problematic. Nationalism has become discredited. It led to two world wars and the Holocaust; it could become a vehicle for racism and xenophobia. And the nation state fails to fit the scale of modern problems: it is too big for the small ones and too small for the big ones. Nations cannot combat global warming, international terror, and the sins of large corporations alone. At the same time, central government feels too remote for problems of social exclusion and inter-ethnic conflict.

More specifically, Britain lost self-confidence. Was it the exhaustion of the war? Was it, as Dean Acheson famously said, that Britain had lost an empire and not yet found a role? Was it the humiliation of Suez, or the fact that British identity was too linked to class consciousness, a hierarchy deeply unsuited to the modern world? Was it the industrial unrest of the 1970s, the strikes, the three-day weeks, the 'Who governs Britain' elections of 1974 and the 1978–79 'Winter of Discontent'? Then there was the twin impact of European Union on the one hand, devolution of Scotland and Wales on the other, inviting us simultaneously to a larger-than-British identity, and a smaller-than-British one: no more Union Jack, no more Britain, just England.

One way or another, by the end of the 1970s there was a feeling that

Britain's greatness lay in the past, to be recaptured in period dramas and memorialized by tele-historians but no longer a living reality. Books have been published with titles like *England: An Elegy*, *The Abolition of Britain*, and *In Memory of England*.[3] Alan Bennett neatly captured the downsized national ego: 'So little, England. Little music. Little art. Timid. Tasteful. Nice.'[4]

It was not always thus. In *Areopagitica* (1603) Milton famously wrote that 'God is decreeing to begin some new and great period in his Church ... what does he then but reveal Himself to his servants, and as his manner is, first to his English-men'.[5] Milton believed that England was the new chosen people: 'Why else was this Nation chos'n before any other, that out of her as out of *Sion* should be proclaimed and sounded forth the first tidings and trumpet of Reformation to all Europ.' In the nineteenth century, Cecil Rhodes said, this time with a more imperial inflection, that 'to be born English is to win first prize in the lottery of life.' In one of Saki's short stories two upper-class gentlemen have time on their hands and want to do something to ease their boredom. 'Let's stroll around looking effortlessly superior,' says one to the other. At times that was a full-time occupation.

No longer. Perhaps the new non-identity has to do with the self-deprecation that is so much part of the English character, and which Kate Fox neatly defines as 'one-downmanship'.[6] But at a certain point, self-disregard becomes dangerous and demoralizing. George Orwell was passionate on the subject, especially in the case of intellectuals before and during the Second World War:

> Within the intelligentsia, a derisive and mildly hostile attitude towards Britain is more or less compulsory, but it is an unfaked emotion in most cases. During the war it was manifested in the defeatism of the intelligentsia, which persisted long after it had become clear that the Axis powers could not win ... English left-wing intellectuals did not, of course, actually want the Germans or Japanese to win the war, but many of them could not help getting a certain kick out of seeing their own country humiliated ... In foreign politics many intellectuals follow the principle that any faction backed by Britain must be in the wrong.[7]

Lionel Trilling and Daniel Bell made the same point about America.[8] Trilling gave it the name, 'the adversary culture', the hostility of intellectuals toward normal feelings of loyalty, belonging and national pride. It continues today in the tendency to see British history as an irredeemable narrative of class, snobbery, imperialism, racism and social exclusion. Hence the equation: British, bad. UnBritish, good.

This applies especially to the religion of Britain: Christianity. This has become almost a national ritual. We have become accustomed to the regular flow of stories of Christianity being marginalized, if not humiliated in the public domain: the places where Christmas has been renamed Winterval so as not to offend non-Christians; the banning of Christian symbols in the public domain; a worker at Heathrow airport forbidden from wearing a cross; hot cross buns discontinued at Easter because their symbolism might distress; Christian student societies at risk because their very existence implies homophobia.

It reached a climax in the run-up to the Millennium celebrations at the Dome. The Millennium was the two-thousandth anniversary of the birth of Christianity. Yet for a prolonged period it seemed as if the ceremony would proceed without a Christian prayer. Repeated representations on behalf of the Church of England failed to change the minds of the organizers. The Archbishop of Canterbury threatened to boycott the event. The press spoke about a constitutional crisis. The Queen was due to be present, yet she was also head of the national church. It was an absurd moment. Without some Christian presence, the Millennium meant nothing other than a page in a diary, the mere passing of time. Eventually the crisis was resolved and there was a Christian prayer, but it was close, and it revealed not only how deeply British elites are alienated from the national religion, but how marginal Christianity has become to public expressions of British culture.

This is not yet, but it comes close to, self-hatred. That is something Jews know about: we can fairly claim to have invented it (Arthur Koestler once memorably said, 'Self-hatred is the Jew's patriotism'). It occurred in mainland Europe in the late nineteenth and early twentieth century, as Jews internalized the negative image others had of them. It represents the breakdown of an identity, and nothing good can come of it.

If that applies to a minority, all the more so to the majority. Tolerance requires self-confidence. Lack of self-confidence generates anxiety and xenophobia. There was a direct connection between Hitler's rise to power and German feelings of humiliation after the First World War. Hitler understood this and was able endlessly to play on it, promising to restore the nation's shattered pride. Nations, like individuals, need self-respect, and may be driven to destructive courses of action to achieve it. Undermining a nation's institutions is playing with fire, as those who do so discover, but always too late.

Nowhere else does multiculturalism reveal its inner contradictions so clearly as here. It began as a commitment to value all cultures. Then it became valuing all cultures equally, a completely different proposition. Then it became valuing all cultures except your own. That is when it becomes pathological. You *cannot* value all cultures except your own – because all other cultures then know that your valuation is worthless.

One who does not respect himself cannot confer respect on others. Lack of self-confidence on the part of a nation is dangerous. When it comes to integrating minorities, it is disastrous.

This is where George Orwell's distinction between patriotism and nationalism is essential.[9] Nationalism, which he opposed, is 'inseparable from the will to power'. Its abiding purpose is to secure ever more prestige for the nation: 'Nationalism is power hunger tempered by self-deception.' Patriotism, by contrast, he defined as 'devotion to a particular place and a particular way of life, which one believes to be the best in the world but has no wish to force upon other people'. That for me is the difference between arrogance and pride. Pride means valuing others because you value yourself. Arrogance means devaluing others so that you can have a high opinion of yourself. National arrogance is unforgivable. National pride is essential.

In Search of Identity

Identity abhors a vacuum. We feel the need to know who we are, of which story we are a part, to which group we belong. We fear 'the forms of things unknown'. We crave 'a local habitation and a name'. In the great encounter at the burning bush, Moses' second question to God was 'Who are you?' His first was 'Who am I?' To know the answer to that question seems for most people to be singularly important. Indeed for some sociologists, this has become the master-question of modernity.

For most of history, people had their identity circumscribed by birth. That determined where you lived, what occupations were open to you, whom you married and what status you held. All of these things were opened up by the various forms of geographic, occupational and social mobility. We have moved, as sociologists say, from status to contract, from fate to choice. Unprecedentedly free to decide what we will become, we seem to need to base our sense of self on something we did not decide, something solid on which to stand in an ever more fluid world. Modernity has been defined as a condition of permanent identity crisis.

Anthony Appiah, Amartya Sen and others have written eloquently on what it means to be cosmopolitan, a citizen of the world, belonging nowhere and everywhere, at home in any place, at ease in any culture.[10] One writer has called this the shift from *pilgrim* to *tourist*.[11] Those who have achieved this state often wonder why others do not aspire to it. Why can't everyone be like that, they ask: a hodge-podge, a mix, a bit of this, a bit of that? Why not be like Walt Whitman: 'Do I contradict myself? / Very well then I contradict myself / I am large, I contain multitudes.'[12] Why can't we live and let live? Why can't we just *get along*?

79

To which the answer is that cosmopolitanism is itself a highly specialized identity, sustained (often in academic life or international business) by close and regular contact with fellow cosmopolitans. Cosmopolitans *don't* get along with non-cosmopolitans. They find them too passionate, too argumentative, too obsessed with minor shibboleths (Freud's 'narcissism of small differences'), too simple-minded, too given to black-and-white, good-and-evil dichotomies, too credulous, too divisive. Cosmopolitanism can be, and often is, its own unconscious form of parochialism.

Whether, as some argue, we retain genetic traces of our hunter-gatherer ancestors, or whether it is simply that we first learn who we are in dialogue with our class-, place- or religiously-selected significant others, we seem to need the binary opposition of us-and-them. From this flow all our feelings of belonging and all our estrangements and fears. The more closely we huddle as Us, the more distant we stand from Them. Identity unites and divides: unites as it divides. You can't, it seems, have one without the other. The good and bad news about identity, the warm fuzzies of togetherness and the cold spikies of separation, go hand in hand.

The Return of the Tribes

What sociologists discovered, beginning in the 1960s, was that ethnic differences were not disappearing, in either Britain or the United States. Neither British, country-house style assimilation nor the American melting pot were functioning as people expected. As war-time national unity began to fade, so suppressed identities re-emerged. One key factor was the black civil rights movement in the States. But other groups – Irish, Polish, German, Dutch, Italian and Jewish – also found their voice. Sociologists began to note that 'the various ethnic varieties of Americans, excepting the intellectuals, tend to remain within their own ethnic group and social class for most of their intimate, primary group relationships'.[13] One of the first to give warning of the possible consequences was Gerhard Lenski:

Our current drift toward a 'compartmentalized society' could easily produce a situation where individuals developed a heightened sense of religious group loyalty combined with a minimal sense of responsibility for those outside their own group. In a more compartmentalized society there is good reason to fear a weakening of the ethical and spiritual elements in religion and a heightening of the ever dangerous political elements.[14]

80

That was in 1961. By 1975, Harold Isaacs was sounding the alarm in his *Idols of the Tribe*: 'Out of the break up of old power systems or the fragile instability of new ones comes the onset of turmoil and instability for all people in all their relationships.'[15] When larger identities, such as national ones, became too amorphous and vague, people would turn to more primordial bonds of belonging, 'vestiges of a more secure past'. Especially in an age of rapid and accelerating change, they felt the need 'to get behind walls that enclose them once more, if only in their minds, in a place where they can feel they belong and where, grouped with their kind, they can regain some measure of what feels like physical and emotional safety.' So, concluded Isaacs, 'we are refragmenting and retribalizing ourselves'.

There was one other factor that, for obvious reasons, interested me. In America, unlike Europe, Orthodox Judaism represented only a minority of the total Jewish population. The reasons for this are complex, but until the 1960s it was assumed that it would die out completely in the United States. Orthodox rabbis ordained before the War felt that their role was to give their faith a decent burial. It could not survive in an individualist, materialist, future-oriented culture. In 1965, sociologist Charles Liebman published an essay, 'Orthodoxy in American Jewish Life' in which he reached the diametrically opposite conclusion: 'The only remaining vestige of Jewish passion in America resides in the Orthodox community.'[16] Liebman was right, as subsequent decades have shown.

Two factors of immense significance were at work here, as in almost every other ethnic identity. The first is that ethnicity per se does not last. It fades over time. First-generation immigrants remember the language, dress, customs and cuisine of home; their children less so. What lasts is religion. This alone can be handed on across the generations. Culture does not command; religion does. Nor does culture define. Enjoying sushi does not make me Japanese; liking Monet does not make me French. But Judaism makes me Jewish, and not Christian, Sikh or Zoroastrian. If I wish to hand on my identity to my children, it will have to have a religious dimension. That is one reason why, in Britain, minorities no longer define themselves in terms of place of origin but by religious affiliation.

The second is that the form of religion most effective in the postmodern world is the one most opposed to postmodernity. So long as national identities were strong, religions tended to emphasize integration. We saw in an earlier chapter how Orthodox Jewish day schools like the Jewish Free School were, a century ago, agents of anglicization. In the curriculum, Shakespeare counted for more than the Talmud. Today the opposite is the case. If national identity is negatively charged, then a countercultural religious identity will take its place.

Here for example is a Muslim writer, Ed Husain, describing his child-hood in state schools in London's East End: 'In the multicultural Britain of the 1980s and 1990s we were free to practise our religion and develop our culture as we wanted. Our teachers left us alone, so long as we didn't engage in public expressions of homophobia or intimidation of non-Muslims. But Britishness and the British values of democracy, tolerance, respect, compromise and pluralism had no meaning for us ... Islamism provided us with a purpose and a place in life.'[17] When the larger culture fails to provide a sense of belonging – when society resembles a hotel – then identity will be found not in integration but segregation.

The Collapse of the Integrationist Ideal

My parents were reasonably religious Jews. Yet they sent me and my brothers to Christian schools. What led them, like many others of their generation, to send their children to be educated in institutions that did not share their faith? First, they wanted us to integrate, to be good Englishmen, to be able to navigate the wider society in which we lived, to take our place in it, be at home in it and make our contribution to it. But there was another reason, no less important.

Schools in those days embodied an ethos profoundly congruent with Jewish values. They taught responsibility, duty, self-restraint, respect for authority, the importance of hard work and honest achievement, and a traditional ethic which included, among other things, a sense of the integrity of marriage and the place of sex within a code of fidelity and commitment. I don't know if my parents formulated these thoughts explicitly, but intuitively they sensed that there was nothing we would be taught that would be detrimental to our growing up as Jews, other than that they did not teach us about Judaism. That, they felt, could be dealt with by supplementary schooling.

Few committed Jewish (or Catholic, Muslim or Sikh) parents would make the same calculation today. Our children's generation passion-ately want to send their children to faith schools. I led a campaign for Jewish day schools,[18] as did my predecessor Lord Jakobovits. We knew they were the key to Jewish continuity. The question a sociologist might ask, though, is why this imperative, which goes back to the dawn of Jewish history, has resonated so strongly in recent decades? Why, generally, have faith schools become so popular in a profoundly secular culture?

One can only speculate. But the following might reflect the thoughts of many traditionally minded parents: The wider society is no longer congruent with our values. We do not want our children taught by fashionable methods that leave them bereft of knowledge and skills. We do not want them to have self-esteem at the cost of self-respect, won by hard work and genuine achievement. We do not want them to be taught that every difference of behaviour reflects an equally valid life-style. We do not want them to be moral relativists, tourists in all cultures, at home in none. We do not want to take the risk of our children taking drugs or alcohol or becoming sexually promiscuous, still less becoming teenage mothers (or fathers).

Many parents do not want there to be a massive gap between their children's values and their own. They do not want moral values undermined by a secular, sceptical, cynical culture. Nor do they believe that the countervailing influences of place of worship, supplementary schooling and home will be enough. For the values of the wider secular culture are not confined to school. They are present in the ever-more-intrusive media of television, the internet, YouTube, MySpace, and the icons of popular culture.

Consumerism, relativism, a moral free-for-all, are not values they want their children integrated into. On the contrary, these are what they want their children to be protected from. You do not have to be deeply religious to recognize that the *Wertfreiheit*, the value-free-ness, of contemporary culture is no match for a religious ethic tried and tested across the centuries. Still less is it likely to give those who internalize it the necessary self-restraint and moral intelligence needed to live a rooted, meaningful, stable life in a rapidly-changing, stress-filled world.

I suspect that people of quite moderate religious convictions – Jewish, Christian or otherwise – look on today's society and wonder whether they really want their children to cohabit without marriage or become parents without a matrix of responsibilities. Perhaps their thoughts are simpler and more direct. They visit local schools and see that those that have a strong religious ethos tend to do better in their academic results, have better discipline, and inculcate a stronger sense of citizenship than those that do not.

In February 2007 a report by the Teacher Support Network showed that 49 per cent of teachers in the UK had been assaulted by pupils.[19] The attacks included stabbing with scissors and nails, attempted strangulation and hands trapped in doors; 39 per cent had had their personal property defaced or damaged. More than one-in-two teachers had considered quitting because of pupil indiscipline. Caring parents do not want their children exposed to a culture without rules, discipline, authority or self-restraint.

So they look elsewhere. Parents even pretend to be religious in order to get their children into a faith school. Voltaire, who did not believe in God (*Écrasez l'infâme*, he said about religion: 'Crush the infamy'), wanted his butler and valet to be religious because he believed that would make them less likely to defraud him. Large numbers of people may have ceased to believe in God, but still believe that religion is the best way, perhaps the only way, of inducting their children into a code and community of values.

So, within two generations, an average Jewish family that once would have had no qualms about sending their children to a non-Jewish school, will today want, even fight, to get their children into the nearest Jewish school. A similar scenario is replicated in other faiths. Segregation is rapidly replacing integration as an ideal. *Communities are turning inward.* As English, or British, identity becomes ever more vacuous, so people search for their values elsewhere, and find them in religious communities.

This would be fine if religious communities were local forms of a nationwide set of ideals. But there is no nationwide set of ideals. It is not that religious people have abandoned society: it is that they feel society has abandoned them. Rightly or wrongly, they feel that society has been hijacked by single-issue lobbies, a cosmopolitan-cynical media elite, and fashionable postmodern doctrines, and that to protect themselves and their children they must turn away from society toward a local community: a church, temple, synagogue or mosque.

Here then is the paradox: the inward turn is good news for Jews, Christians, Muslims, Hindus, Sikhs and everyone else who cares for the continuity of traditional identities. But it is not good news for all-of-us-together. For what it means is that we have ceased to see ourselves as all-of-us-together.

From Nation State to 'Little States'

Two philosophers in particular have issued warnings about this. The first is Michael Walzer. In his *Spheres of Justice* he argued that if a society lacks overall cohesion – he called this a 'neighbourhood' as opposed to a 'club' – then it will generate resistances: 'if states ever become large neighbourhoods, it is likely that neighbourhoods will become little states'.[20] Their members 'will organize to defend the local politics and culture against strangers'. To 'tear down the walls of the state is not . . . to create a world without walls, but rather to create a thousand petty fortresses.' That is exactly what is happening in Britain, indeed across Europe, today.

As the bonds of shared morality, culture and responsibility weaken, so significant numbers of people are turning from society to community, from nation to group, from large- to small-scale associations. Even within groups there is a measurable move from 'church' to 'sect', from inclusive to exclusive forms of belonging. The integrationist ideal is dying. The segregationist alternative is gathering strength. When quite moderate people (those in favour of marriage, for example) begin to define themselves *in opposition to* the prevailing culture, danger signals should start flashing. A society of 'a thousand petty fortresses' is not a society at all.

Walzer's analysis is mild in comparison with Alasdair MacIntyre's already mentioned masterpiece, *After Virtue*. At the end of the book he wrote the following sombre words:

> It is always dangerous to draw too precise parallels between one historical period and another; and among the most misleading of such parallels are those which have been drawn between our own age in Europe and North America and the epoch in which the Roman empire declined into the Dark Ages. None the less certain parallels there are. A crucial turning point in that earlier history occurred when men and women of good will turned aside from the task of shoring up the Roman *imperium* and ceased to identify the continuation of civility and moral community with the maintenance of that *imperium*. What they set themselves to achieve instead – often not recognising fully what they were doing – was the construction of new forms of community within which the moral life could be sustained so that both morality and civility might survive the coming ages of barbarism and darkness.[21]

In other words, when the groups that make up society turn inward, a civilization is in danger of coming to an end.

I do not share MacIntyre's pessimism, but neither do I dismiss it lightly. Twenty-six centuries ago, the prophet Jeremiah sent a letter to the Jewish exiles in Babylon: 'Seek the peace of the city to which you are exiled and pray to God on its behalf, for in its peace and prosperity you will find peace and prosperity.' This is probably the wisest advice ever given to a religious minority. Jeremiah was telling the exiles to work for the common good. Maintaining your own identity is not incompatible with loyalty to, and work on behalf of, the wider society. That is the principle of *integration without assimilation*, working for the good of others without ceasing to be yourselves.

To be a citizen is to 'seek the peace of the city' as a whole. In any society there will be a variety of groups, and their interests will conflict. But the very existence of the *polis* rests on the agreement of all sections to identify with the common good, and to trust in the methods of politics to resolve conflicts without violence, doing justice to the interests of the whole as well as the parts. When a nation loses faith in itself, its citizens find other identities. They turn inward. That, argues

MacIntyre, is not a minor matter. When community takes priority over society and national identity wanes, we are approaching, in his words, 'the coming ages of barbarism and darkness'.

Can this be avoided? If we care for our life together, it must be.

The Argument Summarized

It is time to sum up the argument of this section of the book. The birth of the nation state coincided with the development of a national culture. The question then arose: what is the relationship between the majority and minorities? The first model was the country house. There is a single culture, that of the host country. Those who have a different culture are like guests. They are there but they do not fully belong. The price of belonging – in America, the melting pot, in Britain, assimilation – meant that minorities had to give up their culture. The choice was simple: either they had to cease to be what they were, or they would remain guests, outsiders, not fully at home. Already in the early twentieth century Horace Kallen, the proponent of cultural pluralism, argued that the price of this model was too high. You can change where you are; you cannot change who you are.

Eventually in the 1970s multiculturalism was born, first as a fact, only later as a value. The fact was that societies were becoming more diverse, partly through immigration, partly through the breakdown of old structures of class and religion. The good news about multiculturalism is that it honours multiple identities; the bad news is that it leaves us with too little to bind us together as a society in pursuit of the common good. That is society as a hotel: where we live but not where we belong. The very idea of belonging – of society as home – has become problematic, not just for minorities but for the majority as well.

This is not a superficial problem that can be solved by this government policy or that. I have tried to show how deep are the forces driving us apart. One is the loss of a shared moral code. Another is the combined impact of scientific determinism and a new theory of rights. These have encouraged groups to define themselves as victims of the majority culture, and this poisons relationships between majority and minorities. The third is the new communications technology. Nation states were born in the aftermath of one such technology, the invention of printing. They are endangered by another: satellite television, email and the internet.

The result is the inward turn. That, said Alasdair MacIntyre, is the danger signal. We should heed his warning, but how? One answer, given by Samuel Huntington in the book he wrote after *The Clash of Civilizations*, is to go back to where we were: a Christian nation, essentially a return to the country house. I doubt whether that can be done in Huntington's nation, the United States. It certainly cannot be done in Britain. There is an alternative: to move forward, not back. Society does not belong to any of us, but to all of us. It is the home we build together. What does this mean, in principle and in practice? I consider principle in part 2, practice in part 3.

Society as the-home-we-build-together is a metaphor. But it is also a political philosophy, a way of thinking about the life we share as fellow citizens of a nation. How so? To this question I now turn.

A Theory of Society Creation

Chapter 8

A Forgotten Political Classic

The chief trouble with the contemporary generation is that it has not read the minutes of the last meeting.[1]

Richard M. Weaver

When the times are in joint, when strains on the system are well within the parameters of its tensile strength, then we look for solutions to problems within our conventional way of thinking. The opposite is the case when the times are out of joint, when the world is changing almost faster than people can bear, when in Matthew Arnold's haunting phrase, we find ourselves caught 'between two worlds, one dead, the other powerless to be born'.

That is our situation now. The information technology revolution fuelling global change is one of the greatest transformations in history, as great as the move from the hunter-gatherer stage to that of agriculture, or as the invention of printing that brought the Middle Ages to an end. What the end results will be, we have no way of knowing. History is readable only in retrospect.

Strains are beginning to show in the liberal democracies of the West. The social fabric is fraying. Forces are driving people apart, and all too little binds us together. On the one hand, society is being disaggregated into individuals and groups with no overarching sense of the common good. On the other, resurgent religiosity is leading at least some people to challenge freedom itself, as it has been understood in the West until now.

Politicians have begun to realize that what we face, if we are to defend freedom, is a battle of ideas. Ideas, seemingly useless in the short run, make the difference in the long. We have learned in Iraq and Afghanistan that it is easy to win a war, but hard to win a peace. Removing tyrants is simple; creating a free society is not. That is when what Joseph Nye calls 'soft power', the power of ideas and culture and

91

the moral imagination, are important.[2] They do not replace the need for conventional politics and diplomacy, but they must accompany it.

One of the signs of epoch-making change is that the old formulae no longer work. The conventional solutions are tried. They fail. At such times we arrive at the possibility of what T. S. Kuhn called a paradigm shift. We need a new theory, a new way of looking at things.

New theories can come from unexpected places. Van Gogh was inspired by Japanese painting, Gauguin by the culture of Samoa, Modigliani by the art of Africa. Freud found inspiration in Sophocles and the myth of Oedipus. Psychologists have turned to the Dalai Lama and Tibetan Buddhism. Moral philosophers have often turned to Ancient Greece. Bringing the resources of another culture to bear on the problems of here and now is a creative act, one of the most powerful we have.

When we turn to such resources we are not attempting to recover a past, a lost golden age. We are not engaged in nostalgia. We remain in the twenty-first century with its problems and possibilities. What we are doing is consciously standing outside our current way of thinking, mindful that its resources have been exhausted and what the situation now needs is not more of the same.

I want to take a forgotten political classic and use it to set out a group of concepts that will allow us to think differently about freedom. The contemporary case for liberal democracy is, I believe, inadequate to the challenges that face it in the twenty-first century – challenges that arise from a newly resurgent religiosity. Freedom needs a stronger defence than those currently on offer.

*   *   *

The problem is already implicit in one of the great defences of freedom in the twentieth century, Isaiah Berlin's 1957 essay, 'Two concepts of liberty'. In it he made the case for what he called 'negative liberty', or what we now call liberal democracy: liberty as the absence of coercions and constraints, leaving us maximally free to do what we want. The alternative, ideological politics, freedom to do what we ought, had led in the past to fearful conflicts. Berlin spoke eloquently about 'the slaughter of individuals on the altars of the great historical ideals'. Towards the end of the essay, though, he made a disturbing comment:

> It may be that the ideal of freedom to choose ends without claiming eternal validity for them, and the pluralism of values connected with this, is only the late fruit of our declining capitalist civilisation: an ideal which remote ages and primitive

societies will regard with curiosity, even sympathy, but little comprehension.[3]

So there is nothing inevitable about liberalism and the free society. It took millennia for it to evolve, and there is no guarantee that it will survive. Why so? Because liberalism does not offer, and on Berlin's premises *cannot* offer, an objective justification for itself:

> Principles are not less sacred because their duration cannot be guaranteed. Indeed, the very desire for guarantees that our values are eternal and secure in some objective heaven is perhaps only a craving for the certainties of childhood or the absolute values of our primitive past. 'To realise the relative validity of one's convictions', said an admirable writer of our time, 'and yet stand for them unflinchingly is what distinguishes a civilised man from a barbarian.'

But, as Michael Sandel put it: if one's convictions are only relatively valid, why stand for them unflinchingly?[4] If there is no objective truth in morality, then there is only what individuals decide for themselves. I may choose liberal democracy but you may not. I then have no reason to object to what you do and I find objectionable. You will rightly say to me: on your own account, morality is relative. Therefore you have no reason to object if I see things differently from you. Moral relativism is the worst defence of freedom because it makes freedom itself seem merely relative, hence indefensible.

Imagine a conversation between a political liberal and a religious ideologue, one who believes that religion should govern not only our private lives but also politics and the state. The liberal argues strongly for personal autonomy. Each of us should be free to do whatever we like so long as it is not directly harmful to others. His religious opponent simply disagrees. The supreme value, he says, is heteronomy: obedience to the will of God. Morality is not, and cannot be, a matter of personal choice.

The liberal tries a second approach, familiar to us from John Stuart Mill and more recently Sir Karl Popper.[5] We cannot be sure that our morality is correct. We may be wrong. The best way of pursuing truth is to allow everyone the freedom to enquire, to doubt, to engage in what Mill called 'experiments in living'. This is the argument from fallibility. Morality is like science. It develops through conjectures and refutations, experiments and testing. Like science it needs space for free inquiry.

Again, the religious critic dissents. Morality, he says, is not like science. The proof is that we still read Aristotle on ethics but not on science. There is much in science we do not yet know. But the rules for living a good life have been known for many centuries. They have been revealed. We find them in sacred texts. Our technological powers have grown beyond all recognition, but the human situation has not changed. The right way to exercise power is what it always was. The great religions teach us how to live, and to doubt this is to risk the kind of moral forgetfulness that has derailed many societies in the past.

If these are the best arguments liberal democracy can offer against its critics, it will fail. Freedom needs stronger foundations than this. That is the first problem, but there is another.

*   *   *

Politics is about power. The political classics ask what justifies the creation of a state? What is the nature of political authority? What should be the form of government? To whom is power answerable and how? *These are not our questions.* We have a system of power: parliamentary democracy. It evolved through time. Each stage involved intense political debate. But it is where we are, and we are not about to change it.

The problem we face is about *society*, not the state. It is not about power but about culture, morality, social cohesion, about the subtle ties that bind, or fail to bind, us into a collective entity with a sense of shared responsibility and destiny. It is just this that many political thinkers tend either to take for granted or to dismiss as irrelevant. Yet it is clearly not irrelevant. If society fragments, politics will lose its legitimacy. Why should I honour the laws and government of a society to which I do not feel I belong? No sooner does someone ask this question then we find ourselves thinking about a word not often heard in political debate, namely *belonging*.

More generally it reminds us of something political thought tends to neglect, namely the *third sector* between the individual and the state, often known as civil society. Politics concentrates on relationships between the individual and the state. But when issues of identity enter the conversation, things change. We have seen why. On the country-house model, there is only one identity, that of the dominant culture. If you want to be part of it, you have to assimilate. Minorities must lose their identity in order to belong. Minorities understandably object to this. You can, they say, be British *and* Catholic, or Jewish, or Sikh. If you want people to be loyal to a nation, do not ask them to give up other non-political loyalties.

Historically, this led to the idea of multiculturalism: society as hotel. But on this model there is no notion of loyalty or belonging at all. You pay your taxes, the government provides services, and you are, within limits, free to be whoever you choose. For a while, this seemed to work. After all, the people who made the choices were individuals, and individuals do not challenge the authority of the state. But what if individualism itself is challenged, as sooner or later it must be? For we do not find meaning as individuals. We find it as groups. And groups – especially if they are linked by global communications technology to similar groups throughout the world – can challenge the state. How then do we construct a society so that it is more than the clash of multiple group-identities? The hotel model is inadequate: what we need if we are to mitigate the clash is a sense of shared belonging. And that is what the hotel model fails to create; *on principle* refuses to create. What this leads to, ultimately, is segregation: individuals and groups living in separate rooms with no real values in common, and no real interest in the fate of the hotel.

At this point, contemporary thinkers tend to reply: but at least we hold political values in common; we are all committed to freedom and democracy. But we aren't: that is the point. Freedom is not a value if you believe that the highest human calling is submission to the will of God. Democracy, rule of the people, is not a value if you believe instead in the rule of God. Besides which, the trouble with values as a source of identity is that they are not the source of an identity.

Values are universal; identities are particular. They are about this place, this land, this language, this landscape, this history. They are about somewhere, not everywhere. So we find ourselves back with the limitations of the hotel model. Hotels are fine for cosmopolitans, people who spend their lives travelling, literally or metaphorically. But we are not all cosmopolitans. We can't be. We want, even need, to belong. And if the nation state no longer provides us with an identity, we will look elsewhere, and nowhere more compellingly than to religion. For no systems in history have more profoundly sought an answer to the questions: Who am I? Why am I here? What, therefore, should I do? It is no answer to say that these questions have no answer. Therefore, we need to ask: are there religious, as well as secular, arguments for liberal democracy? And how can we bring together people, religious and secular alike, with strong and clashing systems of belief, into a single, cohesive society?

To answer both, we need to return to three moments in history when specific nations faced the problem of how to unite a deeply divided society. One was England (and Scotland) in the seventeenth century, at a time of conflict and civil war. A second was the United States during periods of mass immigration. America lacked what European nations had: a long-standing history, people held together by memory, custom, conventions and traditions. Americans came from many lands, speaking many languages, united if at all by flight from religious persecution, or the prospect of a 'new world'. That is why society-building is part of American culture in a way it has not been in Europe. The third example is biblical Israel.

* * *

The seventeenth century in Europe was a time of new beginnings. Following the Reformation, Catholic had fought Protestant in a series of bitter confrontations. Out of that crisis came the search for civic peace which eventually laid the foundations for the free and democratic societies we enjoy today. The key figures in this struggle were people such as John Milton, Thomas Hobbes, John Locke, and in Amsterdam, Benedict Spinoza. At the same time, Puritans were making their way across the Atlantic to build a new society in America. They too were in search of freedom. Though they were deeply religious, what they sought was not to impose their views on others but to create a new social order that would make space for religious difference, where men and women who disagreed profoundly on matters of faith could none the less live peaceably together.

All this led to what Lincoln called 'a new birth of freedom', a new kind of liberty: *liberty of conscience*, the idea that religious faith is too important, too sacred to be left to kings, rulers, governments and civil legislation. They built a society of freedom on religious foundations. That is what makes their thought so interesting, so salient, in the twenty-first century. How do you avoid the sectarian violence that today threatens lives in Afghanistan, Iraq, Kashmir, Chechnya and elsewhere? How do you avoid violent protests of the kind that have occurred in Holland, Denmark and France? How do you keep the peace, not between people for whom morality is a matter of personal choice, but between people with strong and absolute religious convictions?

Milton, Hobbes, Locke, and the Pilgrim Fathers of America did not argue in terms of personal autonomy, 'experiments in living' or moral relativism. Nor did they base their case on the classics of the Hellenistic world, such as Plato's *Republic* and Aristotle's *Politics*. The text with which they were in dialogue – Hobbes quotes it in *The Leviathan* 657 times – was one that today we hardly associate with politics at all. It was the Hebrew Bible.[6]

Here I need to guard against misunderstanding. Whether we are religious or secular, we tend to think of the Bible as first and foremost a religious book. That is precisely *not* what I want to explore here. We still turn for inspiration to Plato and Aristotle on politics, education and society, even though we do not share many other aspects of their mental world. We do not believe in Greek myths. We do not share Plato's conviction that society should be stratified into different classes with different functions, or Aristotle's belief that some are born to rule, others to be ruled. We can separate out, as it were, the politics from the metaphysics.

The same is true about the Bible. Its interest as a political text is separate from its religious teachings. I want, for the purpose of constructing a strong defence of liberal democracy, to read it as a political text only, and even then to attend to some aspects of its vision of society but not others. Specifically I want to understand what it was about this book that allowed Britain in the seventeenth century, and America between the seventeenth and twentieth, to create a new kind of social order, one that made space for deep religious differences.

*   *   *

Biblical politics is marked by certain distinctive features. First and most obvious is its insistence on the non-negotiable dignity of the individual. This has, of course, a religious basis. It arises from the idea that we are each – black, white, male, female, young, old, weak, strong – in 'the image and likeness' of God. Immanuel Kant gave the idea its most famous secular equivalent: treat each individual as an end, not a means. This did not immediately give rise to liberal democracy. Yet any system that has this idea at its heart will eventually tend that way. Many political systems do not value the individual. They divide them into classes or castes. They think of them in the mass. They use them as means, rather than as ends. As long as the first chapter of Genesis exists within a culture and people are literate enough to read it for themselves, sooner or later there will be protest. Systems of oppression will crumble. The Bible radicalizes the human spirit with its vision of human dignity.

Second is the prominence the Bible gives to the idea of freedom. Its central story, the Exodus, is about how the supreme Power intervened in history to liberate the powerless. Exodus begins in slavery and ends with people journeying through the wilderness in search of a society where all are equal and none humiliated or exploited. This – the journey from Egypt to the promised land – is Western civilization's meta-narrative of hope, and has never ceased to inspire those who fought for freedom. The night before he was assassinated, Martin Luther King ended his speech with these words: 'I want you to know tonight that we, as a people, will get to the promised land.'[7] No abstract doctrine, no philosophical idea, has the power of that story: freedom as a journey that takes time but never loses faith in its destination.

No less important is the Bible's view of the *place* of politics within the good life. Almost all the textbooks on the history of political thought begin in Ancient Greece and its city states. The Greeks had a unique talent for conceptual thought. They invented philosophy and laid the foundations for modern science. They gave us great political classics and the words we use today, such as democracy. But focusing exclusively on the Greeks at the expense of the Bible gives us a distorted view of Western civilization.

As we will see in chapter 19, liberal democracy is not Athenian democracy. In Ancient Greece the *polis* absorbed the highest energies of the people. The greatest good was participation in public life. Liberal democracy is not like that. It sees politics as necessary but not all-embracing. There is a life outside politics: that is what makes it liberal. The ultimate question is, do people exist to serve the state, or does the state exist to serve the people? That is what differentiated Ancient Greece and ancient Israel. It is also what made the French Revolution different from its English counterpart. French thought emphasized *civic virtue*: service to the state. English and Scottish thought emphasized *civil society*, the groups and associations that exist voluntarily, outside the state.

That difference is still significant today, because it forces us to ask: who creates society? The government, or us? The biblical view of politics is that there is a key dimension of our collective life that is not, and must never be allowed to become, political. The politicization of one area of life after another since the 1970s – sex, marriage, the family, universities, charities, the churches, identity politics and the worst excesses of political correctness – is a sure sign that we are moving from biblical to Hellenistic politics, and with it the danger of a new totalitarianism. The biblical insight is that not everything in our shared life is political. Not everything is a conflict of interests, a struggle for power. There are covenantal relationships, such as love, loyalty, friendship and trust. There is such a thing as society, and it is not identical with the state.

*　　*　　*

So biblical politics is distinctive. But why should it be relevant to the problems of a multicultural society? The answer lies in the Bible's strange but unmistakable fascination with *diversity*. One of the oddest elements of the biblical narrative is the way it describes the Israelites, *not* as a unified nation but as a group of twelve tribes. For a considerable period, prior to the monarchy, the Israelites formed an amphictyony, a loose confederation of separate communities. There is also, in the story of the Exodus, reference to an unidentified 'mixed multitude'.[8] Also within the Pentateuch are repeated injunctions to 'love the stranger'. The later historical works contain references to heroes and heroines who are not Israelite: Jael the Kenite, Uriah the Hittite and so on. Biblical Israel is a nation whose unity is not ethnic but civic. That is why, for example, the 25th chapter of Leviticus is about minority rights. The 'resident alien' is one who does not share the religion of the majority, but does share its political culture.

Contemporary scholars are divided in their views as to the historicity of biblical narrative but they are agreed on this, that Israelite society was an ethnic mix. The Bible does not gloss over this; it seems to go out of its way to emphasize it. That is why it deserves to be read as a political text today. In the ancient world, foreigners were feared. They did not have civil rights. For the Egyptians, they were the *apiru*, for the Greeks they were the *barbarians*. They were a danger; they were inferior; they were outsiders. It is paradoxical that ancient Israel – so often portrayed as a tribal culture – is, especially in its early history, an ongoing reflection on diversity. One of the most famous biblical narratives is a critique of uniformity: the Tower of Babel, which begins with the sentence, 'There was a time when all the world spoke a single language and used the same words.' The result was hubris, then nemesis. Biblical politics is about living with difference. That is what makes it relevant to multicultural societies today.

*   *   *

There are two ways of reading the biblical story. One is as a tale of divine intervention in history. God liberates a group of slaves with signs and wonders. There are miracles, plagues, the division of the Red Sea. God leads the people across the wilderness by a pillar of cloud by day and fire by night. He sends them manna from heaven and water from a rock. That is a religious story that speaks to the religious imagination. It is not my concern here.

But there is another way of reading the story. It is about how Moses turned a ragtag crowd of escaping slaves, fractious, fearful and disputatious, into a cohesive nation with an identity so strong that it was able to survive devastating defeats, as well as a two-thousand-year exile, yet continue to see itself as a nation even when scattered and dispersed across the world. How do you create that kind of identity out of diversity? How do you build this sort of loyalty, this sense of belonging? That was his question, and it is ours.

I suspect we have forgotten how significant the Bible was in shaping the idea of a free society at the birth of modernity. It was, as I have said, the proof-text for Milton, Hobbes, Locke and the founding fathers of America. But it was also, as we will see in the next chapter, a key document for the radical Tom Paine. Most surprisingly perhaps, it fascinated Jean-Jacques Rousseau, the inspiration of the French Revolution. The Bible does not play a role in his *The Social Contract*. But among his unpublished papers, discovered after his death, was the following fragment:

> But an astonishing and truly unique spectacle is to see an expatriated people, who have had neither place nor land for nearly two thousand years, a people mingled with foreigners, no longer perhaps having a single descendant of the early races, a scattered people, dispersed over the world, enslaved, persecuted, scorned by all nations, nonetheless preserving its characteristics, its laws, its customs, its patriotic love of the early social union, when all ties with it seem broken. The Jews provide us with an astonishing spectacle: the laws of Numa, Lycurgus, Solon are dead; the very much older laws of Moses are still alive. Athens, Sparta, Rome have perished and no longer have children left on earth; Zion, destroyed, has not lost its children.
>
> They mingle with all the nations and never merge with them; they no longer have leaders, and are still a nation; they no longer have a homeland, and are always citizens of it.
>
> What must be the strength of legislation capable of working such wonders, capable of braving conquests, dispersions, revolutions, exiles, capable of surviving the customs, laws, empire of all the nations, and which finally promises them, by these trials, that it is going to continue to sustain them all, to conquer the vicissitudes of things human, and to last as long as the world? Of all the systems of legislation which are known to us, some are theoretical creations the feasibility of which is even disputed; others have only produced a few followers, others have never made a well-constituted State, except this one which has undergone all the trials and has always withstood them. Jew and Christian agree in this the finger of God, who according to one is maintaining His nation, and according to the other, punishing it, but any man whosoever he is, must acknowledge this as a unique marvel, the causes of which, divine or human, certainly deserve the study and admiration of the sages, in preference to all that Greece and Rome offer of what is admirable in the way of political institutions and human settlements.[9]

Rousseau was intrigued by the power of Mosaic politics to forge an identity unbreakable by any of the normal forces of history. How did this happen? What was its key idea? To this I now turn.

Chapter 9

Social Contract, Social Covenant

> To be in covenant with other people involves believing that we and they belong to the same moral community; that in this community each person matters in his or her own right and not merely as something useful to the society; that we all participate in the moral community by entrusting ourselves to others and in turn by accepting their entrusting; and that in the moral community each of us has enduring responsibility to all the others.[1]
>
> Joseph Allen

The Hebrew Bible contains two texts that describe the founding of a new political order. What is significant is their juxtaposition. Most political systems have one foundational moment: conquest, victory, revolution, the birth of a new regime. Some have none: traditional societies whose origins are lost in the mists of antiquity. The dual system of the Bible is unusual in its principled duality.

The first text is taken from the book of Samuel.[2] The Israelites, after wandering in the desert for forty years, have arrived in the land and settled it. For several centuries they have been a loose confederation of tribes with no overarching political structure. They have no national leader as such. They have, in effect, local government without central government. From time to time as the need arises, usually when they are attacked by another nation, a charismatic figure emerges to lead the people in battle. These figures were known as 'judges', though not in our modern, legal sense. They were, for the most part, military heroes. The system worked reasonably well for a time, but the strains had begun to show. It was hazardous to rely on the appearance of the right man at the right time. Besides which, society itself was beginning to verge on anarchy: 'In those days Israel had no king; everyone did as he saw fit.'

Eventually there was a crisis. The leader of the day, Samuel, a

101

prophet and judge, was highly regarded. But he wanted his children to succeed him and the people did not. They were corrupt. They accepted bribes. They perverted justice. The elders came to Samuel to tell him that, in their view, the era of rule by charismatic leader was over. They wanted a king 'such as all the other nations have'. The passage that follows is a study in ambivalence.

Samuel was distressed by the petition. He thought the people had rejected him. Not so, said God. It is worse than that: 'It is not you they have rejected, but they have rejected *me* as their king.' They no longer wanted to rely on God to protect them. None the less, God told Samuel to take the people's request seriously. 'Warn them solemnly and let them know what the king who will reign over them will do.' Samuel was to explain what would be involved in having a king. If, despite the warning, they still wanted a king then, said God, that is what Samuel was to give them.

Samuel's speech is a classic text on the dangers of political power:

'This is what the king who will reign over you will do: He will take your sons and make them serve with his chariots and horses, and they will run in front of his chariots ... He will take your daughters to be perfumers and cooks and bakers. He will take the best of your fields and vineyards and olive groves and give them to his attendants. He will take a tenth of your grain and of your vintage and give it to his officials and attendants. Your men-servants and maidservants and the best of your cattle and donkeys he will take for his own use. He will take a tenth of your flocks, and you yourselves will become his slaves. When that day comes, you will cry out for relief from the king you have chosen, and the Lord will not answer you in that day.'[3]

They will pay a high price for monarchy in loss of income and liberty. But the people are unmoved. They still want a king: 'Then we will be like all the other nations, with a king to lead us and to go out before us and fight our battles.' God tells Samuel to go ahead and give them a king.

It is a passage that has puzzled readers and commentators alike. Does the Bible see monarchy as good or bad? If good, then why does God say that asking for a king is tantamount to rejecting him? Why does Samuel try to discourage the people? Why paint monarchy in so negative a light? If it is bad, why does God tell Samuel to heed the people and accede to their request? Already in the book of Deuteronomy, Moses had instructed the people to appoint a king: 'When you enter the land the Lord your God is giving you and have taken possession of it and settled in it, and you say, "Let us set a king over us like all the nations around us", be sure to appoint over you the king the Lord your God chooses' (Deut. 17:14–15). If monarchy is wrong, why command it? The ambivalence is reflected in the medieval Jewish commentators. Some held that appointing a king was obligatory, others that it was optional, yet others that it was a concession to human weakness. So, which was it: good or bad?

The puzzle was solved by the nineteenth-century commentator Rabbi Zvi Hirsch Chajes.[4] What we have in the story of Samuel, he said, is a social contract. It is, in fact, the first recorded instance of its kind. As Hobbes pointed out, by appointing a king – by creating a central structure of power – there is a risk-benefit ratio. We lose, but we gain. We lose a measure of control over our own lives and property. We gain freedom from lawlessness and defencelessness. Kings fight wars and punish criminals. They provide security from threats within and without. But they bring with them heavy costs in taxation and regulation.

That is what Samuel was saying. The people 'under God' have the right to give up some of their freedoms and transfer them to a king who will exercise them collectively on their behalf. Creating a monarchy, though not obligatory, was permissible. The people had been given by God the freedom to choose how they were to be governed. A king would ensure the rule of law. He could conscript an army and defend the nation in battle. The choice was theirs. But the risks were high.

The entire prophetic literature is testimony to Lord Acton's dictum that power tends to corrupt. It can also enslave. It gives the powerful dominance over the powerless. Even when engaged in the holiest of tasks, building the Temple, King Solomon in effect turned the entire people into a corvée, a conscripted labour force, and the kingdom fell apart almost immediately after his death. The biblical ideal is servant leadership: the leader as servant of the people and of God. But how often does this happen? The Bible's answer is: very rarely.

The ideal polity, so the Bible implies, is *nomocracy*: the rule not of men or women, but of law – not law carved in stone or written on scrolls but law engraved in the hearts of the people:

> 'This is the covenant I will make with the house of Israel
> after that time,' declares the Lord.
> 'I will put my law in their minds
> and write it on their hearts.
> I will be their God,
> and they will be my people.' (Jeremiah 31:33)

But this, for the Israelites in Samuel's day, was a utopian aspiration. It still is. So, says God, if you want a king and are prepared to sacrifice some of the freedom I have given you, then appoint a king. But be aware that kings, courts and governments carry a high price. Not for nothing did Hobbes call the central power 'Leviathan' – a monster.

So we find in the first book of Samuel the answer to a question that perplexed the philosophers who followed Hobbes. Was the social contract a historical event or merely a theoretical construct? Did it happen or is it merely a hypothesis? The biblical evidence is that it did happen, very much along the lines Hobbes described, at the transition between the Israelites of the book of Judges and the birth of monarchy.

That, though, is the less interesting fact about this narrative. More significant, and unexpected, is that the social contract appears in the *middle* of the story, not at the outset. It was not the foundational moment of Israelite nationhood. It did not create a body politic. It merely established a system of government – and not even the only system. Israel in the biblical era knew of rule, not just by kings but also by prophets, elders, tribal chiefs, soldiers and scribes. Post-biblically it experienced rule by sages, patriarchs, exilarchs, and town councils. The fundamental issue of politics for the Bible is not, which system of governance is best, but the prior question: how do you forge a nation out of a disparate group of tribes? When that is at stake, social contract is not the first political act but the second.

Social Covenant

The true foundational moment occurred centuries earlier, at Mount Sinai in the days of Moses. God revealed himself to the people and gave them the Ten Commandments. What is important here is not the revelation itself but what preceded it. This is how the Bible describes it:

> Then Moses went up to God, and the Lord called to him from the mountain and said, 'This is what you are to say to the house of Jacob and what you are to tell the people of Israel: "You yourselves have seen what I did to Egypt, and how I carried you on eagles' wings and brought you to myself. Now if you obey me fully and keep my covenant, then out of all nations you will be my treasured possession. Although the whole earth is mine, you will be for me a kingdom of priests and a holy nation." These are the words you are to speak to the Israelites.'
>
> So Moses went back and summoned the elders of the people and set before them all the words the Lord had commanded him to speak. All the people responded as one: 'We will do everything the Lord has said.' So Moses brought their answer back to the Lord. (Exod. 19:3–8)

This, not the social contract in the days of Samuel, was the foundational moment in biblical politics. What God is proposing is not a *contract* but a *covenant.* Covenants were a familiar feature of politics in the ancient Near East. They were secular treaties, usually between a strong nation and a weak one. They set out the terms of a relationship. The strong power would protect the weak, in return for which the weak would pledge its loyalty and fealty to the strong.

The Bible takes this idea and makes revolutionary use of it.[5] It is now conceived of as a partnership between God and a people. God will protect them. They know this because he has already rescued them from slavery. In return, they are to pledge themselves to God, obeying his laws, accepting his mission, honouring his trust. The people are free to choose. Moses brings them God's proposal, and asks them, in effect, to decide whether to accept it or not. The fact of choice is fundamental, for the Bible portrays God not as an overwhelming force but as a constitutional monarch. The supreme power makes space for human freedom. There is no justified government without the consent of the governed, even if the governor is creator of heaven and earth. The people agree. Moses reports their consent. What follows next is the revelation itself, the Ten Commandments, followed by some detailed social legislation, and eventually the covenant-ratification ceremony itself.

There are several remarkable features about this passage. The first is that it makes a very unusual claim about the relationship between God and humanity: God makes space for human freedom and invites an entire people to become, in the rabbinic phrase 'his partners in the work of creation'.[6] The free God desires the free worship of free human beings. God transcends nature; therefore God is not bound by nature; therefore God is free. God sets his image on the human person; therefore humanity is free. The story of the Bible is the tangled tale of the consequences of God's fateful gift of human freedom. Faith, or more precisely, faithfulness, is born where the freedom of human beings meets the freedom of God in an unconstrained act of mutual commitment. That is why historically, wherever the Hebrew Bible has made an impact on political life – usually in some form of Calvinism – it has done so in the name of 'a new birth of freedom'.

Secondly, unlike any other treaty in the ancient world it is made not between two rulers but between God and an entire people, the presence, knowledge and consent of all of whom is essential. It is a point the Bible repeatedly emphasizes: *'All the people* responded as one' (Exod. 19:8); *'All the people* responded with one voice' (Exod. 24:3). In the Hebrew text, the phrase 'the people' appears 17 times in Exodus 19 (the covenant proposed), and 5 times in Exodus 24 (the covenant accepted). This is not democracy in the modern or even the Greek sense. But it is a corollary of the idea that the human person as such is in the image of God. In covenant as the Bible understands it, each individual has significance, dignity, moral worth, the right to be heard, a voice.

Thirdly, the geographical setting is significant. The covenant is made, not accidentally but essentially, in the wilderness. It turns the Israelites from a fractious group of escaping slaves into an *edah*, a nation, a body politic, a 'civil society'. But they have, as yet, no country, no territory, no home. They are in the desert. They have not entered the land. In the history of every other known polity, first comes the territory, then, many centuries later, come the laws. In the case of the Bible, the laws precede the land. The covenant, as Philip Selznick puts it, is 'prepolitical, foundational, and consensual'. The Israelites must have a social *covenant* before they can have a social *contract*.

Setting aside the religious implications of the story, what makes biblical politics unique is its dual theory of how individuals come together to order their collective life. The book of Samuel tells of the birth of Israel as a *kingdom*. The earlier book of Exodus tells of its birth as a *nation*. One is a story about rulers, courts, government and the distribution of power. The other is about rules, relationships, morality and vision. To put it in secular terms: *Social covenant creates a society. Social contract creates a state.*

Thomas Paine on Society and State

Overwhelmingly, the history of political theory has been about the *state*, about how a nation is governed: who rules whom, and how. The great political struggles have been about power. The Bible is full of such stories, as are most other works of history. What is unusual about the Bible considered as a political text is that it regards this as a secondary issue altogether, a distraction from the core business of human inter-action. Its primary interest is *society*. It is there that the great ideals are tested: justice, compassion, human dignity, welfare, relations between employer and employee, the equitable distribution of wealth, and the social inclusion of those without power: the widow, the orphan, the stranger. That, suggests the Bible, requires a different base, another kind of logic. To these issues, social contract is irrelevant. What matters is social covenant.

The first person in modern times fully to understand and articulate the difference was Thomas Paine, one of the most colourful characters England has produced: the only figure to have had a front-row seat in both the American and French Revolutions. Born in Norfolk in 1737 to working-class parents (his father was a corset-maker), Paine tried his hand at several trades without success, and was forced to leave Britain for America to avoid imprisonment for debt. He had a friend there, Benjamin Franklin, through whose influence he became editor of a magazine. In January 1776 he published the book that made him an instant celebrity: *Common Sense*, an argument for American independence that sold no less than 100,000 copies in its first year. He fought with the American army, became Secretary to the Congress's Committee on Foreign Affairs and Clerk of the Pennsylvania Assembly.

Returning to Britain in the late 1780s, he took issue with Edmund Burke's condemnation of the French Revolution and in reply wrote the book that gained him fame and a seat in the National Convention in France: *The Rights of Man*. When the Girondins lost power to the Jacobins and the French Terror began, he was arrested and imprisoned. Eventually he was released and returned to America, but this time he faced a hostile reception. His critique of religion, *The Age of Reason*, had given him the reputation of being an atheist. He died, destitute and disgraced, in New York in 1809.

What Paine understood earlier, and more clearly, than others was the distinction between the two modes of human association. Here is how he set it out at the very beginning of his first great work, *Common Sense*:

> Some writers have so confounded society with government as to leave little or no distinction between them; whereas they are not only different, but have different origins. Society is produced by our wants and government by our wickedness; the former promotes our happiness *positively* by uniting our affections, the latter *negatively* by restraining our vices ... Society in every state is a blessing, but government, even in its best state, is but a necessary evil ... Government, like dress, is the badge of lost innocence; the palaces of kings are built upon the ruins of the bowers of paradise.[7]

Society is one thing, the state – kings, rulers, the lineaments of power – another. Society, says Paine, emerges naturally out of the inability of each of us to supply our wants and needs alone. So we co-operate, divide our labours, trade, form friendships and associations, and establish relationships of trust. Were everyone to play his or her part, there would be no need for government at all. But not everyone does. Some cheat. Some steal. Some invade the territory of others. That is when governments become necessary and when social contracts are made.

Paine's is not the name most often associated with the idea of civil society. That accolade often goes to Adam Ferguson who wrote the first

107

book with that title, or to Hegel who defined it as the realm between the individual and the state. The keenest analyst was Alexis de Tocqueville in his *Democracy in America*. Tocqueville was the first to show how democratic freedom makes demands not only of governments but also of people in their dealings with one another: in families, communities and voluntary organizations, each an exercise in the 'art of association' without which, he believed, democratic societies would eventually fall to the sickness of individualism.

But Paine saw it first – and did so precisely on the basis of a close reading of the Hebrew Bible, which is how he develops the argument in his book. Paine, a natural rebel and a sceptic, was able to read the Bible in a way the more godly did not: as a political document. What he discovered was that the true heroes of the biblical narrative were not kings (government) or priests (organized religion), but prophets: the voice of conscience, the ethical imperative, the people who spoke about the quality of relationships within society. Politics, in the sense of governments and the use of power, is secondary in the Bible. It is a necessary evil. It brings in its wake great dangers. But without it there would be anarchy. Political leaders can rise to greatness: the supreme example in the Bible is King David. But the real arena of collective grace lies with us, the us-together we call, not the state but – society.

Three Types of Polity

Covenant is one of the three broad types of political system.[8] Polities come into being in one of three ways: conquest, slow growth and development, or formal, conscious decision. The first tends to produce a hierarchical society; the second, an organic one; and the third, society-as-covenant.

Conquest leads to *hierarchical societies*. There is a ruler, a court, an administrative and priestly elite, and beneath them the great mass of the people. The key biblical example is the Egypt of the Pharaohs. In hierarchy, power is structured as a pyramid: it is not accidental that the pyramids of Egypt survive as symbols of that empire. More modern examples include Napoleonic France and nineteenth-century Prussia. The hierarchical social order is usually justified by cosmology or myth, in which ranks on earth reflect those in heaven. In *Troilus and Cressida*, Shakespeare gave this one of its most famous descriptions:

> The heavens themselves, the planets and this centre
> Observe degree, priority and place,
> Insisture, course, proportion, season, form,
> Office and custom, in all line of order . . .[9]

108

The second kind of society, one that emerges from long custom and habituation, is usually called *organic*. In an organic society, things are there because they always were. Their origins tend to be lost in the mists of time (though there can be 'invented traditions'). Law, especially common law, is a slow accretion of precedent and tradition. Politics is based less on ideas or specific historic moments than on a sense of natural order, piety and reverence. Organic societies have customs, rituals, uniforms and ceremonials that cast the aura of antiquity and inevitability over the present. Power is less a matter of pyramids than of centre and periphery. Those who wield power meet in clubs, schools, universities, regiments and teams; they cultivate an air of amateurism and frown on meritocracy, effort and enthusiasm. Roger Scruton's *England, an Elegy* is a prose-poem to this kind of society.

The third kind, covenantal society, is formed in a conscious act of new beginnings. The parties come together to achieve what neither can achieve alone (This sounds odd when one of the parties is God, until we remember that there is one thing God cannot do alone, namely live within the human heart: for that he depends on the willingness of humans). In an act of covenant, both parties agree to respect one another's integrity as free agents: this is so even when one of the parties is God himself. The key element in covenant is neither power, nor the past, but a verbal declaration, a mutually binding promise. Covenantal politics is supremely a politics of the word: the word given, the word received, the word honoured in trust.

The parties to a covenant bind themselves to one another in an open-ended bond of mutuality and loyalty. They agree to share a fate. One of the most famous lines of the Bible epitomizes this sentiment: 'Though I walk through the valley of the shadow of death, I will fear no evil for you are with me.' Unlike contracts, which are about *interests*, covenants are about *identity*. They turn a plurality of 'I's into a collective 'We'. The simplest example of a covenant is marriage. Friendship can also take this form. The Bible tells us that 'Jonathan made a covenant with David because he loved him as himself' (I Samuel 18:3). The prophet Hosea gives a striking account of God's covenant with his people as a kind of marriage:

> I will betroth you to me forever;
> I will betroth you in righteousness and justice, love and
>   compassion.
> I will betroth you in faithfulness,
> and you will know the Lord. (Hosea 2:19–20)

Covenants and contracts are different things and address different aspects of our humanity. In a contract, what matters is that both gain.

In a covenant, what matters is that both give. Contracts are agreements entered into for mutual advantage. They are undertaken by individuals or groups on the basis of self-interest. They have specific purposes. They can be terminated by mutual consent. They end once both parties have fulfilled their obligations. By contrast, covenants are moral commitments, and they are open-ended. They are sustained not by letter of law or by self-interest but by loyalty, fidelity, faithfulness. In fact the key word of Judaism, *emunah*, usually translated as 'faith', is better translated as faithfulness.

Social contract creates a state; social covenant creates a society. Social contract is about power and how it is to be handled within a political framework. Social covenant is about how people live together despite their differences. Social contract is about government. Social covenant is about coexistence. Social contract is about laws and their enforcement. Social covenant is about the values we share. Social contract is about the use of potentially coercive force. Social covenant is about moral commitments, the values we share and the ideals that inspire us to work together for the sake of the common good.

Covenant in Western Politics

Covenant played a significant role in European politics in the sixteenth and seventeenth centuries, in Switzerland, Holland, England and Scotland – in fact wherever Calvinism or Puritanism was a presence in the public domain. John Milton was one of its great exponents.[10] His starting point is that we all are born equal, in the image of God. Political society was created when people 'agreed by common league to bind each other from mutual injury and jointly to defend themselves'. It followed that 'the power of kings and magistrates is only derivative, transferred and committed to them in trust from the people to the common good of them all'. Sovereignty lies with the people and 'cannot be taken from them without a violation of their natural birthright'. This is archetypal covenant language.

The idea also played a significant part in sixteenth-century Scotland,[11] through such figures as John Knox, Robert Bruce and Samuel Rutherford. Knox combined the traditional idea of the Scottish band or pact with that of biblical covenanting. During the reign of Charles I, the Scots asserted their independence in 1638 by way of the National Covenant. Eventually they joined the parliamentarians against the king in the English civil war and formalized this in 1643 in the Westminster Confession ('a Confession of Faith for the three kingdoms, according to the Solemn League and Covenant') which became the basis for Scottish Presbyterianism. This was later taken by Scots Covenanters to

America. Among the institutions they created there was Princeton University, one of whose alumni was the political thinker James Madison, who learned Hebrew better to understand the Bible and its politics.

It was in America that covenantal politics received its most complete expression.[12] The first formal act of the Pilgrim Fathers was the Mayflower Pact of 1620: 'We whose names are under-written ... solemnly and mutually in the presence of God, and one of another, covenant and combine our selves together in a civill body politick.' Aboard the Arabella in 1630 John Winthrop similarly declared 'We are entered into covenant with him [God] for this work.'

The United States is unique among modern polities in having the same dual structure as the Bible. It had its own social contract, the Constitution of 1787, which set out the form of government. But prior to that it had its equivalent of a covenant, the Declaration of Independence of 1776, with its great assertion: 'We hold these truths to be self-evident, that all men are created equal, that they are endowed by their Creator with certain unalienable Rights, that among these are Life, Liberty and the pursuit of Happiness' and that 'to secure these rights, Governments are instituted among Men, deriving their just powers from the consent of the governed'. This is as close as politics comes to a nation-making covenant on the biblical model. Richard Niebuhr explains:

> Covenant meant that political society was neither purely natural nor merely contractual, based on common interest. Covenant was the binding together in one body politic of persons who assumed through unlimited promise responsibility to and for each other and for the common laws, under God ... [I]t was not natural birth into natural society that made one a complete member of the people but always the moral act of taking upon oneself, through promise, the responsibilities of a citizenship that bound itself in the very act of exercising its freedom. For in the covenant conception the essence of freedom does not lie in the liberty of choice among goods, but in the ability to commit oneself for the future to a cause.[13]

Why did covenant appear, as it did, specifically in the sixteenth to eighteenth centuries? Undoubtedly part of the answer lay in the spread of Puritanism after the Reformation, helped by the technology of the printed word and the growth of literacy. But there were also compelling social and psychological reasons. The feudal society of the Middle Ages was coming to an end. People were no longer bound to their place and class of birth. Hierarchy, whose supreme expression was the 'divine right of kings', no longer ruled. Tradition – the binding element of organic societies – was growing weaker. Innovation was taking its place. When people become conscious of themselves as individuals, when they insist on personal dignity and freedom, when they seek to be co-architects of their fate, then covenant becomes the most compelling form of politics.

The American political tradition has remained covenantal to the present. Britain, following the constitutional settlement of 1688, retained strong elements of hierarchy and custom. Why then should covenant be relevant to British politics today? The answer, simply, is that Britain today faces the same problem that confronted biblical Israel: how do you create a nation out of many tribes? It also confronted America: how do you unite a disparate population with different places of origin, languages, religions, customs and ideals into a people so that *e pluribus unum*, out of the many, comes one? To that, the answer is covenant, the most powerful way of integrating diversity into national unity without asking anyone to abandon their independence or integrity. Covenants create a new overarching civic or political identity without hierarchy or long-standing tradition. They do so without the use of political coercion. They do so by a simple device. They tell a story.

Chapter 10

Telling the Story

Man is in his actions and practice, as well as in his fictions, essentially a story-telling animal. He is not essentially, but becomes through his history, a teller of stories that aspire to truth. But the key question for men is not about their own authorship; I can only answer the question 'What am I to do?' if I can answer the prior question, 'Of what story or stories do I find myself a part?'[1]

Alasdair MacIntyre

A man is always a teller of tales, he lives surrounded by his stories and the stories of others, he sees everything that happens to him through them; and he tries to live his life as if he were telling a story.[2]

Jean Paul Sartre

At 12.52 p.m. on 20 January 1961, John F. Kennedy, the first Catholic, and youngest man, to be elected as President of the United States, stood on a platform at the east front of the Capitol and delivered his inaugural address. It was one of the finest political speeches of modern times. What is striking from the perspective of British political rhetoric, though, is its religious tone. Kennedy began:

For I have sworn before you and Almighty God the same solemn oath our forebears prescribed nearly a century and three quarters ago. The world is very different now. For man holds in his mortal hands the power to abolish all forms of human poverty and all forms of human life. And yet the same revolutionary beliefs for which our forebears fought are still at issue around the globe – the belief that the rights of man come not from the generosity of the state but from the hand of God.[3]

113

Note the two references to God. The first alludes to the sacred nature of the American covenant as a nation 'under God'. The second refers back to the Declaration of Independence and the phrase 'endowed by their Creator with certain inalienable rights'. The speech ended with these words:

> With a good conscience our only sure reward, with history the final judge of our deeds, let us go forth to lead the land we love, asking His blessing and His help, but knowing that here on earth God's work must truly be our own.

'Conscience', 'history', 'judge', divine 'blessing' and 'help': this is pure covenantal language, deeply reminiscent of the Hebrew Bible, especially those passages in which Moses sets out the concepts of national responsibility and accountability. Four years later Kennedy's successor, Lyndon Baynes Johnson, used even more explicitly biblical language.

> They came here – the exile and the stranger, brave but frightened – to find a place where a man could be his own man. They made a covenant with this land. Conceived in justice, written in liberty, bound in union, it was meant one day to inspire the hopes of all mankind. And it binds us still. If we keep its terms we shall flourish.[4]

Five times Johnson used the word 'covenant'. It was the organizing theme of the entire address. True to its logic he reminded his fellow Americans of the conditionality of their fate. It depended not on wealth or power but on their faithfulness to a moral mission:

> Under this covenant of justice, liberty, and union we have become a nation – prosperous, great, and mighty. And we have kept our freedom. But we have no promise from God that our greatness will endure. We have been allowed by Him to seek greatness with the sweat of our hands and the strength of our spirit ... If we fail now then we will have forgotten in abundance what we learned in hardship: that democracy rests on faith, that freedom asks more than it gives, and the judgment of God is harshest on those who are most favored.

Three and a half centuries after the Pilgrim Fathers, American presidents were still using essentially the same vocabulary of covenant. I want in this chapter to analyse not what Kennedy and Johnson were *saying*, but what they were *doing*. What was happening in these two speeches?

114

History and Memory

Among my earliest memories are those of Passover nights in my grandparents' house. We had come together to celebrate the festival and conduct the *seder*, telling the story of how our ancestors, the Israelites, were slaves and were rescued by God with a series of miracles, and set on their way to freedom. The stroke of genius behind this celebration – and it goes back to the book of Exodus – is that it is set in the home, among families, and it is focused on children. It was my turn, as the youngest child, to ask the traditional 'four questions' beginning with *Mah nishtanah*, 'Why is this night different from all other nights?'

I was being inducted into a people and its memory. I was learning an identity, just as Christian children learn their own identity by telling the story of Christmas and Easter, singing the songs, re-enacting the events, committing to memory the key values: peace on earth, goodwill among men, praying to God to 'forgive us our trespasses as we forgive those who trespass against us'. That is how religions, and cultures generally, shape lives, engraving phrases in the database of memory and giving children the narratives that will frame their understanding of the world and their place within it.

Isaiah Berlin once wrote that 'All Jews who are at all conscious of their identity as Jews are steeped in history.'[5] That, I think, is the wrong word. The authors of the Bible were among the first historians. Two-thirds of the books of the Bible are historical. The prophets of ancient Israel were the first to see God not just in nature but in historical events and to see history itself as a story, a narrative. Yet biblical Hebrew has no word for history. When the language was revived in the nineteenth century, a word had to be borrowed from somewhere else. So history in Hebrew became *historiah*.

In its place, the Bible uses a significantly different word: *Zakhor*, 'remember'.[6]

It appears no less than 169 times in the Bible. It reaches a crescendo in the book of Deuteronomy: 'Remember the days of old; consider the generations long past.' 'Remember the day you stood before the Lord your God at Horeb.' 'Remember what the Amalekites did to you along the way.' 'Remember what the Lord your God did to Miriam.' Above all, there is the constantly reiterated refrain: 'Remember that you were slaves in Egypt.'

There is a difference between history and memory. History is someone else's story. It is about events that happened somewhere else, sometime else. Memory is *my* story. It is about events that happened, in some sense, to me. Hence the rabbinic injunction about telling the story of Passover: 'In every generation we are duty-bound to see ourselves as if we had gone forth from Egypt.'[7] Memory is about identity. It is *the story of which I am a part*. That story may be ancient. In the case of Passover it is very ancient indeed. But I am part of it. That is what identity is – being part of a continuing narrative, one of whose characters I am. Memory is the most powerful form through which group identity is formed and sustained across the generations. We are the story we tell about ourselves.

History answers the question, 'What happened?' Memory answers the question, 'Who am I?' The two are quite different. Reading Greek history does not make me Greek. Reading English history does not make me English. Many social commentators and politicians have argued that British identity should be strengthened by more active teaching of British history in schools. That is desirable in itself. But identity belongs not to history but to memory. It is not a matter of reading texts, learning facts, remembering dates. It is a matter of telling a certain story as our own.

The seder service on Passover, like other rituals in other faiths, is about one generation handing on its story to the next. The fact that this is done at home, within the family, around the table, gives it astonishing power, for family is the most visible symbol of identity and continuity. It is also portable; it survives dislocation. It is not too much to say that this is the answer to Rousseau's astonishment, mentioned at the end of chapter 8, at how Jews were able to maintain their identity for 2,000 years after the destruction of the Second Temple despite the fact that they no longer had a land, a territory, a home. They told their story to their children. On this slender base, identity survived.

Truth as System, Truth as Story

Why a story? With this we come to one of the distinctive features of covenant. It is not an abstract form of politics, based on a cosmological myth or philosophical theory about the human condition. Such things, if they are true, are true universally. They contain no specific reference to this time, that place, these circumstances, this nation. There were societies based on the myth of the 'great chain of being', from higher to lower, in which everyone from king to commoner to serf had their place. Modern liberalism and nationalism were predicated on a philosophical theory about autonomy: individuals and nations should be self-determining. Covenantal polities are not like that at all.

They are rooted in specific historical experience. Covenants are made at particular times, in specific places, for specific reasons. They are predicated on a historical narrative. Such-and-such happened. Because of that, our ancestors came to a collective resolve. They bound themselves and us, their successors, to build a society that would honour a commitment, fulfil a promise, be loyal to certain ideals. We are their heirs, continuing their story, keeping faith with their undertakings, preserving their heritage and handing it on to the next generation.

Covenants are not abstract and only rarely, as in the case of the biblical covenant with Noah (Genesis 9), do they refer to humanity as a whole. That is one of the great differences between political ideologies based on philosophical principles, and covenants based on the Hebrew Bible. *Philosophy teaches truth-as-system, the Bible teaches truth-as-story.* Philosophical truth is timeless, biblical truth is enacted in time. Covenantal societies have their constitutive narratives, stories of early beginnings, hopes, dreams, visions, prophets, heroes, battles fought, victories won, defeats, backslidings and rededications. Usually the story is in the form of a journey, actual or metaphorical: from slavery to freedom, or death to rebirth, or sin to salvation. Story-telling is how covenant is renewed.

Why Telling Stories is Part of Being Human

It is also, in a profound way, how politics is humanized. Jerome Bruner has reminded us of two fundamentally different forms of understanding.[8] One, the 'paradigmatic', seeks to explain the particular by fitting it into a universal structure. Scientific thought is like this. So is philosophy. The standard form of paradigmatic explanation is a general rule: 'If X, then Y.' The other form of understanding is 'narrative'. Unlike science, which seeks the universal, narrative celebrates the particular. A narrative has a specific setting in space and time. It has a cast of characters. They interact in complex and unpredictable ways. The standard form of narrative is, 'Once upon a time X happened, and then Y.'

The 'then' is different in these two sentences. In science and philosophy, the 'then' signals inevitability. If all men are mortal and Socrates is a man, then Socrates is mortal. The conclusion is already implicit in the premises. In narrative, it isn't. That is why we love listening to stories. We want to know what is going to happen next, and *we cannot be sure in advance.* That is why telling stories is part of being human. In narrative, nothing is inevitable. Will the hero find his courage? Will enemies relent and become friends? Will the persecuted escape to freedom? Are we listening to a story of tragedy or hope? Stories celebrate freedom. They remind us that the way human beings respond to a situation can never be fully predicted.

Stories recapitulate the human experience of time: the open future, the outcome dependent on our choice, the alternative possibilities that lie before our imagination and our strength or weakness of will. James

117

Joyce called stories epiphanies of the ordinary.[9] Paul Ricoeur has argued that narrative is essential to our humanity.[10] Stories speak to that dimension of human existence that cannot be reduced to particles of matter in space, selfish genes blindly reproducing themselves, or the iron cage of historical inevitability.

That is what has made biblical narrative, for so many centuries, so appealing to the Western imagination. Its characters for the most part are ordinary people with whom we can identify. Abraham and Sarah, Isaac and Rebecca, Jacob and his family are not epic figures, rulers, demigods, mythic heroes of superhuman strength. Moses has his doubts, David his failings, Jeremiah his questions, Elijah his moral passion, Hosea his tangled loves, Job his burning sense of justice. Unexpected things happen. Great miracles coexist with human fallibility and caprice. Time and again the story is on the verge of being derailed. The Promised Land is surrounded by enemies. The people lapse into idolatry. Prophets warn and are not heeded. Jonah, given a sacred mission, tries to run away.

Yet through it all – through more than a thousand years between Moses and the last of the prophets, Malachi – the themes persist. The vision remains. The call continues to resonate: Can we build a society that is not Egypt, or Babylon? One that does not enslave its inhabitants or sell its soul to decadence? Covenant mirrors the human experience of time, the open future, the contingencies of fate, the dangers that lie along the way on the road to freedom. To enter into a covenant, like deciding to marry or have a child, is to take a risk, an act of faith in an unknown, unknowable future. Alasdair MacIntyre, to whom we owe the renewed interest in narrative as part of ethics and politics, argues that a human life, to be intelligible, must have the form of a story, and that the fundamental form of story is the quest. Covenant is the politics of quest: for the promised land, the place of freedom, the society that honours the dignity of all.

Covenant Renewal

It follows that in covenantal societies, telling the story is always, in some way, a political act. It gives the *polis* and its citizens a historical context. It reminds us of commitments made, promises undertaken, duties accepted, ideals affirmed. A covenanted nation is one in which storytelling is essential.

The Bible gives us several examples. One is Passover itself. Another is the declaration to be made by those bringing firstfruits to the Temple. Those who did so were, according to Deuteronomy, to say the following:

118

My father was a wandering Aramean, and he went down into Egypt with a few people and lived there and became a great nation, powerful and numerous. But the Egyptians mistreated us and made us suffer, putting us to hard labor. Then we cried out to the Lord ... and the Lord brought us out of Egypt with a mighty hand and an outstretched arm ... He brought us to this place and gave us this land, a land flowing with milk and honey; and now I bring the firstfruits of the soil that you, Lord, have given me (Deut. 26:5–10).

This is history-as-memory in its most primal form, a national narrative to be recited by individuals each year.

The most overtly political act of memory was the ceremony prescribed every seven years, when the king was commanded to convene a national gathering at which he read the law (part of the book of Deuteronomy) to the public:

At the end of every seven years, in the year for canceling debts, during the Feast of Tabernacles, when all Israel comes to appear before the Lord your God at the place he will choose, you shall read this law before them in their hearing. Assemble the people—men, women and children, and the stranger living in your towns—so they can listen and learn to fear the Lord your God and follow carefully all the words of this law. Their children, who do not know this law, shall hear it and learn to fear the Lord your God as long as you live in the land you are crossing the Jordan to possess. (Deut. 31:10–13)

We have no historical record of how this was carried out, but we have testimony from the Bible itself of how gatherings such as these took place at critical moments in the nation's history: in the days of Joshua, King Josiah, and after the Babylonian exile in the time of Ezra and Nehemiah. These were ceremonies of covenant renewal. On each occasion, the leader recalled the nation's history, restated the terms of its existence as a community of faith under the sovereignty of God, and reaffirmed its commitment to the future.

That is what is happening in the speeches of John F. Kennedy and Lyndon Johnson. The American Presidential Inaugural Address every four years is the functional equivalent of the king's reading of the law specified in Deuteronomy. It is in effect a ceremony of covenant renewal, a public ratification of the nation's terms of existence, its moral commitment to 'the rights of man' and to 'liberty, justice and union'. The result, from George Washington onward, is the most sustained example of covenant-thinking in modern times. Ironically, the country that committed itself in the First Amendment to the separation of Church and State, produced the most religious political narrative in the modern world.

Britain does not have a national narrative. Its political rhetoric contains nothing resembling the American Inaugural Address, and it is important to understand why. It is not because Britain is less religious than the United States, though it is. It is because British politics is not covenantal. It once was, in the seventeenth century, and when it was, this is how British politicians spoke. After the settlement of 1688, however, Britain reverted to its earlier hierarchical and organic character, and the result is that Britain does not have a national narrative.

It may, however, need one, for two reasons. The first is that in an age in which liberal democracy is under threat, it can no longer be taken for granted. We need to know, perhaps even as children, why Britain is as it is. It would be a narrative of freedoms fought for, liberties won, injustices remedied and wrongs righted. It should be an inclusive narrative, telling among other things of how people from many different places and faiths came here and added greatly to our collective life. Stories ground liberty on something more stable and compelling than abstract concepts or the shifting sands of moral relativism. They also address directly the challenge of integrating minorities. Stories unite. They tell us who 'we' – all who live in this place – are. They become essential when a nation no longer shares a common ethnicity or a single overarching religious system of belief.

Stories create memory, and memory creates identity. That is why covenant and narrative are at the heart of nations consciously created out of diversity. Given the centrifugal forces at work in an era of globalization, this ancient form of society-building may be necessary if we believe, as many do, that liberal democratic politics needs a sense of collective belonging. This, at any rate, is the conclusion drawn by the eminent historian of nationalism, Anthony Smith, in his recent book *Chosen Peoples*:

> Where a given community manifests a clear sense of itself as 'chosen' for a task or covenant, where its members are firmly attached to homeland and soil, where they seek to emulate the virtues of past golden ages, and where their members are prepared to make personal sacrifices, if not of life, then of time and effort for the future of the community and the yet unborn, there we may expect to find a lively sense of national identity, one able to withstand the dangers and temptations of rapid change in a more interdependent world.[11]

There is, of course, a danger in the very idea of a national destiny, and it must be confronted head-on. The concept of a 'chosen people' is ostensibly similar to that of a 'master race'. These two ideas are, however, opposites. A chosen people is defined by a task, a master race by a sense of innate superiority. A chosen people feels called to serve; a master race to dominate. The characteristic emotion of a chosen people is humility; the virtue of a master race is pride, in Latin *superbia*. A master race sees victory in terms of its own merits; a chosen people attributes it to God or providence or history, not itself. A master race sees defeat as humiliation; a chosen people sees it as a call to repentance. A master race commemorates its victories in monumental architecture and ceremonial inscriptions. A chosen people does the opposite: it records its defeats and shortcomings. There is no more self-critical literature than the Hebrew Bible – an ongoing story of failures, backslidings and derelictions of duty.

A chosen people lives under the constant possibility of judgement, and thus also of rededication, repentance, *metanoia*. Lincoln was the great prophet of this theme. John Schaar sums up Lincoln's faith in these words:

We are a nation formed by a covenant, by dedication to a set of principles and by an exchange of promises to uphold and advance certain commitments among ourselves and throughout the world. Those principles and commitments are the core of American identity, the soul of the body politic. They make the American nation unique, and uniquely valuable, among and to the other nations. But the other side of the conception contains a warning, very like the warnings spoken by the prophets to Israel: if we fail in our promises to each other, and lose the principle of the covenant, then we lose everything, for they are we.[12]

This too is part of American political discourse: a constant recall to first principles, moral commitments. So a society predicated on a covenant is one that tells a certain kind of story about itself – a story of moral purpose and ideals, of founding moments and promises undertaken. It tells and retells that story, not always in the same words but with the same themes, at ceremonial occasions which become acts of rededication. That story is the basis of its collective identity as a nation, and of individuals as citizens, and the nation takes care to teach it to its children.

Covenantal politics is the most powerful form of identity creation because it does not depend on custom, habit or tradition-for-the-sake-of-tradition. Nor does it rest on an ideology, a philosophical system, a theory about power, wealth or the human condition. It honours the great truth of human identity, that we are not *human beings in general*,

121

nor are we citizens because we are of this race or that creed. We are part of a story, begun by those who came before us. They have entrusted us to write its next chapter in such a way as to do justice to, and keep faith with, what went before. We cannot change our colour; most of us do not wish to change our religion; but we can learn a new story and teach it to our children. That is why, when nations have stories, they can be inclusive. They invite newcomers to make it their own.

The French philosopher Jean-Francois Lyotard once defined post-modernism as 'the death of meta-narrative', meaning that we don't have, or don't need, the big stories any more – the ones that tell us who we are, where we came from, and what we are called on to do. He was wrong.[13] Without memory, there is no identity, and without identity we are cast adrift into a sea of chance, without compass, map or destination.

Chapter 11

The Responsible Society

If I am not for myself, who will be? But if I am only for myself, what am I?[1]

Hillel

The more we rely on ourselves, the smaller our need for the state; the smaller the state, the more we will learn to work together.[2]

Jonathan Freedland

A covenantal politics is, by definition, a *politics of responsibility*. It is created by an act of commitment. The people undertake to abide by a moral code, pursue a moral vision and create a society built on justice, compassion and respect for human dignity. This is not a side-effect, something that happens along the way. It is the foundational act of a covenantal society – what Philip Selznick aptly describes as a 'self-conscious moral order'.[3] It happens when a nation 'under God' resolves to take fate into its own hands and build a society on the basis of something other than wealth or power. It is, to quote Selznick again, 'an act of faith and resolve, a self-defining commitment.'

This is what makes covenant distinctive as a basis for politics. Unlike other systems it does not take social structures for granted. It does not see them as written into the fabric of the universe or consecrated and legitimated by antiquity. Unlike the politics of organic societies, the parties to a covenant do not say, 'This is what we do because this is how things have always been done'. Nor, unlike the defenders of hierarchical societies, do they see differences in class, rank and power as given by birth or the natural order of things. Covenants arise among people strongly committed to freedom, equality and dignity. Often, as in Puritanism, they make their appearance as a protest against societies whose inequalities have become morally untenable.

At the heart of covenant is the profound realization that society is

123

what we make of it. The way things are is not necessarily the way things ought to be. Covenant is born when a free people question the established order and conclude that there is a better way. They seek to create a society that refuses to divide humanity into rulers and ruled, those who command and those who obey. It is a collective moral undertaking on the part of 'We, the people', *all* the people, rich, poor, weak, strong, powerful and powerless alike. It says, in effect: there is no one else to do it for us, and we can achieve together what none of us can do alone. It is built on the idea that we are individually and collectively responsible for our future. We each have a part to play. Covenant is the conscious decision to create a society in the light of shared ideals.

Covenant is politics with a purpose. It sees history as a journey – long, slow, fraught with setbacks – toward a destination perhaps never finally reached but glimpsed from afar. It recognizes that we are fallible, frail, prone to every kind of moral failing, but it refuses to give way to cynicism or despair. It is built on faith of an unusual kind. A religious way of putting it would be to say that it is faith that God has faith in us. God empowers us to become 'his partners in the work of creation'. A secular way of saying it is to refuse to believe that *Homo homini lupus est*, 'man is a wolf to his fellow-man', is the last word about the human condition. One of the great exponents of covenant politics, the late Robert F. Kennedy, said in his tribute to the assassinated Martin Luther King, that the aim of politics is 'to tame the savageness of man and make gentle the life of this world'.[4] It is the combination of high ideals, together with a candid acknowledgement of human weakness, that is the common factor in prophetic Judaism, seventeenth-century Calvinism, and the biblical strand in early American politics.

The idea that covenantal politics is an expression of human responsibility may sound odd to those who recall its religious roots. Is not the biblical narrative precisely based on *not* exercising human responsibility but rather on leaving fate to God? Was it not he who brought his people to freedom, divided the sea, led them across the wilderness, and gave them manna from heaven and water from a rock? In fact, however, it is just this story that most powerfully explains why human responsibility is essential. In the early years of their history, when God did everything for the Israelites, they remained in a state of arrested development. They quarrelled, were ungrateful and rebelled. They displayed all the signs of a dependency culture.

Slowly over the centuries, the miracles became rarer. The people suffered division, defeat and exile. Eventually, in the days of Ezra and Nehemiah, the people of their own accord renewed their covenant with God, and from then on they never worshiped idols again. The story of the Hebrew Bible as a whole, extending across a thousand years in real time, is of the progressive withdrawal of divine intervention and the transfer of responsibility to human beings.

The politics of responsibility was born when the transcendence of God allowed people to see the relativity, the man-made quality, of all social structures. The only thing that satisfies the prophetic imagination is a society of free individuals, each respecting the non-negotiable dignity of others, who come together in freedom to pledge themselves to work together to build a gracious, just and compassionate world. That is our task. God does not do it for us. He teaches, guides, warns, instructs, inspires, gives us strength when we are weary and hope when hope seems lost, but he does not do the work for us. Instead, the Creator calls on us to create. The Shaper of history summons us to shape history.

A covenantal society is a moral community, future-oriented, goal-directed, whose citizens are on a journey toward a destination. That does not mean that people agree. On the contrary, Americans fought a civil war over the question: Does the phrase 'all men are created equal' include blacks? Does it permit slavery? Covenantal societies are argumentative societies. What they share, though, is their emphasis on responsibility, personal, mutual, reciprocal and collective. As Judaism's second-century sages put it: 'All Israelites are responsible for one another.' It is we, together, who make society.

It is this combination of personal and collective responsibility that gives covenantal societies their energy. They enlist their citizens. They generate ideals. They see us all as co-builders of the social order. That is the egalitarian thrust of the biblical phrase 'a kingdom of priests'. All ancient societies had priests, but they were a minority, an elite. A kingdom of priests is one in which all bear the burden; all are guardians of the collective conscience. Covenant democratizes responsibility. It creates active citizens. It is a politics of empowerment. It sees society as the home we build together.

Structures of Grace in Society

It is hard to make comparisons across the centuries. Yet what is striking about both the Hebrew Bible and early Christian ethics is their emphasis on personal responsibility for the structures of grace within society. It is the individual, not the state, who is commanded in the Bible to care for the poor, pursue justice, release people from debt every seventh year, and let employees rest every seventh day. It is the individual who is told:

> Do not take advantage of a hired man who is poor and needy, whether he is a brother Israelite or a stranger living in one of

125

your towns. Pay him his wages each day before sunset, because he is poor and is counting on it ... Do not deprive the stranger or the fatherless of justice, or take the cloak of the widow as a pledge ... When you are harvesting in your field and you overlook a sheaf, do not go back to get it. Leave it for the stranger, the fatherless and the widow, so that the Lord your God may bless you in all the work of your hands. (Deut. 24:14–19)

The book of Ruth, in which Boaz looks after his relative Naomi and her daughter-in-law Ruth, gives us a glimpse of this ethic in action. The Bible calls it *chessed*, usually translated as 'loving kindness' or perhaps more accurately, 'covenant love'.

The prophets, without exception, see the moral texture of a society as the critical variable in its fate. Their sharpest words are reserved for those who believe you can serve God without caring about your fellow human beings. These passages are among the most incandescent in the Bible. Amos castigates the people: 'You oppress the righteous and take bribes, you deprive the poor of justice in the courts ... Let justice roll down like a river and righteousness like an ever-flowing stream' (Amos 5:12, 24). Isaiah, in God's name, delivers the great indictment:

> When you spread out your hands,
> I will hide my eyes from you;
> even though you make many prayers,
> I will not listen;
> your hands are full of blood.
> Wash yourselves; make yourselves clean;
> remove the evil of your deeds from before my eyes;
> cease to do evil, learn to do good;
> seek justice, correct oppression;
> bring justice to the fatherless,
> plead the widow's cause. (Isaiah 1:15–17)

The point is that this is not the responsibility of any particular group within society, but of everyone. That is what citizenship in a covenantal society is: co-responsibility for justice, equity, kindness and compassion. A free society, implies the Bible, is a moral society, for if there is corruption and injustice, there will no longer be social cohesion. The powerful will oppress the powerless. The rich will be at best indifferent to, at worst exploitative of, the plight of the poor. Each will seek his or her own advantage rather than the common good. Society will become demoralized, people will not rally to its defence, and it will either fall to an enemy without or it will implode from within.

126

Nowadays we tend to make a sharp distinction between religious ritual and social inclusion. Yet the two are often intimately intertwined. The Bible says, for example, about religious festivals: 'You shall rejoice on your festival, you, your son and daughter, your male and female servant, the Levite, the stranger, the fatherless, and the widow who are within your towns' (Deut. 16:14). On this, Maimonides, the twelfth-century codifier, writes: 'As well as eating and drinking, it is your duty to feed the stranger, the orphan and the widow, and other poor and unfortunate people, for if you lock the doors of your courtyard and eat and drink with your wife and family without giving anything to the poor and bitter in soul to eat and drink – this is not rejoicing as a religious commandment but mere gastronomic pleasure ... Rejoicing of this kind is a disgrace to those who indulge in it.'[5]

What we see in these texts is that the festivals are not just religious rituals. They are acts of *community-creation*. A decent society, the Hebrew Bible implies, is one in which people at the margins, the poor, those from fractured families, and the 'stranger' (what we would now call a member of an ethnic minority) are not to be excluded from communal celebrations. It is not only their legal and economic situation the Bible cares about, but also their psychological needs for friendship and inclusion. There is something here that still speaks to our situation today.

A very similar spirit animates the New Testament.[6] Jesus tells his disciples to feed the hungry, give drink to the thirsty, clothe the naked, visit the sick, and give hospitality to the stranger. Between Judaism and Christianity, and between both and Islam, the theology may be different but the ethic is the same.

It is anachronistic to compare these ancient texts with a welfare state in which basic provisions are the responsibility of the government and its agencies. We did not have a welfare state in Britain until 1945. Governments until then were more limited in scope. Yet the concept of centralized welfare is not wholly absent from the Bible. In one of its more famous stories we read about how Joseph, foreseeing seven years of famine, stored grain in the years of plenty and gave it to the people of Egypt during the lean years.

It is a very pointed story, and like many biblical narratives it is far more subtle than a surface reading suggests. On the face of it, Joseph has saved a whole nation from starvation. He says so to his brothers: God has brought about the strange sequence of events by which he became second-in-command in Egypt, 'to save many lives' (Genesis 50:20). Yet Joseph at the same time centralizes the whole economy of Egypt. To pay for the food, the people give money, then their livestock, then their land and labour. The Egyptians become, in effect, slaves to their own government, just as the Israelites were later to do. There is surely a critique here, as we saw in Samuel's speech warning against the appointment of a king, of 'big government', the over-intrusive state.

Putting all this together, a picture begins to emerge. The Hebrew Bible, as we saw, distinguishes between covenant and contract, society and the state. We now see why. Society is about the quality of human relationships within families and communities. It is local, small-scale, inter-personal. It has a human face. The state is central, impersonal. It levies taxes, it provides services, but there is nothing voluntary about its operation. It uses power, not goodwill. So if the state grows at the cost of civil society, something is lost. When taxes replace generosity, and social workers replace caring neighbours, a dimension of social life atrophies and wanes. Instead of individuals being linked horizontally to one another in bonds of reciprocal responsibility, they are linked vertically to the state. They become passive recipients instead of active citizens. And though there are many gains – equality of provision, consistency, reliability – there is also a loss. The fabric of community wears thin.

An Age of Volunteering

One of the remarkable features of Victorian England was the huge growth in volunteering and philanthropy. Frank Prochaska tells us that most communities would have 'various schools for the poor, visiting societies, working parties, mother's meetings, and temperance societies'.[7] There were voluntary groups for everything: 'soup kitchens, maternity charities, crèches, blanket clubs, coal clubs, clothing clubs, boot clubs, medical clubs, lending libraries, and holiday funds'. Charity was not a middle-class preserve. Workers formed societies for mutual aid in times of sickness or unemployment or injury. Navvies created sick clubs and visiting societies. Friedrich Engels, Karl Marx's colleague, was struck by the kindness of the poor to the poor: 'although the workers cannot really afford to give charity on the same scale as the middle class, they are nevertheless more charitable in every way'. People were involved in the fate of their neighbours and co-workers. The historian A. J. P. Taylor called them, not unkindly, 'a great army of busybodies'.[8]

Much of this sense of responsibility had religious roots. William Wilberforce called it 'Practical Christianity'. Anglicans fought slavery and distributed Bibles. The Unitarians and Quakers favoured educational projects. Baptists and Congregationalists promoted temperance. Methodists pioneered in district visiting, going out to the poor in their homes. And they were all involved in education through charity schools, ragged schools, Sunday schools and Bible classes. The

Victorians knew that there was something special about this. The *Nonconformist* declared in 1842: 'In no other kingdom under the sun is there such a periodical gathering of benevolence and piety.'

There was more at stake here than alleviating poverty and ignorance. The Victorians, like their American contemporaries, had a strong sense of freedom. They did not like excessive government intervention. They preferred to exercise responsibility themselves. They believed, as Samuel Smiles put it in 1859, 'in helping and stimulating men to elevate and improve themselves by their own free and independent individual action'. They recognized that there is a limit on what governments and laws can achieve. They can provide services, but they cannot change lives. For that you need education, moral ideals, and networks of support. Far from being content with the status quo, the Victorian volunteers championed the cause of those who lacked a voice: the poor, minorities, women, neglected or abused children and the working class. Charles Dickens drew attention to many social injustices through his immense literary power.

John Stuart Mill realized that one of the best defences of freedom was to get people involved in solving their own problems through collaborative activity at a local level. He argued that governments should encourage citizens 'to manage as many as possible of their joint concerns by voluntary co-operation' rather than relying on the state. They should restrict 'to the narrowest compass the intervention of a public authority in the business of the community'. Excessive state intervention, he believed, anaesthetizes the spirit of liberty. Collective self-help energizes it:

> In proportion as the people are accustomed to manage their affairs by their own active intervention, instead of leaving them to the government, their desires will turn to repelling tyranny, rather than to tyrannizing: while in proportion as all real initiative and direction resides in the government, and individuals habitually feel and act as under its perpetual tutelage, popular institutions develop in them not the desire of freedom, but an unmeasured appetite for place and power.[9]

The man who saw this most clearly was Alexis de Tocqueville, the French diplomat who made a study of American society in the 1830s. Tocqueville believed that democracy was vulnerable to individualism. People might prefer private satisfaction to public service. The one antidote was local civic engagement. This taught people the 'habits of the heart' necessary to protect freedom. Otherwise there was a perennial danger that people might leave everything to government, and find eventually that they had lost the power to govern themselves. In a famous passage he draws a picture of how liberty could be killed by kindness on the part of the state:

> Above this race of men stands an immense and tutelary power, which takes upon itself alone to secure their gratifications and to watch over their fate. That power is absolute, minute, regular, provident, and mild. It would be like the authority of a parent if, like that authority, its object was to prepare men for manhood; but it seeks, on the contrary, to keep them in perpetual childhood: it is well content that the people should rejoice, provided they think of nothing but rejoicing. For their happiness such a government willingly labors, but it chooses to be the sole agent and the only arbiter of that happiness; it provides for their security, foresees and supplies their necessities, facilitates their pleasures, manages their principal concerns, directs their industry, regulates the descent of property, and subdivides their inheritances: what remains, but to spare them all the care of thinking and all the trouble of living?[10]

By taking on itself ever more responsibilities, democratic government gently, benignly, imperceptibly robs citizens of the exertions of altruism and self-help that are essential to the maintenance of a free society.

Victorian England understood the difference between state and society, contract and covenant. There are things that can be achieved by government action and others that can only be achieved by patient face-to-face voluntary engagement with people.

Social Capital

Economists have a name for this: they call it 'social capital'.[11] By this they mean the habits of co-operation, reciprocal altruism and trust that occur when people work (or play, or pray) together.

Modern societies have an enormous dependence on two institutions: the market and the state. Both are contractual institutions that people engage with in pursuit of self-interest. Both involve competition, in one case for wealth, in the other for power. But societies cannot be built on competition alone. For without trust, societies eventually break down. If I cannot trust you to honour your word, then I cannot trade with you or vote for you without relying on massive systems of surveillance, regulation and enforcement. That is not a trust society but a risk society.

Any group – even in the case of social animals like primates and dolphins – needs habits of co-operation as well as competition. And habits of co-operation depend on covenantal virtues: faithfulness, loyalty, honesty, integrity, friendship, collegiality, trusting others and acting so that others trust you.

Social capital is not created either by the isolated individual or the mechanisms of the state but by the activities focused on in this chapter: friendships, communities, voluntary activities, philanthropy, all the relationships where we put aside considerations of power or personal advantage and are bound instead by a sense of duty or fellowship, sympathy or a simple desire to help.

Societies rich in social capital tend to have high morale, a strong sense of belonging, lower crime and less inter-group tension. Where habits of caring for others are strong and widely diffused, collective identity is also strong. The Victorians understood this. Sociologists and politicians rediscovered it in the 1980s when they asked why huge programmes of welfare had not conquered poverty. That was when they began to realize that social problems often have a personal, psychological and communal dimension as well as an economic one. We need networks of support. Without them people feel vulnerable and alone, and it is hard to solve personal crises alone.

Social capital is not, in and of itself, a complete solution to social ills. Communities can be narrow and exclusive as well as generous and inclusive. Strong communities can come into conflict with one another; hence the warning about the 'inward turn' in chapter 7. Nor are they evenly distributed throughout the country and the population. Relying on voluntary help can leave some far less supported than others. That is why state action is necessary. The Bible itself recognizes this. Hence the laws about cancellation of debts in the seventh year and the return of land to its original owners in the Jubilee. Private charity and communal provision are not in themselves sufficient to correct the huge inequities and inequalities that arise from any economic order. What is important is the balance. State must be supplemented by society, and contractual relations by covenantal ones. A good society needs both justice and compassion. Justice can be established by law; compassion flows from the human heart.

In this regard, Britain is well poised to take this further. It has huge reservoirs of social capital. Today there are more than 160,000 charities and more than 200,000 other non-charitable voluntary and communal organizations. Sixteen million people engage in voluntary work: nearly two adults out of every five give of their time to help others. In recent years the same has been true among new ethnic minorities, Muslim, Hindu and Sikh. They have founded hundreds of new charities and voluntary groups, and that too will play its part in helping them feel secure and supported. Volunteering remains one of Britain's greatest strengths and helps explain why community relations are better, and

131

ethnic and religious tensions lower, here than in most other places in Europe.

A Culture of Responsibility

I have tried to show in this chapter how the biblical emphasis on society as well as state is translated into practice, in biblical times and today. It comes about through a culture of responsibility, in which we see ourselves as implicated in the fate of others. A large part of what makes for societal grace cannot be done by governments, impersonal agencies and centralized provision. It depends on us, all of us, through habits of help and hospitality, giving and getting involved. Civil society is the sum of all these myriad interactions happening every day between neighbours and strangers.

Judaism and Christianity embody a strong ethic of practical engagement, as does Islam with its principle of *zakat*, alms-giving to the poor. Nor is this a religious imperative only. The hundreds of thousands of secular charities remind us that this is part of the human condition. The best way of breaking down barriers between people or communities is through simple, unforced acts of kindness. One act can undo years of estrangement. Civil society humanizes our collective life.

This helps explain a curious feature of biblical ethics. It is striking that the Bible has no word for 'rights'. It sets forth its moral vision entirely in terms of duties, obligations, responsibilities and commands. Quite clearly, the Bible *presupposes* rights. The idea that all of us are 'in the image' of God implies a right to human dignity. The command, 'Justice, justice shall you pursue' entails the right to a fair trial and to the rule of law. The duty to set aside portions of the harvest for the poor represents a right to welfare. Yet rights are not part of the biblical vocabulary. Why so?

We tend to think that rights and responsibilities are correlative, two sides of the same coin. If I have a right to X, someone has a responsibility to ensure that I have X. But this is not quite so. Rights and responsibilities belong to two different systems. Rights are enshrined in law. Responsibilities, for the most part, are born in the moral imagination. There are some responsibilities that can be legislated: a parent is responsible for the conduct of a child, a driver is responsible for staying awake, alert and sober. But in a deeper sense, responsibility depends on education, culture and the human personality. There are individualist cultures in which people say, 'Why should I get involved? It's your problem, not mine.' There are familial cultures in which people feel responsible for kin but not for strangers. There are tribal cultures in which a clear distinction is made between duties to 'us' and unconcern for 'them'. The Bible rules that a stork is an unclean animal, yet its name in Hebrew is *chasidah*, 'the compassionate one'. A disciple once asked a rabbi why an animal with so lovely a name is unclean. The rabbi replied, 'Because it shows compassion only for its own.'

So rights depend on law, responsibility on culture. But without responsibility, rights are a cheque on an empty account, a song on an iPod whose battery is dead. On 10 December 1948 the United Nations made its momentous declaration of Human Rights. Yet human rights abuses have not visibly diminished since. That is why the Bible is more concerned with cultivating habits of responsibility than merely prescribing rights. Rights are legislated by states. Responsibility is created by society. You cannot have one without the other. A system of rights must be accompanied by a culture of responsibility.

Responsibility cultures are sustained tutorials in human freedom. They locate change 'in here' rather than 'out there'. They do not see the individual as powerless, caught in a vast swirl of forces beyond their control. Instead, they understand that change requires effort, and great change requires collective effort. Therefore, I must search for ways through which I can establish co-operation with others, trusting them and earning their trust, so that we can work together for common goals while respecting one another's freedom and dignity. A society that honours rights will be one that encourages responsibility.

That is why I have argued for a metaphor of society as the home we build together. It focuses on our individual and collective responsibility for the social order. We did not make the country house: we were guests there. We did not make the hotel: we were visitors there. Both of these models locate responsibility for society *somewhere else*, and that is a disempowering way of seeing things. The home we build together is one in which I have the dignity of co-authorship. I helped plan and build it. I invested my time and energies into it. Because of this it holds a special meaning for me. It is where I belong. It is home.

Chapter 12

The Home We Build Together

A passenger on a boat began to drill a hole under his seat. The other passengers protested. He replied, 'What business is it of yours? I am drilling a hole under my seat, not yours.' The others replied, 'But the water will rise and flood the boat for all of us.'[1]

Rabbi Shimon bar Yochai

Call them not 'your children' but 'your builders'.[2]

Talmud

I have argued that the Hebrew Bible deserves to be taken seriously as a political text, because it answers the question that is ours: how do you construct a society that respects cultural and religious diversity while at the same time promoting civic equality, social cohesion and a sense of the common good. Most political theories are about the state, not society; about the configuration of power not the shape and influence of culture. Plato was interested in culture, as was Aristotle, and Hegel. But they and others who thought about it took it for granted that society, or at least those who had rights within it, would share a single culture. For them it was only a monoculture that sustained the state. Organic societies share a culture, but they generate a strong, sometimes dangerously exclusive, nationalism. Hierarchical societies sometimes impose a culture. In other cases they admit diversity, as did the Ottoman Empire with its millet system, but what they then cannot admit is equality. That is what makes covenantal politics of special interest today.

The Bible is, of course, a religious document, but that is not my concern here, nor was it the concern of Hobbes, Locke, Spinoza, Rousseau or Tom Paine. They read it because it was about politics: kings, priests, prophets, corruption in high places, the constant call for a return to justice, equality, dignity and compassion, internecine rivalries, national defeats, exiles, returns, rededications. It is about how individuals conduct their lives together, sometimes with violence, sometimes with duplicity, but it never lets these failings be the final word about the human situation. We can live graciously together in families, communities, societies – even, in Isaiah's most daring visions, as all humanity. But that requires a highly specific way of thinking about relationships, through covenant, the voluntary association of free and independent agents through the mutual exchange and honouring of promises. That alone allows freedom and order to coexist.

The Israelites whose early history is told in the books of Exodus, Numbers and Deuteronomy, lacked a national identity. They had been slaves. They were conscious of ethnic and religious diversity: that is the point of the Bible's emphasis on the 'twelve tribes' and the 'mixed multitude'. They had, as yet, no land, no state. They were a group of asylum-seekers on the move. Out of this inchoate and fractious group, Moses had to create a sense of common purpose and belonging. That is what makes exodus politics, the politics of covenant, so germane to our situation today. When societies seek unity out of diversity, while at the same time honouring the dignity of difference, they turn to covenant. That is what the English, Scots and Americans did in the seventeenth century, and what the Dutch and Swiss had done a century before.

The Tabernacle

There is, though, one detail I have deliberately saved till last. Read the book of Exodus and you will see that the early chapters are all about the politics of freedom. They tell of slavery, oppression, the mission of Moses to Pharaoh, the ten plagues, liberation, the division of the Red Sea and the revelation at Mount Sinai. All of this is a sequential story about liberty. But the last part of Exodus – roughly a third of the book as a whole – is taken up with an apparently minor and irrelevant episode told and retold in exhaustive detail: the construction of the Tabernacle.

This was the first house of worship made by the Israelites. It was a modest affair, made of poles, beams, skins and drapes that could be taken apart, carried on their journeys, and re-assembled at their next encampment. It had, or so it seems, no lasting significance. Once the Israelites had entered the land, the Tabernacle was left in Shilo for several centuries until King David established Jerusalem as the capital of the newly united kingdom, and his son Solomon built the Temple. So why is the story of the Tabernacle told at such length?

The question becomes all the more acute when we realize that the narrative is deliberately constructed in such a way as to create a set of linguistic parallels between the Israelites' construction of the Tabernacle and God's creation of the universe. The key Hebrew words – for *make, see, complete, bless, sanctify, work, behold* – are the same in both texts. The effect is to suggest that making the Tabernacle was the human counterpart of the divine creation of the universe. But now compare the length of the two texts. The creation of the universe takes a mere 34 verses (Genesis 1:1 – 2:3). The making of the Tabernacle takes several hundreds of verses – more than fifteen times as long. The Bible is clearly intimating something important, but it is hard to see what it is. What has making a portable sanctuary to do with exodus, freedom and national identity?

The Hebrew Bible is, as already stated, a political as well as a spiritual text, and it tells a political story. Despite the miracles, the essential narrative is remarkably human. The Israelites are portrayed as a querulous, almost ungovernable group. Moses, their deliverer, comes to them with the news that they are about to go free. His first intervention, however, only makes things worse, and the people complain. Eventually the people leave, but Pharaoh and his army pursue them. They are trapped between the approaching Egyptian chariots and the Red Sea, and again they complain. Moses performs a miracle. The sea divides. The Israelites cross through on dry land. They sing a song of deliverance. But three days later, they are complaining again, this time about the lack of water.

Some six weeks later, at Mount Sinai, they receive the great revelation. God speaks directly to the people. They make a covenant with him. Moses reascends the mountain to receive the tablets on which the covenant provisions are engraved. While he is away, the Israelites commit their greatest sin. They make a golden calf and dance before it, saying, 'These are your gods, Israel, who brought you up out of Egypt.' The episode of the golden calf is told in Exodus 32–34, in the middle of the account of the making of the Tabernacle, so clearly there is some connection between them.

Putting all this together we arrive at the boldest of all Exodus' political statements. A nation – at least, the kind of nation the Israelites were called on to become – is *created through the act of creation itself.* Not all the miracles of Exodus combined, not the plagues, the division of the sea, manna from heaven or water from a rock, not even the revelation at Sinai itself, turned the Israelites into a nation. In commanding Moses to get the people to make the Tabernacle, God was in effect saying: *To turn a group of individuals into a covenantal nation, they must build something together.*

Freedom cannot be conferred by an outside force, not even by God himself. It can be achieved only by collective, collaborative effort on the part of the people themselves. Hence the construction of the

Tabernacle. A people is made by making. A nation is built by building. What they built was a 'home' for the Divine presence. The Tabernacle, placed at the centre of the camp with the tribes arrayed around it, symbolized the public square, the common good, the voice that had summoned them to collective freedom. It was a visible emblem of community. Within the Tabernacle was the ark, within the ark were the tablets of stone, and on the tablets of stone were written the details of the covenant. It was the home of their constitution of liberty. Here, then, is the source of the title of this book. *Society is the home, the Tabernacle, we build together.*

It was built out of difference and diversity. That too is the point of the narrative. Each of the Israelites brought his or her own distinctive contribution. Some brought gold, others silver, others bronze. Some gave jewels, others animal skins, and others drapes. Some gave of their skills and time. The point is not what they gave but that each was valued equally. As the Bible says about the half-shekel contribution: 'the rich not more, the poor not less'. The Tabernacle was built out of the differential contributions of the various groups and tribes. It represented *orchestrated diversity*, or in social terms, integration without assimilation. That is the dignity of difference. Because we are not the same, we each have something unique to contribute, something only we can give.

Moses was faced with a problem not unlike ours. How do you turn a group of people – in his case, liberated slaves – into a nation with a collective identity? His answer – God's answer – was dazzling in its simplicity. You get them voluntarily to create something together. The voluntariness is essential: Moses was commanded to ask for contributions 'from each whose heart prompts him to give'. At the same time, of course, he had to create a mood, a cultural climate, in which giving was expected. The story of the construction of the Tabernacle has an inescapable political dimension. It is about how you create a sense of national belonging. The best way of making people feel 'I belong' is to enlist them in a shared project so they can say, 'I helped build this.'

The Tabernacle is a symbol of society. And once we recognize the linguistic and literary parallelism between the making of the Tabernacle and the creation narrative in the first chapter of Genesis, we understand the immense implication: *Just as God creates the natural universe, so we are called on to create the social universe* – a universe, like that of the planets and stars, that is ordered, rule-governed, a space of integrated diversity, a world we can see and say, as God saw and said, that it is good.

Milton and the Temple

John Milton understood this and said so in his great defence of free speech, *Areopagitica* (1644).[3] His problem, like other seventeenth-century writers, was how to move beyond the sectarian wars that had destroyed the peace of Europe for a century. How could you create social cohesion out of the clash of religious beliefs, not only between Protestants and Catholics, but also between other, smaller radical groups of the time like the Quakers, the Diggers, the Ranters, the Levellers, the Fifth Monarchists, the Socinians and the Muggletonians, each with its own interpretation of Scripture, its own version of utopia?

How do you defend freedom of speech, and ultimately liberty of conscience, in a religious age, using religious texts? How in an age of conflict do you justify a society in which there is space for difference on matters of ultimate concern? Milton's argument is that God wants difference, for it is only through the clash of opinions that truth is honed and refined. 'Where there is much desire to learn, there of necessity will be much arguing, much writing, many opinions; for *opinion in good men is but knowledge in the making*'. The path to truth passes through the city of many voices. The strength and vigour of argument within a culture is a measure of its spiritual health.

Yet Milton was aware that many of his contemporaries disagreed. They believed that society requires us all to hold the same faith. Milton's refutation is based on the building, not of the Tabernacle but the Temple. It is absurd to insist on uniformity, as if:

> while the Temple of the Lord was building, some cutting, some squaring the marble, others hewing the cedars, there should be a sort of irrationall men who could not consider there must be many schisms and many dissections made in the quarry and in the timber, ere the house of God can be built. And when every stone is laid artfully together, it cannot be united into a continuity, it can but be contiguous in this world; neither can every peece of the building be of one form; nay rather the perfection consist in this, that out of many moderat varieties and brotherly dissimilitudes that are not vastly disproportionall arises the goodly and gracious symmetry that commends the whole pile and structure.

Society, for Milton, is the arena in which all sorts of groups, different yet linked in a collective task, each have a contribution to make to 'the whole pile and structure'. It is precisely this integrated diversity that gives society its complex beauty, its 'goodly and gracious symmetry'. Society, for Milton, is the Temple we build together.

139

Metaphors affect the way we think. Unlike the country-house model, society as Tabernacle speaks about genuinely shared identity, not about hosts and guests, insiders and outsiders, centre and peripheries. And unlike society-as-hotel, society as Tabernacle is a place that holds special significance for us because we helped build it. We gave, we contributed, we shared in the making; in it we invested something of ourselves. Covenant is about how to create identity through collaborative activity and collective responsibility.

The distinctive features of the Tabernacle model are:

- Identity is achieved. It is not granted. We are what we do.
- There is an integral connection between giving and belonging. Because we are co-creators of society, we are members of it in a strong sense.
- It is a model that focuses on responsibilities, not rights.
- It focuses on altruism rather than – as in the social-contract model – the convergence of multiple calculations of self-interest.
- It focuses on the future, not just the past. The national narrative, which includes the people's past, is still being written and we are its co-authors.
- It is teleological. It focuses on purpose, not status. Every contribution counts.
- It carries with it a strong sense of the common good: the Tabernacle is a symbol of collective dedication.
- It is not *ethnic* nationalism. Race, colour, place of origin and length of residence are irrelevant.
- It is not *faith-based* nationalism, a creedal community. Identity is about doing, not believing.
- It is a strong form of *civic* nationalism, based on participation in the national project, and seeing society as a work in the making.

Society is made out of the contributions of many individuals. *What* they give is unimportant; *that* they give is essential. Society is what we build together – and the more different types of people there are, the more complex and beautiful will be the structure we create. The important thing is that we build together. A nation is made by contributions, not claims; active citizenship, not rights; what we give, not what we demand. A national identity can be made out of the contributions of many cultures, many faiths. What matters is that together we build something none of us could make alone.

Voluntary and Non-Voluntary Contribution

There is one last twist in the story. It took place almost five hundred years after the construction of the Tabernacle. Milton spoke about the Temple, as if it and the Tabernacle were similar things. In one sense they were. They were both places of worship, at the symbolic centre of society: the Tabernacle in the midst of the camp; the Temple in Jerusalem. Both involved the contributions of many kinds of people. Both were projects of society as a whole.

There was, however, one difference. The Tabernacle was made out of voluntary contributions. The Temple was not. To build it, Solomon had to turn the Israelites into a vast labour force:

> King Solomon conscripted laborers from all Israel – thirty thousand men. He sent them off to Lebanon in shifts of ten thousand a month, so that they spent one month in Lebanon and two months at home. Adoniram was in charge of the forced labor. Solomon had seventy thousand carriers and eighty thousand stonecutters in the hills, as well as thirty-three hundred foremen who supervised the project and directed the workmen. At the king's command they removed from the quarry large blocks of quality stone to provide a foundation of dressed stone for the temple. The craftsmen of Solomon and Hiram and the men of Gebal cut and prepared the timber and stone for the building of the temple. (I Kings 5:13–19)

But is this not precisely what the Israelites left Egypt to avoid, becoming a mere labour force for a ruler engaged in a grand project, even if it is the holiest of holies? Is this not, albeit temporarily and for a sacred cause, a new form of slavery?

No less fascinating is the explanation given in the second book of Samuel for why God, when David first mooted the idea of a Temple, said No. This is the message he sent through the prophet Nathan:

> Go and tell my servant David, 'This is what the Lord says: Are you the one to build me a house to dwell in? I have not dwelt in a house from the day I brought the Israelites up out of Egypt to this day. I have been moving from place to place with a tent as my dwelling. Wherever I have moved with all the Israelites, did I ever say to any of their rulers whom I commanded to shepherd my people Israel, "Why have you not built me a house of cedar?"' (2 Samuel 7:5–7)

God tells David that his son will build the Temple. The book of Chronicles (I Chron. 28:3) gives a completely different explanation.

141

David had been a warrior. He fought wars and shed blood. Only a man of peace can build a temple to God. Yet the earlier contains a tantalizing suggestion: that God does not seek the glory of great buildings. It is only the barest hint, but it lingers in the mind.

What was the result? After Solomon's death, the people came to his son and successor, Rehoboam, and staged a protest. 'Your father put a heavy yoke on us, but now lighten the harsh labor and the heavy yoke he put on us, and we will serve you.' The elders who had counselled Solomon told Rehoboam to grant their request. Rehoboam's young friends, however, told him to refuse. Rehoboam did refuse. The nation split in two, the ten northerly tribes declaring an independent kingdom under Jeroboam. It was the end of the united kingdom. No subsequent ruler was able to reunite the tribes.

This too is a political statement of the highest order. What can be done voluntarily cannot necessarily be done coercively. The Tabernacle, built out of voluntary contributions, united the nation. The Temple, built by conscripted labour, divided it.

In contemporary language: society is not the state. Civil society, where the covenantal virtues are exercised, is made up of voluntary associations. When the state takes over the work of civil institutions, it is not the same thing under a different name: it is a different thing entirely. That is the difference between contract and covenant, between what people do because the government decides, and what they do out of a sense of shared commitment. Society is what we make together, all of us, without delegating away responsibility to others. Governments administer states. We, the people, build societies.

The Argument Summarized

With this I come to the end of this section of the argument. In it I have set out a cluster of political ideas based on the concept of covenant. As it appears in the Bible it is a religious idea. But it started life as a secular one: covenants were an ancient Near Eastern form of treaty between states. There is nothing inherently religious about covenant. What makes it distinctive is that it is about relationships – within a family, a community, or a society. Essentially it is about creating a relationship of trust. Those bound by a covenant, voluntarily undertake to share a fate. They choose to link their destinies together. They accept responsibilities to and for one another. Covenants redeem the solitude of the 'lonely crowd'.

Our political vocabulary has become impoverished, and may not be strong enough to sustain liberal democracy through the challenges that lie ahead. Liberal societies cannot be built on the assumption that everyone within them is liberal. I am not. As one who takes religion seriously, I do not believe that personal autonomy is the highest value. Indeed, I find the whole concept incoherent. Morality is not what I decide; it is what holds a group together. A private morality is as inconceivable as a private language that only one person understands. Yet I am a profound believer in liberal democracy. The reason is that morality is not politics; politics is not morality. Liberal democracy is a political phenomenon, not a moral one. It is the best system yet devised to allow different groups of people with strong, and strongly clashing, beliefs to live graciously together.

The less liberal people become in their moral and religious beliefs, the more they need liberal democracy. That is what is happening today. While many are drifting into a libertarian culture in which they find it hard to articulate any non-relativistic values, others are turning to highly non-liberal religious identities. They want to be chosen, not to choose. They seek meaning, not just explanation. They prefer community to autonomy, commitment to shifting allegiances. They want to live for something higher than consumerism, more inspiring than lowest-common-denominator politics, more demanding than relativism, and more altruistic than individualism. They seek something worth dedicating a life to. They believe in a universe in which we are more than dust on the surface of infinity. In a world of constant, accelerating, bewildering change, they seek to discern that which does not change. You cannot build a life, let alone a home, without foundations.

Covenant has proved its power whenever it has been tried. It was initially addressed to a group, the Israelites, who did not yet have a state. So effective was it that it allowed the nation so formed to survive for two thousand years, dispersed across the world, everywhere a minority, with its identity intact. If any political idea has been put to the test and succeeded, covenant is such an idea. Our problem today is different but similar. In Britain we have a state. What we lack in certain areas – inner cities, areas of ethnic concentration, economic deprivation and high unemployment – is a way of sustaining society as opposed to 'parallel lives', 'segregation' and 'conflicting ghettoes'. Covenant is the most compelling theory of society-building.

Unlike a social contract, which is an arrangement between self-interested individuals, a covenant is about creating a 'We' out of multiple 'I's'. It is about common identity, shared destiny, collective responsibility, moral reciprocity. It is about the deep human need to live in groups on whose support we can trust in times of crisis. If these do not exist at a society-wide level, then many people will turn away from society and focus instead on a religious, ethnic or neighbourhood community. I quoted Alasdair MacIntyre's chilling warning that this

143

inward turn is the first sign of the end of a social order. For him it is the danger signal par excellence.

Covenant is built not on personal autonomy and moral relativism but on strong ideals: human dignity, freedom and an equality of human worth. Only strong ideals can counter other strong ideals. There is a telling definition of a liberal as 'someone who can't even take his own side in an argument'. That is the weakness of basing liberalism on relativism. It renders it indefensible. It lasts only as long as it is not seriously challenged. It needs a stronger basis than this.

Because covenant is about identity, it involves telling a story. Covenants are not abstractions. They begin at a specific time, in a particular place. The story has to be told and retold, on special dates and ceremonial occasions. There are many advantages of a politics of narrative. Stories unite without creating uniformity. We each interpret a story our way. The Passover ritual speaks explicitly about 'four children', each of whom understands the story differently. Stories lend themselves to endless re-interpretation without ceasing to be the same story. They create *continuity through change*, which allows us to adapt to change without fearing that we are thereby losing our identity.

In particular, stories bring to our shared life the dimension of time, and time – open, unpredictable – is essential to a humane political order. Change does not happen overnight, and we need to write patience into the political culture. A consumerist culture has difficulty with time. Its slogans are, 'Takes the waiting out of wanting', 'The must-have's', and other variants of I-want-it-now: instant communication, search-engines that take microseconds, cars that accelerate ever faster, political soundbites and attention-spans that grow shorter by the year. Freud defined civilization as the ability to defer the gratification of instinct. By that measure we are rapidly becoming de-civilized. We need to bring back the dimension of narrative time, the time that takes time without losing hope.

Covenant restores to society the salience of responsibility, not just rights. It reminds us that someone else's rights are my responsibility. Those who need to take can do so, because we have all been educated to give. Rights are noble things, essential to human dignity, but without the widespread diffusion of responsibility they are undeliverable. Bentham called them 'nonsense on stilts'.

Lastly, covenant makes the connection between giving and belonging, between saying 'I helped build this' and saying 'I belong here'. That is why the country-house model of a single dominant culture, and the hotel model of non-communicating cultures, do not meet our needs. They do not generate a sense of shared, inclusive belonging. In the country house, minorities are outsiders. In the hotel, everyone is an outsider – at best, a cosmopolitan tourist ready to take the next plane

144

to a better salary or retirement home, practising postmodern irony, unable or unwilling to make a commitment.

What the covenant model reminds us is that there is a limit to state action in a liberal democracy. States cannot make marriages, build communities, shape cultures, generate commitments, or form meanings. They shouldn't try. That is the enduring truth of liberal democracy, with its sharp distinction between politics and the pursuit of meaning. We find meaning in community. We exercise power to resolve conflict, ensure fairness, create justice, and address need. There are things only the state can do, and there are others only we can do, in concert with others with whom we build relationships of trust. John Donne was right: 'No man is an Island, entire of itself ... any man's death diminishes me, because I am involved in Mankind'.[4] That is as good a definition as we will get of the politics of covenant, of collective belonging and solidarity. Society is the home we share because we build it together.

Part 3

Where Next?

Chapter 13

The Uses of Covenant

In practice, the essence of the common good is to secure in social life the benefits of voluntary cooperation.[1]

Michael Novak

I have argued for covenant as a way of thinking about contemporary society. It addresses problems other theories do not, especially how to create cohesion in a society of multiple ethnicities and diverse cultures. Covenant entered the West through religion, but it is not an essentially religious concept. An analogy is forgiveness, which also began life as a religious idea, but which now addresses all of us, regardless of faith. Thinking in terms of covenant does not presuppose an actual, historical agreement any more than social contract presupposes an actual, historical contract. It is simply a way of thinking, a habit of heart and mind that shapes our understanding of social realities. I want in the remaining chapters of the book to look at how it might help us think differently about the issues that confront us in liberal democracies today.

Beyond the State and the Market

Overwhelmingly in the past half-century, two ideas have dominated thinking about society: the individual and the nation, and two institutions: the market and the state. The market relates to us as individuals. We choose, we spend, we buy as we wish and can afford, and in so doing we think primarily of ourselves. The state relates to us collectively as a nation. We vote, we pay taxes, and we expect the state to provide us with services in return.

These institutions account for the two words we apply to the kind of society in which we live. It is *liberal* and *democratic*. Democracy refers to

149

the state. How should power be exercised, and by whom. By a ruler? A group? By all of us together? Representative democracy says that whoever rules should be accountable to all of us, by way of free and regular elections in which all of us, regardless of colour and creed, have a vote.

But democracy does not guarantee freedom. Tyrants have come to power by democratic election: Hitler did. So there is a second question: How far should power extend? Democracy means rule by the people, which in effect means by the majority of the people. The danger is that this can lead to 'the tyranny of the majority'. The majority can seek to impose its will on others, thereby denying them freedom and rights.

The answer lies in ring-fencing an area of life beyond the reach of politics. This, we recall, was the original meaning of the word 'rights', defined by the 1948 United Nations Universal Declaration as including the right to life, liberty and security of person; equal treatment and protection by the law; freedom of thought, conscience and religion; of opinion and expression; peaceful assembly and association, and so on. These are inalienable in the sense that they cannot legitimately be intruded on by the state. John Stuart Mill provided a more extensive definition that included anything that does not do harm to others. This is a large area of freedom: hence the word 'liberal' in liberal democracy.

Since the nineteenth century we have tended to think that these are all we need by way of broad principles governing our collective life. But they are not, for there is a third word that accompanies 'liberal' and 'democracy', namely 'society' itself: that which holds us together as a body politic. This relates not to the accountability of power (democracy) and its limits (liberalism) but to something which precedes them both: the idea of society as something that binds us together in a set of reciprocal relationships and responsibilities.

Societies can be held together in a number of ways: by a shared religion, a hierarchy of class, or by habit and long association. But these no longer apply to the liberal democracies of the West. We no longer share a religion, we do not believe in privilege and class, and we are no longer a tradition-directed society. When these bases fail, we need covenant.

There is an illusion that we can do without this third dimension. Surely liberty and democracy are enough. We elect governments, and set a limit to the areas of life in which they can intrude. Why do we need anything more?

We need more because without society, politics itself begins to lose its legitimacy. Why should we make sacrifices for others? Why should we pay taxes to ensure that education and healthcare are available to everyone? Why not let us keep the money and arrange schools and

150

hospitals for ourselves? Answer: because this would benefit the rich and harm the poor. But why should the rich care about the poor? At some level we need to draw on a sense of collective solidarity. We care about others because they are not just others. They are, in some sense, 'us'. But in what sense?

That is when we arrive at the concepts of society and the common good, and without them – relying on power and wealth, politics and economics alone – we will not arrive at a just society, a community of human dignity. It was the contribution of the ancient prophets to argue that society is built on moral foundations, equity, justice, loving-kindness and compassion. The prophets, though they were idealists, were also political realists, and they were proved right. A society that lacks the dimension of care for others cannot long survive on the basis of wealth and power alone. We need a third dimension.

The Logic of Covenant

The market, the state, and covenant are three different approaches to social life and the logic of association. I live in the world together with others. I have wants, but so do they, and our wants clash. How can I avoid conflict? I have needs, so do they, but none of us can provide all our needs alone without help from other people. How can we create co-operation?

There are two ways of getting other people to do what we want. We can force them: that is the answer of power. Or we can pay them: that is the answer of the market. But neither involves treating other people with dignity and respect. Neither satisfies Kant's criterion of a moral relationship: treat other people as ends, not means. If I force you, or pay you, to do what I want, then I am using you as a means, not an end.

Covenant is the third possibility. We create co-operation not by getting you to do what I want, but by joining together in a moral association that turns You and I into 'We'. I help you, you help me, because there are things we care about together. Covenant is a binding commitment, entered into by two or more parties, to work and care for one another while respecting the freedom, integrity and difference of each. Covenant is politics without power, economics without self-interest. What difference does it make? For one thing, it gets us to think about the common good, the good of all-of-us-together.

The Common Good

Think for example about a beach. In some places, beaches are part of the national heritage. They are public: accessible to everyone on equal terms. They cannot be bought or sold. In other places, there are private beaches, owned by hotels or individuals. Access to them is restricted to those who can pay. A public beach represents the common good. A private beach represents the market. A country in which all beaches were sold on the open market would be one in which all citizens would be impoverished, not materially but culturally, perhaps even spiritually. There are, we feel, some things that should not be sold to the highest bidder because they should not be sold at all. They are the property of all of us, which is to say, of none of us. They are there to be enjoyed, not owned.

Liberal democracy has tended to concentrate on the individual and on one particular power, the power to choose. Courtesy of the market, I can choose what to buy. Thanks to the liberal state, I can choose how to live. Surely everyone gains in such a situation. True, but only up to a point. We gain as individuals; we lose as a society. There are, we feel, things so important to human dignity that they should be available to all, not just those with wealth or power. That is when the concept of covenant comes into play: the idea that all of us must come together to ensure the dignity of each of us. Covenant is the politics of the common good.

We need the concept of the common good to make sense of a responsible society. It is clear, for example, that we are going to have to change our habits of consumption if we are to protect the environment from global warming and climate change. But why should I care about such things? It will affect life long after I am gone. In what sense do I have obligations to generations not yet born? Besides which, what difference does it make if I act in ways that are not environmentally friendly? There are six billion other people on the planet, and the impact of my behaviour is infinitesimal.

The answer is the common good. That is what binds me to the fate of people in other places, other times. Without it, economics alone will not lead me to care about the environment, nor will there be a political consensus to take the measures necessary to protect it. There is such a thing as society; there is a common good, available to each of us because it belongs to all of us. And if the word 'society' is to have any salience at all, other than as a mere abstraction, then we will have to protect certain spaces – not just physical spaces, but social, intellectual, moral spaces as well – from the intrusions of the market on the one hand (buy what you like), and the liberal state (do what you like) on the other.

Covenant makes sense of the common good in a way economics and politics – the pursuit of individual self-interest – cannot. We each pledge to act for the benefit of all in matters that affect us all. The 'all' of covenant is wider than the electorate because it includes the dead, the living, and the not yet born. Covenant is commitment extended through time. It includes the duty to preserve the best of the heritage of the past, as well as to act in the interests of the distant future. That is why we conserve historic buildings and plant forests for generations to come.

Hence the latent tension in the phrase 'multicultural society'. For society is made by its public culture. Multiculturalism, at least in some of its forms, seems to deny that there is a public culture. It doesn't take the beach and sell it to the highest bidder. Instead it parcels it out to a number of groups, some ethnic, some religious, some gender-based, some lifestyle-based. This space is ours; that is yours. But the fact that the owners of the beach are now groups, not just private individuals, does not mitigate the fact that it has ceased to be ours, all-of-us-together. And that must be an impoverishment of our public life.

Some things must stand outside the state and the market if we are to breathe the air of togetherness at all. Why should it be so important? Because there are things that belong to us not because we are this or that, but simply because we are human, and the more extensive and beautiful they are, the more human we will feel. The texture of our public spaces is what gives us civic pride or its absence. A 2004 British survey revealed that 85 per cent of respondents said that they believed that the quality of their public spaces had a strong impact on their quality of life.[2] A city of magnificent houses and private gardens but no public parks might be rich in individual satisfaction but poor in collective grace.

The common good used to be predicated on a shared religion: the principle, established by the Treaty of Augsburg, of *cuius regio, eius religio,* that the inhabitants of a region are bound by the religion of its ruler. Then, as toleration was extended to other faiths, it became a matter of a shared moral code, often given expression in civil law. In an earlier chapter I showed how this principle was gradually eroded in the second half of the twentieth century, first by the liberal revolution of the 1960s, then by the multicultural revolution of the 1980s. The first extended moral liberty to the individual; the second, to the group. Both were compelling because society as it was then was too exclusionary. It was white, Anglo-Saxon, Church of England, and those whose colour or ethnicity or faith were different were outsiders, guests. The host was generous, and many of the guests felt grateful for the hospitality. But after the terrible consequences of European nationalism, who in honour and decency could speak of hosts and guests any

more? So society was parcelled out, first to individuals, then to groups, and became a hotel.

But hotels are not public spaces. Yes, they have lounges and bars and restaurants and conference rooms, but the guests do not see themselves as a community. They are not bound to their fellow guests by anything like collective responsibility. If someone spills a drink, there will be a waiter to mop it up. That's what we pay for. In a hotel we delegate responsibility away. That is part of the social contract. A public beach is not like that. We try not to drop litter. We may even, if we are public spirited, pick up the litter we find – for we are jointly responsible for the beach. Public spaces depend on people voluntarily honouring a code: don't pick the flowers in a flower bed, don't drop lighted matches in a forest, don't leave the remains of your lunch on the grass. They require a widely diffused sense of responsibility. The common good is less like a hotel than a public beach. So what happened in the 1960s and 1980s, turning society from a country house into a hotel, meant an inevitable loss of the idea of the common good.

Loyalty

Another fundamental virtue of covenant is loyalty, a concept hard to account for in terms of economics and politics alone.[3] Consider, for example, the modern phenomenon of 'kiss-and-tell' memoirs or disclosures to the press. Almost anyone in the public eye nowadays risks the possibility that someone he or she considered a friend will betray a confidence if the reward of so doing is sufficiently high. Why was this once considered unforgivable but is now, if not acceptable, at least accepted?

The answer, surely, is that the market has come to have greater salience in people's lives than virtue. Virtue benefits us; the market benefits me. When large personal gain outweighs unquantifiable public loss of trust, the result is the slow death of loyalty, discretion and the entire sensibility that once went with a code of honour. Discretion may be the better part of valour, but indiscretion pays a better price. Where there is no loyalty, there is no friendship; where no friendship, no trust; and where no trust, no true relationship. Today Mephistopheles would be too late to tempt Faust. Faust would already have an agent who handles these things.

Friendship depends on loyalty. So do marriage, community and most other social institutions. If all we have is the market and the liberal state, loyalty will cease to exist as a virtue. What will count is personal gain: money or the pursuit of power. Nations cannot survive without loyalties. Yet the market undermines them. It constantly invites us to

the new product, the better deal, the more attractive option. It says, 'Forget about them, think about yourself, because you're worth it.' Loyalty is for wimps. But we cannot live without loyalties. A world without them is one without relationships of long-term commitment. It is inevitably a world without grace.

Complex Identities

Covenant is also an idea for our time because it is supremely suited to a world of multiple identities. Who are we nowadays? English? British? European? Just a human being? Devolution has split Britain into four: England, Scotland, Wales and Northern Ireland. At the same time, the European Union has drawn us into a larger grouping that may, in some cases, circumscribe national sovereignty. A case involving human rights, for example, can be taken to the European Court. So who are we?

One of the most powerful features of covenant is that it is made for a question like this. Unlike most forms of identity, it is not a Yes-No, Us-Them, If-I-am-right-you-are-wrong way of partitioning reality. It recognizes that we have multiple identities and loyalties. That is because it is not ontological but relational. It doesn't speak about essences – either I am this or I am that. It speaks about commitments, pledges, responsibilities.

So, for example, the Hebrew Bible recognizes three different levels of covenant: the universal (made with Noah), the personal (with Abraham), and the national (with the Israelites at Mount Sinai). I am a human being, bound to others in a covenant of human solidarity. I am a child of Abraham, and thus have something in common with Christians and Muslims who also trace their identity, literally or metaphorically, back to the biblical patriarch. And I am a Jew. I have other covenantal bonds as well: to my wife, through the covenant of marriage; to my children, through the covenant of parenthood; to my local community through the covenant of neighbourliness; and to Britain through the covenant of citizenship.

A covenantal politics in Britain is made for the new devolution: the Scottish Parliament, the National Assembly for Wales and the Northern Ireland Assembly, alongside the Parliament of Westminster. Recall that the 1643 union between Scottish Covenanters and the English Parliamentarians was in the form of a Solemn League and Covenant, which declared among other things:

> we have now at last (after other means of supplication, remonstrance, protestation, and sufferings), for the preservation of

ourselves and our religion from utter ruin and destruction, according to the commendable practice of these kingdoms in former times, and the example of GOD'S people in other nations, after mature deliberation, resolved and determined to enter into a Mutual and Solemn League and Covenant, wherein we all subscribe, and each one of us for himself, with our hands lifted up to the Most High GOD, do swear ...[4]

Covenants are invaluable when we seek to create federal structures. Indeed the word 'federation', from the Latin *foedus*, means 'a covenant'. Recall that in a covenant, the several parties agree to work together while respecting their distinct identities. None is subsumed in the others. There is no assimilation or melting pot. Covenants create co-operation while honouring difference. And what works for Britain makes equal sense for Europe as a whole: *Europe des patries*, a Europe of separate nation states none of which seeks to give up its identity in the larger whole.

It is also perfectly suited to a society in which there are many faiths. Leaders of the various religions in Britain should be able to come together to create a covenant of their own. It would not be a declaration of faith, for we each have our own faith. It would be, instead, a declaration of collective commitment to the values of citizenship, belonging, respect for diversity, tolerance and the common good.

Covenant also speaks to our place within the human community worldwide. The covenant of human solidarity is based not on military, political, economic or cultural imperialism but on the fact that we are human. We are all in God's image; life is sacrosanct; so is human dignity. We have a collective responsibility for the future of the planet, for seeking peace, protecting the environment, ensuring human rights and caring for those who lack the minimum necessary for dignified existence. We cannot in good conscience pursue our own affluence while a billion people are living in absolute poverty and 30,000 children die every day from preventable disease.

Covenant generates a politics of complexity because human life is complex. It is utterly opposed to the kind of nationalism or absolutism in which loyalty to the state (or faith, or ideology) is everything, and other human loyalties nothing. But it is equally opposed to postmodern detachment, in which the very concepts of loyalty and commitment are attenuated and eventually cease to exist.

The Necessity of Cohesion

Social contract and social covenant are both necessary, but they are different. Social contract is about the relationship between the individual and the state, mediated by power. Social covenant is about relationships between people and the groups they form through the values they share. The common good is covenantal, not contractual. It belongs to society, not the state. There are political regimes in which the state creates and enforces the common good, but only by being authoritarian and eventually totalitarian. That is the danger when society fails and the bonds of trust between people begin to fray. No one said this more clearly than Bertrand Russell in the Introduction to his *History of Western Philosophy*:

> What had happened in the great age of Greece happened again in Renaissance Italy. Traditional moral restraints disappeared, because they were seen to be associated with superstition; the liberation from fetters made individuals energetic and creative, producing a rare florescence of genius; but the anarchy and treachery which inevitably resulted from the decay of morals made Italians collectively impotent, and they fell, like the Greeks, under the domination of nations less civilized than themselves but not so destitute of social cohesion.[5]

Societies cannot do without a sense of social cohesion. Without it they fragment into groups and lonely individuals, each of whom is more concerned with what is good for me or my group than what is good for all of us together. They become anxious, vulnerable, easily given to anxiety and a sense of persecution. Conflicts that in another age might have been resolved by listening and compromise become instead scenes of angry confrontation: between pro- and anti-abortion lobbies in the United States, pro- and anti-fox hunting groups in Britain, conservatives and gay and lesbian sympathizers in the churches, green activists against governments, anti-globalists against international corporations, animal rights campaigners against pharmaceutical companies, single-issue lobbies against the rest.

Hasty decisions are made for the sake of restoring order. The political process is increasingly bypassed in favour of the media-attention-catching gesture. Little by little the carefully woven fabric that once threaded us together unravels. We are left with a risk-society instead of a trust-society, and barely concealed hostilities in place of habits of co-operation. Order is maintained by an ever more visible police presence. Surveillance increases and privacies are lost. Fraternity gives way to an ever greater risk of fratricide, and civilization gradually subsides into the sea with all the dignity of the Titanic, and all the tragedy likewise.

We either make social cohesion, or its absence unmakes us. The common good cannot be legislated. It cannot be brought into existence by government fiat. In fact, like happiness, it cannot be aimed at directly. The paradox of happiness, as Aristotle knew and contemporary psychologists have rediscovered, is that it occurs as a by-product of something else, something that absorbs our energies and challenges our skill. Belonging, loyalty and a sense of the common good emerge as by-products whenever individuals and groups come together to face a common challenge.

Every child in Britain should be taught two skills: contract-making and covenant-making. Contract is about association for self-interest; covenant is about association in shared identity. Both are important life skills. Contract teaches us the logic of non-zero-sumness. Life is not a match in which you either win or lose. Creative, lateral thought can often create win-win scenarios. Covenant teaches us about relationships: love and loyalty, commitment and responsibility. Teaching children about covenant-making will help them in later life to build families and communities, based on a regard for the other as well as self. It will also help them answer one of the most difficult of life's questions: Who am I?

Chapter 14

Who Am I?

England was not a nation or a creed or a language or a state but a home. Things at home don't need an explanation. They are there because they are there.[1]

Roger Scruton

Political community depends on the narratives by which people make sense of their condition and interpret the common life they share ... At a time when the narrative resources of civic life are already strained – as the soundbites, factoids, and disconnected images of our media saturated culture attest – it becomes increasingly difficult to tell the tales that order our lives. There is a growing danger that, individually and collectively, we will find ourselves slipping into a fragmented, storyless condition. The loss of the capacity for narrative would amount to the ultimate disempowering of the human subject, for without narrative there is no continuity between present and past, and therefore no responsibility, and therefore no possibility of acting together to govern ourselves.[2]

Michael Sandel

Moses' second question to God at the burning bush was, 'Who are you?' His first was, 'Who am I?' He meant, of course, who am I to be equal to the task you have set me, of leading a people to freedom. But he was also asking the question of identity. Moses' identity was anything but straightforward. Brought up as an Egyptian prince, he had spent his adult life as a shepherd among the Midianites, one of whom he had married. He was also, by birth, a member of the Israelites, then being held by the Egyptians as slaves. So the question was real. To which group did he belong? To whom did he owe loyalty? That is a question we all face nowadays.

For most people at most times, identity was not problematic. You were born into a place, a culture, a religion, a class, and these circumscribed your possibilities. Movement from one place, culture, religion or class to another was rare – so rare as not to enter into your frame of reference. Today, at least in the West, many of those certainties are gone. We are mobile. We face multiple possibilities. We are what we decide to be. That is what sociologists mean when they say we have moved from fate to choice. It is what the existentialist Jean-Paul Sartre meant when he said that for human beings 'existence precedes essence'. Modern identities are deeply problematic. If everything about me – where I live, what I do, which segments of culture I attend to – is a matter of choice, then who or what is the 'I' that does the choosing? That, in part, explains the power of religion in the postmodern world. It offers, as much of contemporary culture does not, an answer to the question, Who am I?

The way a society frames this question-and-answer is immensely consequential. So, for example, the European Enlightenment emphasized the universal. Montesquieu placed loyalty to humanity above loyalty to the nation, and loyalty to the nation above loyalty to the family. Shelley spoke of 'man / equal, unclassed, tribeless and nationless'.[3] But most human beings cannot live at this level of abstraction. The result in Europe in the nineteenth century was the return of nationalism with a vengeance, a nationalism that swallowed up all other loyalties.

Today we rightly distrust this kind of exclusive claim on who we are. But we have not returned to the universalism of the Enlightenment. That is precisely the difference between modernism and postmodernism. Modernism worshipped the universal. Postmodernism worships nothing at all. Some postmodernists doubt that we have an identity – a soul, a self – at all. We are just a succession of experiences with nothing to connect them. Hence Michel Foucault's famous statement that 'man is an invention of recent date, and one perhaps nearing its end'.[4] Again, that is a reason for religion's return as a reaction against 'the unbearable lightness of being' in a world without certainties and identities.

That is another reason why the concept of covenant is helpful, especially at a time when people ask 'Who am I?' and find it hard to give an answer. As I explained in the previous chapter, covenant is not an all-or-nothing approach to identity. It sees it in terms of moral commitments. I am a Jew, a rabbi, a child of my parents, a husband to my wife, a parent to my children. Some of these I chose; others – my parents, my religion – I did not. Each, though, is part of who I am. Each involves responsibilities, and they can clash. Should I go to the conference abroad or stay to be with our daughter who is about to have a

160

baby? Conflicts of duty are not rare: they are part of the essence of the moral life. So covenant steers a course between fate and choice and allows me to see the multiple strands of identity without lapsing into postmodern identity-less-ness.

Where then does national identity fit in to all this? The nationalist answer is that it dominates all else. It was this that the novelist E. M. Forster was protesting against when he said, 'If I had to choose between betraying my country and betraying my friend, I hope I should have the guts to betray my country.' I don't think he was proposing treason: he was merely reminding us that there are other values and commitments in life.

The cosmopolitan answer is the opposite: nations are not everything, but nothing. I am a citizen of the world. But this too is too extreme. I have to belong somewhere if I am to be recognizably human at all. A life without commitments is possible but it is an impoverished thing, a speck of dust blown by the wind, finding no resting place, no home.

The covenantal answer is that being a citizen of a nation is part of the complex web of obligations that makes me who I am. It is not everything, but it is certainly not nothing. The nation is where I live: it is in the landscape I inhabit, the language I speak, the culture that surrounds me and the society of which I am a part. It makes almost everything else in my life possible, for without a political system I would have no power. Without an economy I would have no job. Without a government, my education, healthcare, welfare and retirement would be entirely in the hands of chance or fate. I owe it, not everything, but much.

Nations are predicated on societies, and societies are built on the mutual acceptance of a code of law-abidingness and restraint that allows us to go about our business with a maximum of order and a minimum of fear. Our very freedom depends on other people honouring their responsibilities. So, for example, the peace and quiet I enjoy in a public park is predicated on the fact that you are not about to disturb it by playing loud music on your ghetto-blaster. My freedom depends on your self-restraint, as yours does on mine. That is a covenantal approach to national identity: neither nationalistic nor cosmopolitan, but civic and moral. I have a duty to play my part in sustaining the human environment within which I and my fellow citizens live. In covenant, identity is not a matter of race or ethnicity but of loyalty and responsibility.

Being Bilingual

It also, especially for minorities, involves being bilingual. A simple example: a lawyer or doctor in the company of fellow professionals uses a technical language outsiders find hard, even impossible, to understand. In dealing with clients or patients, though, he or she will use a simpler language, less precise perhaps, but at least intelligible to a layperson. The same is true of every cognitive minority, including religious or ethnic groups within a largely secular society. If we seek integration without assimilation, we must learn to speak a first language of citizenship, together with a second language of ethnicity and faith.

The two are different, and this sometimes confuses people. So, for example, when I am in a pulpit, preaching to a congregation, I speak as a Jew to fellow Jews, a believer to fellow believers. I use many phrases – some in Hebrew – that will be intelligible to my audience but not to a non-Jewish visitor. They are part of our shared vocabulary as a faith. I don't need to explain what they mean. Communities are always like this. There are jokes that are amusing when said by 'one of us', that would be offensive if told by an outsider. That is the difference, and it is *all* the difference, between the ability to laugh at yourself, and being laughed at by others. What makes us a faith community are the texts we share, the songs we sing, the rituals we observe, the references we can take for granted.

When, though, I broadcast on national radio or television or write for the national press, I have to use a different vocabulary. I am speaking to an audience 99.5 per cent of which is not Jewish. So the language is different; so is the tone. That is one of the key differences between *Gemeinschaft* and *Gesselschaft*, 'community' and 'society', a relationship between friends and one between strangers. One of the key differences, about which I will say something in chapter 16, is *civility*. What people notice when they make the move from village to city, religious community to wider society, is the politeness, the distance, the formality. Often they find it off-putting. Where is the passion, the fire, the authenticity? Eventually they work it out: civility is a code for minimizing friction between strangers. Until they understand this, it all seems like a foreign language. John Murray Cuddihy accurately described the process through which immigrant or minority groups must go, as 'the ordeal of civility'.[5]

It is a necessary ordeal. To live together as citizens of a liberal democracy, we have to use the language of *public reason*, language people outside our group will understand. I can't say to non-Jews, 'Do this because the Bible says so'. A Muslim can't say to non-Muslims, 'Do this because the Koran says so'. That is not because we live in a secular society, though we do, but because this is the only way we can hold fast to our faith and yet still be part of the national conversation together with those of other faiths or none. I hope to persuade other people of the truth of my point of view, but I must live with the possibility that I may fail. Society is like football: I support my team and hope it will win. But I recognize that the rules of the game take priority over which team I support, because without rules, there is no game, and without the game, there is no team.

So being British is like keeping to the rules of the game. It is what allows me to be a Jew, you a Christian, someone else to be a Muslim, and all of us to live together in peace. We have our team, but we also have a loyalty to the rules, the people who make them, and the people who administer them. That is what being bilingual means. We have an in-group way of thinking and talking, but when we take to the field, we honour the rules, because they bind all of us equally, and without them there is no game. That is what national identity is in a multicultural society. It also, crucially, involves telling a story. That has not been part of the British tradition, but it must become so now.

The National Story

Whenever I visit Washington DC I make a point of going to see the presidential memorials, Jefferson's, Roosevelt's, and Lincoln's. Each carries inscriptions taken from their words: Jefferson's 'We hold these truths to be self-evident ...', Roosevelt's 'The only thing we have to fear, is fear itself', and Lincoln's Gettysburg address and his second Inaugural, 'With malice toward none; with charity for all ...' London has no equivalent that I know of. There are memorials and statues everywhere, each with a brief inscription saying who the statue represents, but no speeches, quotations, soundbites. Even the memorial to Churchill, whose speeches rivalled Lincoln's in power, is a statue without a text.

This phenomenon is of a piece with the fact that the clubs and gathering-places of Britain's governing elite have no signs or name-plates. You only know where they are if someone in the know shows you. It is as if, in Britain (or is this confined to England?), if you have to ask, you don't belong. Knowledge that in America is publicly displayed, is in Britain tacit and taken for granted. Those who need to know, know.

America tells national stories, Britain doesn't. The reason, as I explained in chapter 10, is that the two nations have different political cultures. America's is based on covenant, Britain's on hierarchy and tradition. The difference is precisely set out in the two quotations that head this chapter. Roger Scruton's is a statement of what it is to belong to an organic society. Michael Sandel, of Harvard, is eloquent on what it is to be an American. Sandel says, in effect, we can't live as citizens without a narrative. Scruton says we can and do. These are quite different ways of seeing society-as-home.

British identity is based on the fact that it has been here a long time. That is fine as long as identity can be taken for granted. It is highly problematic when it can't. When asked, 'What is it to be British?', we find it hard to give an answer. That is a serious deficiency when a sense of the common good, so necessary for social cohesion, comes under strain. Shared responsibility needs shared identity, which needs collective memory, which needs a narrative. Britain hasn't had a narrative, but circumstances have changed.

'Telling the story' is at the heart of covenantal politics. It sustains identity and creates a sense of collective belonging. It binds the generations, reminding us of where the nation came from and is going to. It locates national identity in a set of historic events, speaking of the values for which those who came before us fought, and of which we are the guardians for the sake of the future. It must be an inclusive narrative, capable of being owned by newcomers as well as by those whose families have been here for many generations.

Inclusivity is of the essence in covenantal narrative. It says to everyone, regardless of class or creed: this is who we are, and it is your story too. Story-telling binds without dividing. It creates a sense of common identity that transcends other identities. That is why, for example, Martin Luther King was able to use it to such effect in some of his greatest speeches. He was telling his fellow African Americans to see themselves as an equal part of the nation. At the same time, he was telling white Americans to honour their commitment to the Declaration of Independence and its statement that 'all men are created equal'. Narrative politics, telling the story, is egalitarian without being confrontational. That is its strength.

Americans are used to telling the story because that has been part of their political culture from the beginning. Their key narrative is the biblical story of the exodus. Successive generations defined themselves as a people who had come from an old land to a new, from slavery to freedom, from persecution to liberty. They had crossed a sea, journeyed through the wilderness, and had arrived in what Washington called 'the almost promised land'. This carried, and still carries, responsibilities: to honour the freedom of others, to care for the poor, the weak and the old, to practise justice and compassion.

America has not always done so. It has had notorious failures. But it can always be recalled to its foundational commitments. That is because narrative politics is moral politics, politics with a purpose, failure to honour which brings a nation under judgement. For it is a

164

nation 'under God', meaning that it can be called to account for its shortcomings. It is answerable not just to the electorate but to the sacred pledge of its founders. Covenant writes into national self-consciousness the need for self-criticism and rededication. If handled with responsibility – a big 'if' to be sure – it can generate humility, the only real antidote to the standing temptations of 'mission drift' and the arrogance of power.

This has not been part of English political culture because until recently it was structured around class and tradition. Hierarchical and organic societies do not rely on narrative. Hierarchy is predicated on a sense of natural order. Organic societies depend on the aura of inevitability that comes with being, or seeming, very old. The Houses of Parliament, for example, are quite new: they date from the mid-nineteenth century. Most of the earlier buildings were destroyed by fire in 1834. Barry's and Pugin's designs were consciously antiquarian, designed to make the edifice look older than it is. Britain does 'old'. What it doesn't do is narrative.

Description and Narrative

A case study may make this clearer. In 1924 Baldwin, then Prime Minister, made a speech that subsequently became famous, on the sights and sounds of England. For him, England was:

> ... the tinkle of the hammer on the anvil in the country smithy, the corncrake on a dewy morning, the sound of the scythe against the whetstone, and the sight of a plough team coming over the brow of the hill ... The wild anemones in the woods in April, the last load at night of hay being drawn down a lane as the twilight comes on, when you can scarcely distinguish the figures of the horses as they take it home to the farm, and above all, most subtle, most penetrating and most moving, the smell of wood smoke coming up in an autumn evening, or the smell of the scutch fires ... [6]

This is fine prose, but it is not a narrative. It is a series of impressions. It evokes a sense of place, not history or destiny. It precisely matches Roger Scruton's remark that 'England was not a nation or a creed or a language or a state but a home.' Home is what you conjure up through images and the mystic chords of memory. The same applies to George Orwell's equally famous description, twenty years later:

> The clatter of clogs in the Lancashire mill towns, the to-and-fro of the lorries on the Great North Road, the queues outside the

Labour Exchanges, the rattle of pin-tables in the Soho pubs, the old maids hiking to Holy Communion through the mists of the autumn morning ... solid breakfasts and gloomy Sundays, smoky towns and winding roads, green fields and red pillar-boxes. It has a flavour of its own.[7]

The description, the metonymic details, are different. Orwell spoke of town not countryside, and from the perspective of a member of the working class, not Baldwin's landed elite. But the genre is the same, an evocation of 'home'.

In 1993 the then Prime Minister, John Major, gave a speech in the same tradition: 'Fifty years from now, Britain will still be the country of long shadows on county grounds, warm beer, invincible green suburbs, dog lovers and pools fillers and – as George Orwell said – "old maids cycling to holy communion through the morning mist".'[8] This is superbly well done, but the environment had changed. Jeremy Paxman, for example, said about it: 'Where on earth did all this stuff come from? Which corner of England was the Prime Minister talking about where life proceeded in this quaint, prelapsarian way?'[9]

The problem is not which sights and sounds you choose. It lies in the very attempt to evoke a sense of belonging by conjuring up a landscape of the mind. Baldwin, Orwell and John Major were all trying to capture *genius loci*, the spirit of a place. Baldwin could do it in the 1920s. Orwell could still do it in the 1940s. No one can do it now except, as filmmakers do, by way of period drama. 'The past is a foreign country.' Foreign, not home.

In a multi-ethnic society, you can no longer evoke identity by painting a picture. You have to tell a story. Narrative is central to America, as it was to the biblical Israelites, because both were faced with the problem of how to create unity out of diversity: *E pluribus unum.* For America it was successive waves of immigration, for the Israelites, the twelve tribes and the mixed multitude. Britain too is now a land of diverse cultures and multiple minorities. It is no longer an organic society linked by memories of wild anemones and old maids hiking to Holy Communion.

British Values

How then do you create a national narrative? You begin with a ritual: a day, a date, a commemoration. The American narrative emerged through the institution of the Presidential Inaugural Address. Hence the call by a number of politicians for a Britain Day. That, I believe, is right. Ritual precedes myth. First comes the occasion, then the story.

We need moments of collective celebration, a strengthening of bonds between groups, national and local, and a focus of belonging that is forward-looking and built around shared values and ideals. Jonathan Freedland gets to the heart of the matter when he says that 'when we have a national project, we will have national pride.'[10] That is civic identity.

The result will be the slow coalescence of a national narrative. Culture shifts take time, and must be undertaken at many levels by many institutions. Schools have a major part to play, not just in history and citizenship classes but at school assemblies and other ceremonial occasions. The media too must be enlisted. Some of the best work on identity in recent years has been done by tele-historians retelling the story of the nation. Businesses should be encouraged to find ways of celebrating national and local identities as part of their code of corporate responsibility, just as they have factored in environmental and health concerns ('organic') and awareness of international poverty ('fair trade' labelling).

Faith groups must be brought into the process. There was a fine example of this during the Millennium celebrations. On 3 January 2000, there was a ceremony involving all of Britain's major faiths: Christian, Jewish, Muslim, Hindu, Sikh, Buddhist, Jain, Zoroastrian and Bahai. It was held in religiously neutral space, the Royal Gallery in the Houses of Parliament, and it was televised. It celebrated citizenship. Some representatives made short speeches; others sang songs or made music. The themes were thanksgiving and belonging. Three generations of a Hindu family from Newcastle stood together while the youngest granddaughter read a poem about the good things in her life – her family, her town, her country. A Jewish choir sang a verse from Psalm 133: 'How good and pleasant it is when brothers live together in unity.' It was a good model and should serve as a precedent for other such occasions, centrally and locally.

We each have a story to tell about what Britain means to us. For me, Britain is the nation that gave freedom a moral dimension. It is there in the writings of the Scottish Enlightenment as well as English thinkers from Milton to Locke to John Stuart Mill. The social gospel is an integral part of British Christianity, from Methodists to Evangelicals, Baptists to Quakers. You find it in novelists such as Charles Dickens, George Eliot and Elizabeth Gaskell; in the great Victorian philanthropists such as Lord Shaftesbury, Octavia Hill, Charles Booth and Thomas Barnardo; as well as in radicals such as Tom Paine, Robert Owen, William Lovett, John Ruskin and William Morris. Gertrude Himmelfarb reminds us that it was in Britain that the 'passion for compassion' first arose, and its transformation from private sentiment to public virtue was 'the unique contribution of the British Enlightenment'.[11]

Britain is where intellectuals spoke a language people could understand. No world class philosopher ever wrote more clearly than Bertrand Russell, and none kept their sense of humour more vividly alive (Russell said that he only once caught G. E. Moore telling a lie – when he asked, 'Moore, have you ever told a lie?' and Moore replied, 'Yes'). British thought never sought refuge in intellectual impostures or impenetrable abstractions. You can judge a nation by its language. If it says what it means, it is an honest culture. If it hovers above the threshold of intelligibility, beware (What is the difference, British academics ask, between a postmodernist and a member of the Mafia? The Mafia make you an offer you can't refuse. A postmodernist makes you an offer you can't understand).

Martin Heidegger, the greatest German philosopher of the twentieth century and the most incomprehensible, was an enthusiastic member of the Nazi party, which he joined in 1929. That kind of thing didn't happen here – because British thought emphasized sense over sensibility, the concrete and empirical over the theoretical and ideological. When Bishop Berkeley wondered how you could refute subjective idealism – the idea that nothing is real outside the mind – Dr Johnson kicked a stone and said, 'Sir, I refute it thus'. A language that encourages people to think straight and talk simply is the best defence against evil in a high-minded cause.

Britain does not have a literature of hate. Yes, there is prejudice as well as pride, but it did not become part of public discourse as it did in so many other countries. It is where colour never became the divisive issue as it did in the United States. When Enoch Powell made his famous 'rivers of blood' speech, he became, for most Britons, a political pariah. After the 7/7 terror attack, the nation, far from erupting into race riots, was united in simple, moving grief.

For me Britain is where the son of a Polish immigrant who had to leave school at the age of fourteen, could go to university and be treated by others as an equal. My university supervisors could not have been less like anyone I had ever met before. One, Jimmy Altham, was an Old Etonian. Another, Roger Scruton, was a fox-hunting Tory. A third, Sir Bernard Williams, was a lapsed Catholic and a principled atheist. Not once did they attack my beliefs, faith or way of life, or treat me with less than total courtesy and respect. I learned from them that the pursuit of truth demands qualities of character as well as of intellect. That is why I am so distressed at the politicization of British universities today. For me, this is a betrayal of one of Britain's finest traditions.

Britain is the nation – perhaps the only one in the world – where the leaders of all the major faiths know each other as personal friends, where Christians, Jews, Muslims, Sikhs and Hindus, caught up in conflicts elsewhere in the world, meet in warmth and mutual respect. It is where I, as a rabbi, am encouraged to speak to people of all faiths and none, not just my fellow believers. I do not know of anywhere else where this happens to quite the same degree.

That is what Britain means to me. And yes, it has many faults, but so does everything anyone loves. And yes, being British and Jewish (or Hindu, Muslim, Sikh or any other adjective) involves a delicate balance. Integration without assimilation – national identity without loss of other, more specific identities – is not an easy option. It is merely better than the alternatives. Kierkegaard said that 'purity of heart is to will one thing'. But to will one thing is to deny the complexity of the world and the claims it makes on us. So I will several things, of which being British and Jewish are two. I cherish the compliment once paid me by Clifford Longley in a preface he wrote to one of my books, that 'he's a next-door neighbour, a fellow Englishman, one of us', and then added, 'and even when he's boring, he's boring in an English sort of way.'

From Values to Stories

Identities are built on values, but they need narratives to make them come alive. Values are universal, narratives are particular. Britain is a democracy, but so are many other countries. It believes in freedom, but who does not? That is why we need a story that links us to this place, this people, this land. Jack Straw, who has written thoughtfully on this subject, suggests a narrative that wends through 'the Magna Carta, the civil war, the Bill of Rights, through Adam Smith and the Scottish Enlightenment, the fight for votes, for the emancipation of Catholics and non-conformists, of women and of the black community, the Second World War, the fight for rights for minority groups, the fight now against unbridled terror.'[12] That, it seems to me, is as good a starting-point as any.

The narrative I have told in this book is more generic, but it goes like this:

Once upon a time there was a country house called England. Over time, three wings were added, Scotland, Wales and Northern Ireland, so that the house was now a quadrangle with a courtyard. The owner was the king; around him was a court; there were colonial administrators who managed the king's other properties; there was a large group of labourers who tended the fields; and there were guests, many of whom had been there so long that they were indistinguishable from the rest, though some remained different and were looked on suspiciously by others.

Those who lived in the country house had many likeable features. They had a stubborn streak of independence and individuality. They had all sorts of rules, most of which had developed over the course of time without any general theory behind them. They valued liberalism, tolerance, fairness, open-mindedness, freedom of speech, courtesy, respect and social responsibility. Much of the work on the house was done voluntarily and not on the king's instructions. They loved the house and its traditions and celebrated them in elaborate and gracious ceremonies.

But economic fortunes changed. The king's other properties had to be sold back to their original owners. The country house itself was sold to an international corporation which turned it into a hotel. That, though, did not seem to work. The place was impersonal and far too commercialized. The heritage theme seemed more contrived than natural. The grand dining hall had become a restaurant – small tables, choice of menu, no host, no banquet, no ceremonial meals – neat, nice, but not the same.

Eventually the hotel was sold to a charity, known as Citizens of Britain. They decided that the buildings would become a national heritage. One section would be the home of the king, the rest would be open to the public, free. Around them, they would build a town. Everyone would help in the building. Many people were attracted to the project: those who had lived there before, together with others from many different countries, each with their own customs and traditions. They worked together for years; the project bonded them; the old-timers brought back some of their ceremonies; the newcomers taught them new songs, new recipes, new ways of doing things. The house was old, the homes were new, and there was a good balance of continuity and change. What stayed the same, though, were the values: the freedom, the independence, the tolerance, the respect for difference. Those, most people felt, were non-negotiable. They were what gave the place its core identity and without them the project wouldn't work, wouldn't even be worth doing.

Some of the people who remembered the old country-house days found it hard to adjust. Even they, though, preferred the new arrangements to the days when it had been a hotel. Many of the old-timers realized that in many ways things were better now than they were before. Then only a privileged few ever saw the best rooms. Now they could be visited by everyone. Then the country house was a closed community; now it was an open one. There were no longer ranks or hierarchies of privilege and power. Everyone gave voluntarily to the community because it was theirs, and they knew that every new plant in the garden, every

170

new tree in the orchard, every new painting in the gallery belonged to all of them, together.

And in a strange, unexpected way, news of the new community spread. Other owners of country houses and hotels were fascinated by the new project and came to see how it worked. Some liked what they saw and thought about doing it themselves. So the place recovered some of its former glory, though in a different way. Then it was about grandeur and magnificence. Now it was about community and belonging. But now, as then, what made the place special was that it was right for its time. Without knocking down any of the old buildings, people had given them a new meaning at the heart of their new project. They called it The Home We Build Together.

To which I would add two lines from Wordworth's *Prelude*:

What we love, others will love
And we will show them how.[13]

Chapter 15

Face-to-Face, Side-by-Side

Thus it is that men possessing quite different, even opposite metaphysical or religious outlooks can converge, not by virtue of any identity of doctrine, but by virtue of an analogical similitude in practical principles, toward the same practical conclusions, and can share in the same practical, secular faith, provided that they similarly revere, perhaps for quite diverse reasons, truth and intelligence, human dignity, freedom, brotherly love, and the absolute value of moral good.[1]

Jacques Maritain

The most brilliant act of creative diplomacy I encountered was undertaken by the late Lord (Victor) Mishcon. He cared passionately about peace in the Middle East, and in the early 1980s he realized he had the chance to do something about it. He knew the then ruler of Jordan, King Hussein. Their children had gone to the same school and the families had become friends. He also knew the Israeli Foreign Minister, Shimon Peres, because he was his lawyer.

He decided to bring the two of them together. He invited both to dinner at his apartment. The evening proceeded agreeably until the two got up to leave. They thanked their host for his hospitality. Mishcon put on an air of surprise. 'You can't leave yet,' he said. '*What about the washing up?*' 'Are you serious?' they said. 'Absolutely,' Mishcon replied. And so the two men removed their jackets, rolled up their shirtsleeves, went into the kitchen and did the washing up.

People bond when they do something together. So, the king of Jordan washing, the Israeli foreign minister drying, a friendship was struck between the two. The result would have been a peace treaty between Israel and Jordan had it not been overruled by the then Prime Minister of Israel. But the treaty did eventually happen, in 1994, and in 1995 Mishcon was awarded the Star of Jordan by King Hussein.

173

Sometimes side-by-side – working together – is more effective than face-to-face – talking together.

I-and-Thou

Implicit in the metaphor of 'the home we build together' is a certain way of thinking about relationships between different groups in a diverse society. If the great defenders of freedom in the twentieth century – Karl Popper, Friedrich Hayek and Isaiah Berlin – have one thing above all others to teach us, it is the importance of non-utopian approaches to social transformation. Utopias are beautiful in theory but at best ineffective, at worst disastrous, in practice. How do you translate high ideals into a workable code of action that takes account of human fallibility?

In this chapter I want to propose a different way of thinking about inter-group and interfaith relationships than the one that has captured people's imagination for the past sixty or so years. The author of that vision was Martin Buber, one of the best known Jewish thinkers of the twentieth century. Buber understood that Judaism is less about metaphysical creeds than about the quality of relationships between people. Drawing inspiration from prophetic texts and the tales of the Hassidim, he spoke about the immediacy of human encounters at their most intense and non-judgemental. All else falls away when two people meet and each is fully open to the other. We cease to be bearers of adjectives and nouns – this race, that faith – and become simply selves, personal presences, singular, unique. He believed that the Divine presence lives in such meetings. He called them I-and-Thou.

What happens when two selves truly meet is *dialogue*, not in the Platonic sense of a collaborative search for truth, but in the more mystical sense of an unscripted encounter in which we cross the abyss separating self from self and meet in *das Zwischenmenschliche*, the interhuman or intersubjective, where one loneliness meets another and finds grace. Neither attempts to change the other, but both are changed by the very act of reaching out.

After the Holocaust, this came to be seen as an answer to the single most perplexing problem in human civilization. How do we break the connection between religion and conflict, between group identity and hostility to outsiders? It remains to this day a problematic question as to how far the Nazi programme of genocide was made possible by earlier Christian hostility to Jews. One thing, though, seemed certain, that somehow the rift between Christianity and Judaism had to be healed.

Buber's concept of dialogue seemed the perfect answer. What could be more healing than for Jews and Christians to meet in I-and-Thou encounter, neither attempting to convince or convert the other but merely seeing in one another the face of the human, which is the image of God? And so, quietly at first and with slowly growing momentum, Jews and Christians met, and talked, and discovered one another's deeply held beliefs, and began to recognize the contours of one another's humanity. More recently, dialogue has embraced other faiths: Islam, Hinduism, Sikhism, Buddhism and so on. It is a lovely programme. In one or other form I have been involved in it for years.

I mean to detract nothing from its beauty when I say that, none the less, it is an elite pursuit, for it demands a high degree of confidence, knowledge, openness, breadth and generosity of imagination to come face to face with one whose beliefs are radically opposed to those on which you have staked your life. Interfaith dialogue has enormous achievements to its credit. But it tends to take place among the few, in settings far removed from the faultlines and frontlines of conflict. I support it, value it, and practise it. But some sixty years of dialogue have not yet yielded a world of peace between faiths.

The concept of dialogue is utopian. And just as the Western imagination would have been impoverished without its prophetic utopias, so would it be without the hugely important idea of I-and-Thou. The question is not, Can we do without dialogue? To that, the answer is No. The real question is: Can we also do something else, something *non-utopian*, practical, small-scale, local, nationwide that calls for no exceptional capacities for tolerance and mutual understanding? We can, if we understand the difference between face-to-face and side-by-side. This was tested in a remarkable experiment carried out in 1954 by Muzafer Sherif, known as 'The Robbers Cave'.[2]

The Robbers Cave

Sherif wanted to understand the dynamics of group conflict and prejudice. To do so, he and his fellow researchers selected a group of 22 white, eleven-year-old boys, none of whom had met one another before. They were taken to a remote summer camp in Robbers Cave State Park, Oklahoma. They were randomly allocated into two groups. Initially neither group knew of the existence of the other. They were staying in cabins far apart. The first week was dedicated to team-building. The boys hiked and swam together. Each group chose a name for itself – they became the Eagles and the Rattlers. They stencilled the names on their shirts and flags.

Then, for four days they were introduced to one another through a series of competitions. There were trophies, medals and prizes for the winners, and nothing for the losers. Almost immediately there was tension between them: name-calling, teasing, and derogatory songs. It got worse. Each burned the other's flag and raided their cabins. They objected to eating together with the others in the same dining hall.

Stage 3 was called the 'integration phase'. Meetings were arranged. The two groups watched films together. They lit Fourth-of-July firecrackers together. The hope was that these face-to-face encounters would lessen tensions and lead to reconciliation. They didn't. Several broke up with the children throwing food at one another.

In stage 4, the researchers arranged situations in which a problem arose that threatened both groups simultaneously. The first was a blockage in the supply of drinking water to the camp. The two groups identified the problem separately and gathered at the point where the blockage had occurred. They worked together to remove it, and celebrated together when they succeeded.

In another, both groups voted to watch some films. The researchers explained that the films would cost money to hire, and there was not enough in camp funds to do so. Both groups agreed to contribute an equal share to the cost. In a third, the coach on which they were travelling stalled, and the boys had to work together to push it. By the time the trials were over, the boys had stopped having negative images of the other side. On the final bus ride home, the members of one team used their prize money to buy drinks for everyone.

Similar outcomes have emerged from other studies. The conclusion may seem obvious, but it is nothing short of revolutionary. The faultlines between groups is not, as it has so often been thought, an inexorable fact of human nature, hardwired into our genes. We do indeed feel hostile to the outsider, the other, the stranger, the alien. That is written into our evolutionary psychology, and it will surface whenever it is given the chance.

But the boundaries can be redrawn so that you and I are on the same, not opposite, side of the table. All it takes is a shared task that both of us can achieve together but neither of us can do alone. It does not need an elite encounter, a dialogue. Sherif found that the 'integration phase', his equivalent of dialogue, did not, in and of itself, reduce conflict or change perceptions. What broke down the walls of estrangement and inter-group hostility was simply the necessity of working together to solve a shared problem. That is a paradigm-shifting insight. Side-by-side works better than face-to-face.[3]

Non-utopian Peace

Compare two texts about peace. The first is from the book of Isaiah:

The wolf will live with the lamb,
  the leopard will lie down with the goat,
  the calf and the lion and the yearling together;
  and a little child will lead them ...
They will neither harm nor destroy
  on all my holy mountain,
  for the earth will be full of the knowledge of the Lord
  as the waters cover the sea. (Isaiah 11:6, 9)

The second is from the Talmud:

For the sake of the ways of peace (*darkhei shalom*), the poor of the heathens should not be prevented from gathering gleanings, forgotten sheaves, and corners of the field. Our masters taught: for the sake of the ways of peace, the poor of the heathens should be supported as we support the poor of Israel, the sick of the heathens should be visited as we visit the sick of Israel, and the dead of the heathens should be buried as we bury the dead of Israel.[4]

The first is inspirational, visionary, hope-giving. The second is a prosaic programme for good community relations. The trouble with the Isaiah passage is that it hasn't happened yet and is unlikely to do so within the foreseeable future (There is of course the story of the zoo keeper who proudly displayed to a visitor a cage containing a lion and a lamb living peacefully together. 'How do you do that?' asked the visitor. 'Simple', replied the keeper. 'You just need a new lamb every day'). The formula of the sages did happen for the better part of twenty centuries, and within limits, it worked.

The prophets have always received a better press than the rabbis, for an obvious reason. They were the first and greatest social critics, fearless in speaking truth to power, unafraid to confront corrupt kings and indolent priests, tireless in their call to integrity and justice. Their success was, however, limited. In fact, with the sole exception of Jonah, the only prophet sent to a Gentile city, we know of none who actually brought about social transformation. The rabbis did succeed. Under their tutelage Jewry became one of the most obstinately faithful of all religious groups. The way of life of rabbinic Judaism was so compelling that Jews survived, their identity intact, in exile and dispersion, for longer and under more adverse circumstances than any other.

The reason was that the rabbis were not utopians. Without losing sight of the end of days, they legislated for the here-and-now. Without relinquishing the prophets' dreams, they translated them into codes of practice, learnable behavioural norms. They put their faith in education. They brought heavenly ideals down to earth, creating a

177

redemption of small steps. They took a realistic view of humanity. They acknowledged human failings and found ways of turning them to good purposes. Even if people initially do good for ulterior motives, said the rabbis, if they do it long enough they will eventually come to do it for its own sake.

The prophets spoke poetry, the rabbis prose; but the rabbis succeeded where even the greatest of the prophets failed. *When it comes to realizing high ideals among ordinary human beings, choose non-utopian solutions.* They are more effective, and more humane.

What guided the rabbis was probably the best advice ever given to a minority community. It had been set out in the seventh century BCE at the time of the fall of Jerusalem to the Babylonians. The Temple had been destroyed. Large and influential sections of the people had been taken to Babylon in captivity. That was when the prophet Jeremiah sent a letter to the exiles. Jeremiah has often been branded as a prophet of doom. He was, in fact, a prophet of hope. But he was also a political realist. He knew there was no chance, at that time, of Jews defeating the Babylonians. What mattered was preserving their identity in a strange land, and waiting until the political climate changed. Some half-century later, when Cyrus of Persia conquered Babylon, it did. Jews were allowed to return to their land. Jeremiah was proved right.

In the meantime, said Jeremiah, make yourself a constructive part of the society to which you have been taken captive. He wrote:

This is what the Lord Almighty, the God of Israel, says to all those I carried into exile from Jerusalem to Babylon: 'Build houses and settle down; plant gardens and eat what they produce. Marry and have sons and daughters; find wives for your sons and give your daughters in marriage, so that they too may have sons and daughters. Increase in number there; do not decrease. Also, seek the peace and prosperity of the city to which I have carried you into exile. Pray to the Lord for it, because if it prospers, you too will prosper.' (Jeremiah 29:4–7)

Take the city's welfare as your own. Work for it, pray for it, contribute to it, and don't see yourselves in opposition to it. Keep your faith. Preserve your identity. Stay true to yourself but be a blessing to those among whom you live. Pursue integration without assimilation. The rabbinic 'ways of peace' were a translation of Jeremiah's injunction into a simple set of guidelines. Do acts of kindness to your non-Jewish neighbours as you would to your Jewish ones. Share your food, give charity, visit the sick, and make sure that the dead are given a decent burial.

The 'ways of peace' are a code of good neighbourliness, active citizenship. They are perhaps the first provisions on record for promoting good community relations and social cohesion. They form the rudiments of a code of conduct between different ethnic or religious groups. Isaiah spoke of utopian peace. The sages sought ways of achieving a lesser, more immediate goal, namely *civil peace*, cohesiveness and an absence of strife between different groups within a single society. The 'ways of peace' is a non-utopian programme for peace in the imperfect world of the here-and-now. It also addresses one of the fundamental problems social theorists have identified in modern societies.

Bonding Capital, Bridging Capital

Religions, like other civil associations, are outstanding at creating 'social capital', relationships of trust and goodwill which flow from a sense of shared identity and mutual responsibility. We saw how, in nineteenth-century Britain, Christian groups created an entire social infrastructure of voluntary and charitable organizations, educational, social and welfare. They brought people into contact with one another, created friendships, alleviated ills without recourse to state action, and humanized the often dehumanizing effects of industry, urbanization and income inequality.

Driven by strong faith and a sense of social solidarity, Christians of all kinds visited the sick, comforted the bereaved, supported people in need, created schools for the poor, and generated funds to help the unemployed. The system was not perfect. It did not guarantee equality of provision, nor was it equal to all the social challenges. So, after 1945, the welfare state was born. But social capital remains important. Charities and faith communities can do what governments cannot. They change lives. They humanize forms of care that might otherwise be impersonal. They teach people to give, and be lifted by the act of giving.

But the great theorist of social capital, Harvard political scientist Robert Putnam, made a significant distinction between *bonding* and *bridging* capital.[5] Bonding capital is a form of relationship *within* a community. It is what binds the members together. The word 'religion' itself comes from a Latin root meaning 'to bind'. So, members of a congregation, or a neighbourhood, or a trade, or a profession, help one another. That is the point of their association.

But there is a downside to communities so formed. Their members can be friendly to one another while being hostile, or indifferent to, members of another community. They can be parochial, even socially divisive. That is where we need *bridging* capital, acts of friendship across communal boundaries.

179

Bridging capital is essential in highly divided societies. We need to meet across boundaries and faultlines and discover our common humanity as well as our differences. The more fissured society becomes, the more suspicious we are of strangers, the more stereotyped our images of those not like us, and the lower our levels of trust. That is what makes the 'ways of peace' so interesting a case study, because it is just that: a programme of bridging capital, specifically designed to bring Jews into contact with non-Jewish neighbours through acts of kindness.

In 2002 we had the opportunity to put a national project of bridging capital into action, based on the idea behind the 'ways of peace'. The Queen was celebrating her golden jubilee, and together with the Archbishop of Canterbury and other faith leaders, we decided to mark the occasion by asking the members of our respective communities to undertake acts of kindness to people who were *not members of our faith* – to reach out a hand of friendship across boundaries. The Prince of Wales gave it his backing and personal participation. The programme – called 'Respect' – was launched in England in the spring of 2002, and later in Scotland. All nine of the major religious groupings in Britain participated – Christian, Jewish, Muslim, Hindu, Sikh, Buddhist, Jain, Zoroastrian and Bahai. It expressed the idea that civic peace demands more than tolerance. Tolerance is passive; kindness across faiths is active. It takes the threads of our respective communities, in their variegated colours, and makes them part of the social fabric we weave together.

That, it seems to me, should be part of a new covenant between the faiths. Faiths, as we know, unite and divide. They unite by dividing: by identifying an 'us' as opposed to 'them'. Hence both the good and harm they do come hand-in-hand. We are the children of light; they are the children of darkness. That generates light but also darkness.

There is only one non-utopian way of creating the good without the harm, and that is to create programmes of what in Hebrew is called *chessed*, in Latin *caritas*, or in English, loving kindness, across boundaries. We must love strangers as well as neighbours, in the simple sense of love-as-deed, practical help. That imperative flows from the covenant of human solidarity, and in a national context, from the covenant of citizenship.

That is one way in which faiths could take a lead in healing some of the tensions that currently exist within the liberal democracies of the West. Each church, synagogue, temple or mosque should have some project of kindness to strangers: unconditional kindness, with no element of evangelism or hope of conversion, that we extend to people simply because they are human and have needs, not all of which they can satisfy themselves.

I have tried to illustrate in this chapter what a covenant of active citizenship might look like, taking as a model the rabbinic idea of the ways of peace. The kind of ethnic segregation that the Cantle Report called 'parallel lives' can be addressed by programmes of cross-community outreach. This is the side-by-side approach, as opposed to the face-to-face of dialogue. It is modest, local, and makes no pretension to be an I-Thou encounter. It embodies no high aspiration that one day all the differences between faiths will prove illusory and we will find ourselves in the peace envisioned by Isaiah. It is simply working together across divides to solve the simple, practical problems we all face. It worked in the experiment involving the Eagles and the Rattlers. It almost brought about a peace deal between Jordan and Israel. Its strength is its ability to touch deep chords of common humanity.

For we are cast into this world together. We have souls, we have religions, and they are different. But we also have bodies and they have needs: for food, shelter, clothing, education, access to medical care, protection from the thousand shocks that flesh is heir to, sometimes even the simple fact of company. These are human universals that cut across cultural dividing lines, and they suggest a model for benign coexistence.

It lies in redrawing the boundaries between Them and Us. As long as the Eagles and Rattlers were competing, there was a boundary between them. As soon as they faced problems they could only solve together, the boundary moved. They both became 'Us' facing a recalcitrant world. It is easier to change mental boundaries than to change human nature. That is what Jeremiah meant when he told the exiles, 'Seek the peace and prosperity of the city'. Do not see yourselves and the Babylonians as on opposite sides. Religiously you may be, but civically you are not. You share the same interest in the common good. That is the covenant of citizenship: prosaic, non-utopian, but effective, gracious, and ultimately an acknowledgement that though our faiths may be different, our fate is one.

The most lateral solution I ever encountered to a potential interfaith problem happened in North London. A community there had allowed the grounds around the synagogue to grow unattended for several years. They were frankly unsightly. Opposite the synagogue lived a Christian lady who wondered how she might improve the situation. The proposal she came up with was a stroke of genius. She asked for a meeting with the synagogue lay-leaders. 'I would like', she said, 'to help you make a biblical garden. Let me work with your children to create it. They will learn about the plants of the Bible. They will also learn about gardening. I think they will enjoy it.' And so it happened.

She worked with the children of the synagogue Hebrew Classes for a year. They studied the flora of the Bible and planted as many of its plants as they could. There were bulrushes, for the young Moses floating down the Nile. There were wheat and barley and pomegranates. There were two types of 'burning bush'. The project was magnificent. The children learned more that year than any other. At the opening ceremony they spoke with passion and impressive knowledge. They gained, the synagogue gained, and the Christian neighbour now had a beautiful garden to look at.

Sometimes working together side-by-side achieves miracles. Making things together turns strangers into friends.

Chapter 16

Civility

Civility is a belief which affirms the possibility of the common good; it is a belief in the community of contending parties within a morally valid unity of society.[1]

Edward Shils

Civility ... is the sum of the many sacrifices we are called on to make for the sake of living together.[2]

Stephen Carter

Some years ago I was in Jerusalem to receive the Jerusalem Prize. The custom is that after the ceremony, which takes place in the Knesset, the Israeli parliament building, the President of Israel gives a reception for the winners. At that time the President was a robustly secular Israeli known for his forthrightness. He spoke about the winners and why they had received the prize. When he came to my name he said, 'I see that the Rabbi has been awarded the prize for his contribution to religious education in the Diaspora.' He paused, then continued, 'Religious education is certainly better than nothing, but ...' He then proceeded to deliver a diatribe against religion, saying that what were really needed were secular schools that taught the Hebrew language. It was certainly a debatable point, but this was possibly not the most appropriate moment to make it. When I returned, I said to the Israeli ambassador, 'Now I understand why, after four thousand years, the Hebrew language still does not have a word that means tact.' He thought for a moment, then said, 'In Hebrew, the word for tact is *tact.*' To say it, he had to use the English word.

I spoke in the last chapter about the covenant of citizenship. That can be understood in two ways, depending on whether we think of state or society. In relation to the state, citizenship is about voting, keeping the law, knowing your rights and understanding Britain's political structures. In relation to society, citizenship is quite different. It involves helping others, giving to charitable causes, volunteering and community service. Society, unlike the state, calls for covenantal virtues, and we defined these as habits of character that did not involve money or power, but instead friendship, trust, loyalty and compassion. Covenantal virtues are intensely vulnerable. They need protection against being politicized or economized. If you turn everything into money or power, you kill covenantal virtues and the institutions they create: you destroy marriage and the family, friendship and community. There are two defences against this: one an arena, the other a habit. Lose these and you will eventually lose liberal democracy. The arena is called *civil society*; the habit is *civility*.

Not all cultures develop the habits and conventions of civility.* The British, however, developed it to a fine art. I used to love the way Sir Humphrey – the top civil servant in the comedy series about British politics, *Yes, Prime Minister* – would signal his disagreement to his political masters. 'You are completely wrong' became 'Up to a point, Prime Minister.' 'That would be a disastrous mistake' became 'Courageous, Prime Minister.' To a journalist, 'Yes' was translated into 'I couldn't possibly comment on that.' Civility is of the essence when it comes to peaceful coexistence between different ethnic and religious groups, but it hasn't always existed. When did it develop and why?

It all began, according to Norbert Elias, with the fork.[3] Until the seventeenth century standards of public behaviour were different from what they later became. People ate with their hands and a knife. Plates and dishes were lifted to the mouth. It was not unusual for someone to wipe his nose on the tablecloth. In his 1523 treatise *Diversoria* Erasmus described a typical scene in a German inn where people are eating together. One washes his clothes and leaves them to dry on the stove. Another is cleaning his boots on the table. People spit everywhere. No one uses a fork. There are no forks.

Apparently they existed centuries before among the Byzantine nobility. In the eleventh century a Venetian doge married a Greek princess who brought with her a fork and used it at meals. This was regarded as scandalous by the Venetians: 'This novelty was regarded as so excessive a sign of refinement that the dogaressa was severely

---

* I once conducted a public conversation at an Israeli university with the novelist Amos Oz. Oz is a well-known secularist, and we wanted to show that secular and religious Jews could conduct a respectful conversation. It was a marvellous occasion, but I could not help noticing that it was held under the auspices of a chair of 'civility' endowed by an American philanthropist. There is no Hebrew word that precisely captures the meaning of this word. It was translated as *Ezrachut*, i.e. 'citizenship', which is not the same thing at all.

rebuked by the ecclesiastics who called down divine wrath upon her.'
Not until five centuries later did it begin to appear among the upper
classes in Italy, then France, then England and Germany. As late as the
nineteenth century Americans regarded it as a European affectation.
Using it, said one, was like 'eating soup with a knitting needle'.

It appeared as part of what Elias calls an 'increasingly strong tendency to remove the distasteful from the sight of society'. Civility
emerged with the break-up of the Middle Ages, the development of
trade, free markets, the division of labour and, especially, the growth of
a middle class. Etiquette that had previously been associated with royal
courts (thus 'courteous') began to filter down more widely. There was a
general softening and gentling of manners. Codes of behaviour are
profoundly linked to social structure and hierarchies of power. When
these change, so does behaviour. Hence the fork. When society is built
on trade, and merchants adopt the habits of the nobility, it becomes no
longer polite to eat with your hands.

The word civility, like civilization and citizen, comes from *civis*, the
Latin for town. Politic and politics likewise derive from the Greek word
for a city, *polis* (the word polite comes from a slightly different root
meaning 'to polish'). These derivations suggest that the cluster of virtues they represent have their origin in the distinctive life of cities. For
it was there that, in ancient times as well as today, people from many
different countries and cultures came together to do business. Villages
were places where people knew one another, had grown up together,
shared a culture, and interacted repeatedly. Familiarity, brusqueness,
rough and ready manners, were the result. You don't have to be on best
behaviour among people who know you well. Civility, therefore, is an
ethic for dealing with strangers, people who may have a quite different
background from yours. It is a code for the gracious coexistence of
difference.

It is particularly associated with trade. In ancient times it could be
found in the maritime cities of the Mediterranean. From the seventeenth century onward it followed the great trading centres: Italy, the
Netherlands, France and England. Max Weber famously argued that
there was a connection between 'the spirit of capitalism' and the Protestant ethic. There was, though not necessarily in the way he described
it. His case was that Protestants, especially Calvinists, were driven to a
combination of industry and frugality by their belief in predestination
and the view that this-worldly success was a sign of other-wordly bless-
edness. Another and no less significant factor, though, was that Prot-
estantism *internalized ethics*. Ethical norms moved from 'out there' to
'in here', from socially-enforced code to personally enforced
conscience.

In the medieval economy, where most dealings were between people who knew one another, what were most important were customs, traditions, conventions. That changed with the growth of the free market. It meant that trade was no longer primarily between family and friends but between strangers. What mattered therefore was *trust*. How do I know I can trust you? Only if I know that your word is your bond. Character then becomes important, and the various markers through which character can be judged. In their famous study of changing American culture in the 1950s, *The Lonely Crowd*, David Riesman, Nathan Glazer and Reuel Denney argued that pioneer societies need not tradition-directed or other-directed personality types but inner-directed individuals who carry their conscience with them as a kind of internal compass.[4]

Civility therefore emerges at a particular stage in the development of a society and its economy, when the individual becomes more important than the group, and trade more important than war. Military society with its codes of honour and chivalry gradually makes way for a commercial society with its quite different virtues of prudence, industry and trustworthiness. One of the first to chart the change was Adam Ferguson in his *Essay on the History of Civil Society* (1767).[5] 'Polished manners' appear, he notes, when people begin to 'find, in the mutual desires of tranquillity, which come to possess mankind, and in those public establishments which tend to keep the peace of society, a repose from foreign wars, and a relief from domestic disorders.' That is when they 'learn to decide every contest without tumult, and to secure, by the authority of law, every citizen in the possession of his personal rights'. *Gemeinschaft*, the life of close-knit communities, gives way to *Gesellschaft*, a society of strangers, whose interactions are protected against friction and unpredictability by internalized rules covering everything from honesty to table manners.

Civil Society

Civility is connected with the no less important idea of *civil society*. As people begin to move from villages to towns, so they experience the need for networks of support no longer provided by their neighbours. Hence the astonishing growth, in nineteenth-century Britain and America, of charities, fellowships and friendly societies. The great chronicler of this process was Alexis de Tocqueville, who saw it as one of the most striking features of American society. Americans of all ages and classes, he said, form associations on the slightest provocation:

They have not only commercial and manufacturing companies, in which all take part, but associations of a thousand other kinds, religious, moral, serious, futile, general or restricted, enormous or diminutive. The Americans make associations to give entertainments, to found seminaries, to build inns, to construct churches, to diffuse books, to send missionaries to the antipodes; in this manner they found hospitals, prisons and schools. If it is proposed to inculcate some truth or to foster some feeling by the encouragement of a great example, they form a society. Wherever at the head of some new undertaking you see the government in France, or a man of rank in England, in the United States you will be sure to find an association.[6]

Tocqueville saw this as the great strength of American society. I have argued that it is Britain's strength as well. Tocqueville called it an 'apprenticeship of liberty', an ongoing seminar in citizenship, the one antidote to what he saw as the great danger of liberal democracy: individualism. Individualism makes people more interested in private satisfaction than public duty. When this happens, they leave the work of helping others to the government. They lose the capacity for collective action; they no longer think of the common good; they become passive recipients as opposed to active participants in the work of community building. The result, Tocqueville thought, would be disastrous: 'No sooner does a government attempt to go beyond its political sphere and to enter upon this new track, than it exercises, even unintentionally, an insupportable tyranny.'[7]

Hence the importance of these institutions as a means of cultivating public virtue, checking the growth of the state, and building a sense of responsibility. Often they are connected to the local place of worship. There is hardly a church or synagogue that does not have dozens of such groups, and the same is true in other faiths. Together they constitute one of the greatest contributions of religion to liberal democratic societies.

Religious or secular, their significance is that they are the primary arena of covenantal relationships, based on friendship, altruism, the sense of self that expresses itself in service to the larger group to which I belong. In a liberal democracy they are the great – often the only – counterweight to the state and the market, politics and economics. Tocqueville's associations, Burke's 'little platoons', sociology's 'mediating structures', are the third sector between the individual and the state, and they protect covenantal relationships from being contractualized into temporary allegiances based on self-interest.

The mark of totalitarian societies is that such groups don't exist. Rousseau saw that they compromise total loyalty to the state, and he was against them for that reason. You don't betray your friends or your co-religionists to the police. Hence a police state must be vigilant against friendship, religion or anything else that brings people together in free association. The absence of civil society is one of the reasons people in former tyrannies or totalitarian states find it difficult to establish a democracy. They are not used to doing things for themselves, in concert with others, without recourse to the state. Tocqueville intuitively saw that civil society – the complex, multiple arena of voluntary engagements – is liberty's best and last defence.

Civility and civil society look like different things. One is a personal matter of manners, sensitivity, politeness, tact. The other is a social phenomenon: associations, congregations, communities of commitment. What connects them is *concern for the welfare of others*, a refusal to let everything be determined by politics or economics, an insistence that human beings owe one another a respect that is not coerced or paid for, but simply because they are human beings. Civility and civil society represent the power of the personal in a world of impersonal forces. They create friendships in societies where we are thrown together as strangers. They are oases of togetherness in the anonymity of urban life and the lonely crowd. They cut across conflict and competition. If we lose civility, and if civil society becomes politicized, the future of freedom is in danger.

Losing Civility

Both are happening now. We are living through the death of civility. It is an extraordinary transformation. In 1944 George Orwell could speak about 'the gentle-mannered, undemonstrative, law-abiding English of today',[8] noting that an 'imaginary foreign observer would certainly be struck by our gentleness; by the orderly behaviour of English crowds, the lack of pushing and quarrelling'. In 1955, in his *Exploring English Character*, Geoffrey Gorer wrote:

> In public life today, the English are certainly among the most peaceful, gentle, courteous and orderly populations that the civilized world has ever seen ... this orderliness and gentleness, this absence of overt aggression calls for an explanation.[9]

Today it is commonplace to encounter road rage, muggings, street crime, drunkenness, lager louts, hoodies, yobbishness and 'laddishness'.[10] Teachers are attacked in the classroom. Nurses encounter violence from their patients. The English have acquired a worldwide reputation for football hooliganism, and this applies to players as well as fans. In first-class football matches in 1946–47, 10 players were sent off; by the mid-90s the number had reached 451.

Incidents of violent crime have soared. There were 4,221 such incidents in 1898, 331,843 in 1998–99: adjusting for population growth, a 47-fold increase. A 2002 survey of tourist offices in 17 countries found that, for loutishness, British visitors were top of the league. A 1999 European Union survey showed that 41 per cent of English youngsters between 15 and 16 had tried cannabis, the highest rate in Europe. Alcohol abuse has spread to women: British women lead the field in Europe.

There are broadcasters famous for their aggressiveness. A few years ago I was taking part in a televised discussion about religion in contemporary society. One of my fellow panellists, a well-known television personality, was making his case against religion with withering sarcasm. I sat through it unmoved. Unable to shake my confidence he suddenly let out a stream of wild abuse, accusing Jews of being worse than the Nazis. Had he been drunk or a member of the British Nationalist Party, it would have been understandable. He was neither; he was and is an eminent scholar. Since the discussion was being filmed and was due to be televised, I told the presenter that I would only continue if I was given an undertaking that the outburst would be edited out. After prolonged consultation with the editor, he gave me the assurance and we continued. It was my first encounter with rage as a substitute for argument, and it was disturbing.

The death of civility is serious. It may seem slight, mere etiquette, what Hobbes called 'small morals' as against more substantive virtues. But it is a precondition of liberal democracy in a diverse society. Any free society will contain disagreements on everything from school uniforms to abortion. Civility allows us to negotiate such disagreements without ceasing to be friends. It signals respect for the other person even in the absence of shared values and beliefs. It means that though we disagree, we are part of the same moral universe. We share a commitment to the common good. We are part of something that embraces us both. We recognize that we may win some arguments and lose others, but – by choosing to live in this particular society – we honour its protocols of conflict resolution.

Civility means that we reserve an area of respect that is not politicized. What allows us to do this – what gives liberal democracy its attractiveness to those who come from traditional cultures where strife may be the norm – is that we know our view will be listened to. We will have a fair hearing, the chance to articulate our convictions and concerns. We know that we are dealing, for the most part, with people who respect the deeply held views of others. Civility, said Edward Shils, is 'a belief which affirms the possibility of the common good; it is a belief in the community of contending parties within a morally valid unity of society.'[11]

Neutral Spaces

Civility also needs civil society. Specifically it needs *neutral spaces*, places where people gather as friends, co-equals, united in a fellowship of respect and trust. That is what charities, churches, schools, universities and professional associations ideally are. We come together in pursuit of an ideal and to do this we set certain considerations aside. The rich are not respected more, nor the poor less. We honour the aims of the organization; we leave politics aside. That is what gives such associations their dignity and integrity. They represent values that cannot be decided by vote or bought by money. Within them we leave behind the clamour and conflict of the outside world and honour our joint commitment to a cause, a calling or an ideal.

As I mentioned earlier, my first doctoral supervisor was the late Sir Bernard Williams, at the time described as the most brilliant mind in Britain. I had just returned from a religious seminary. He, a lapsed Catholic, was a principled atheist. Nor was this irrelevant to my doctorate, since I was trying to write about the concept of authenticity, which has both religious and secular undertones. Yet in all the times we met, he never once challenged my religious beliefs. That, for me, was one of the greatest lessons I ever learned at university: what it is to come together with others in the pursuit of truth, laying personal convictions aside and concentrating on evidence and logic, clarity, coherence and consistency.

One of the most disturbing features of the past few years has been the erosion of civil society by the systematic politicization of what were once neutral spaces. One after another, universities, NGOs, charities, professional bodies, and churches have been drawn into overtly political activity: boycotts, bans, exclusions, disinvestment campaigns, and politically partisan websites. These activities, some of which are undertaken for motives that are pure, have the effect of isolating, and even driving out, people whose political opinions or attachments are different. The result is that they cease to be institutions of civil society and become pressure groups, lobbying for change in government policy in areas that have nothing to do with the purposes for which these groups are constituted. As soon as they do this, they lose – one is almost tempted to say, betray – the function they once had of bringing people together across divides and become, as Tocqueville warned, as divisive as politics always is and always will be.

A church that undertakes a disinvestment campaign, for example, will cease to be able to function as an agent of local community cohesion. By allying itself to one group, it distances itself from another. It thereby forfeits its real and local power to unite by setting politics aside, and becomes instead one political voice among many. It erodes,

190

instead of enriching, civic space. It loses whatever moral authority it once had by virtue of the fact that it stood above the fray and could therefore be trusted by others to listen impartially to their hopes and fears.

Often this is done in the name of 'the prophetic voice'. The prophetic voice is indeed essential to the moral health of a society. As Michael Walzer has pointed out in several books, however, the prophets had moral authority precisely because they stood within the society they criticized.[12] They spoke out of loyalty to their people and the principles by which they believed society should be governed. That was what Dietrich Bonhoeffer did in Nazi Germany, Martin Luther King in America and Desmond Tutu in South Africa. There is a difference between the prophet who lives 'in the midst of his people' and the armchair critic who passes judgement on another people from afar.

When neutral space is politicized, it ceases to be neutral. When covenantal institutions are politicized, they are destroyed. That happened in France during the Dreyfus affair. It happened in Germany in the early years of fascism. Racism found some of its most trusted allies among judges, doctors, university professors and high-ranking members of the armed forces. It happened in the United States in 1941 when Bertrand Russell was barred from taking up an academic position at City College, New York, because of his views on sexual ethics.

Ideological politics – the politics that seeks to invade and conquer the totality of public life – is incompatible with civil society: on that, Rousseau and Tocqueville, from their opposite perspectives, were agreed. Civility makes space for difference. Ideology aspires to eliminate difference. To quote Edward Shils again: 'Civility and ideological radicalism are irreconcilable'.[13] Ideology is 'at war with the rest of society'. It finds abhorrent 'the very notion of a common interest, of a concern for society as a whole'. Convinced that it alone has the truth, it has no patience for impartiality, fair procedures, reasoned debate. It speaks; it does not listen. It knows; it has no space for doubt. It sees the even-handedness of civil discourse as a weakness to be exploited, not a strength to be respected.

We have forgotten how many battles had to be fought before civility prevailed and civil society emerged. There is nothing inevitable about 'the mutual desires of tranquillity' about which Adam Ferguson wrote, nor about the habits that enable human beings 'to decide every contest without tumult'. On the contrary: writing as he did in the eighteenth century they struck him as new, unprecedented, strange. The descent from civility to barbarism can happen with surprising speed, if we fail to honour the institutions and habits that allow people to disagree while remaining friends.

The media have a part to play in this as well. It is striking, for example, how when faith leaders agree, when they exercise civility, it is impossible for them to capture media attention, especially on television. Extreme voices, yes; moderate ones, no. The result is that the extremists become heroes to some and villains to others. The image conveyed is of a society polarized between religious and secular radicalism – and what is appearance today becomes reality tomorrow, because we are dependent on the media to hold up a mirror to ourselves. Its image becomes ours, and that in turn affects what we do.

Consensus, say the media, is boring. Conflict is exciting. And surely that is so. But as the novelist Amos Oz points out, the difference between Shakespeare's tragedies and Chekhov's is that in Shakespeare, by the end of the play, the stage is strewn with dead bodies. In Chekhov, the characters are thoroughly miserable, but they live. Sometimes conflict resolution is boring. But freedom depends on people preferring the boredom of peace to the excitement of war.

If we are to defend liberal democracy, we will have to recover civility and civil society. Civility means, among other things, the willingness to listen respectfully to those with whom we disagree. It means forgoing tendentious use of language, *ad hominem* attacks, the delegitimation of unfashionable opinions, and the substitution of anger for argument. Civil society involves protecting non-political associations against being hijacked for political ends. To use the terminology of Richard John Neuhaus, the West once had a *sacred* public square, from which dissent, deemed heresy, was excluded.[14] It then had the *naked* public square, society as hotel with no shared values. What we now need is the *civil* public square, where strong disagreement is contained by a yet stronger commitment to public reason, where the rules of the game matter no less than which team wins.

Chapter 17

Multiculturalism or Tolerance?

For it is unreasonable that any should have a free liberty of their religion who do not acknowledge it as a principle of theirs that nobody ought to persecute or molest another because he dissents from him in religion.[1]

John Locke

How, Schopenhauer once asked, do porcupines live together in winter? If they huddle too closely they harm one another with their spines. If they are too distant to give each another warmth, they freeze. The solution will always be a matter of balance between closeness and distance.

That is the basic problem of human association. We value our independence but we recognize our interdependence. We need one another for warmth, friendship, support. We are social animals. In the wild, an animal that gets separated from the group dies: it is easy prey to a predator. Our ancestors too lived and hunted in groups for the same reason. The need to be with others is hardwired into our brains.

At the same time, too much closeness creates tension. We need private space if we are to develop our individuality. Life in a village where everyone knows everyone else's secrets can be claustrophobic. Much of urban life has been a steady pursuit of privacy as a defence against the sheer physical proximity of so many other people. So, like porcupines, we try to strike a balance. Too much togetherness leaves us little space to be ourselves. Too much isolation breeds loneliness, isolation, alienation and despair.

The name we have given to this problem is *tolerance*, a key virtue in liberal democracies. However, the concept is fraught with difficulties, some of which I want to analyse in this chapter. My argument will be twofold. First, I want to distinguish tolerance as a moral virtue and as a political one. The two are not the same, and failure to distinguish them

193

leads to confusion. The second is terminology. In the seventeenth century people like Locke spoke about 'toleration' not 'tolerance'. More recently we have become accustomed to use the word 'multiculturalism' rather than tolerance. Are these three words for the same phenomenon – a willingness to live and let live? Or are they different things entirely? Clarity here is of the essence, for tolerance comes wrapped in mists of vagueness and leads to conflicting expectations.

What we can say in advance is that tolerance is not a timeless and universal virtue: it is a time-bound and particular one. It did not exist prior to the seventeenth century, and attempts to read it back into ancient texts are anachronistic. Societies have taken different views at different times as to how close or how distant they want their bonds to be. In general in the past they were tighter. Groups were held together by shared kinship, ethnicity or faith. Toleration was born as a virtue out of specific circumstances in Europe in the seventeenth century. The liberal democratic state is one of the results.

The Elusive Virtue

What is toleration?[2] It is, philosophers tell us, an 'elusive virtue'. Bernard Williams put it more strongly: it seems, he said, to be both necessary and impossible. How so?

Toleration has been defined as the virtue of refraining from exercising one's power with regard to others' opinions or actions even if they deviate from one's own view over something important and even if one morally disapproves of them.

Taking this bit by bit: toleration arises when I have the power to stop something but I choose not to do so. If I have no power, the question does not arise. I cannot claim credit for putting up with something I can't prevent: loud music from car stereos, for example. It isn't tolerance but impotence that characterizes my attitude. I would ban it if I could, but I can't.

There are also things with which I disagree, and could prevent, but don't, not because I am tolerant but because I judge them to be not significant enough in the scheme of things. I disapprove of people cutting ahead of me in queues, but life is too short to argue the point. 'Wisdom', said William James, 'is learning what to overlook.'

Tolerance is also the wrong word when what is at stake is not morality but aesthetics, a matter of taste. You prefer Mozart; I prefer Mahler. You like chocolate fudge ice cream; I prefer malt whisky. That we put up with such differences is not toleration. That's just how life is: my taste is this, yours is that. That's what makes taste different from moral judgement.

So tolerance arises when I think you are morally wrong about a matter of some consequence. None the less I forbear to do what I can to prevent you doing it, because I am tolerant. I believe in making space for difference. I recognize the existence of deep moral disagreements which lead to my thinking X is wrong, but you sincerely believing otherwise. Therefore, though I disapprove of what you do, I do not attempt to stop you doing it.

But this is where difficulty arises. In what sense do I believe that X is wrong? Often people defend tolerance on the ground that there is no one conception of the good. The Ancient Greeks believed that infanticide was permissible. We do not. Almost everything that one culture has found repugnant, another has permitted. And if people can differ across space and time, why not in roughly the same space at the same time? You think one way. I think another. There is no neutral way of deciding which of us is right. Therefore we agree to disagree. Is this tolerance?

No, for this is the doctrine known as moral relativism. It makes disagreements about morality like disagreements about taste. I prefer this; you prefer that. A relativist culture is not a tolerant but a post-tolerant one. If I do not think you are wrong to do what you sincerely believe to be right, then I do not tolerate you. I simply accept that there is no accounting for conscience, the way there is no accounting for taste.

So let us go back to genuine, substantive moral disagreement. Let us say that I believe that abortion is, under all circumstances, wrong. You disagree. I believe the foetus has a right to life; you believe that a woman has the right to choose. Here is a genuine situation calling for tolerance. But why should I be tolerant? In what sense can this be a virtue?

Toleration is sometimes argued for in the following terms. Imagine a society in which roughly half the population believe in the right to abortion on demand, and half do not. They believe, to the contrary, that abortion is morally wrong, the unwarranted destruction of a human, or potentially human, life. Surely – so the argument goes – everyone is better off in a situation in which we are each free to act in accordance with our consciences. Those who think it permitted can have an abortion. Those who do not, will not. As the American bumper-sticker put it: 'If you disagree with abortion, don't have one.'

Yet this cannot be right. Imagine being present in Rwanda in April 1994. Hutus are murdering Tutsis. I find myself in a situation in which I can prevent a murder. I decide to do nothing. I think murder is wrong, but I also recognize that some people believe otherwise. Is this toler-ance? Surely not. It is dereliction of moral duty. In Jewish law, for example, I am morally accountable for the wrong I could have prevented but did not. How can inaction – being a passive witness to evil – be considered a virtue?

Not so, you say. Tolerance recognizes an important fact about the moral life. Morality requires autonomy. To be moral I must do what I believe to be right. Autonomy, or self-legislation, is the precondition of any virtue. Therefore a tolerant society – one that gives maximum liberty to individuals to do what they think right – will be more moral than one that imposes conformity.

This argument, deriving from Immanuel Kant, is so deeply embedded in our culture that it can be hard to see how absurd it seems to someone who comes, as it were, from another tradition. Let's do a thought experiment involving the philosopher's friend, a visitor from Mars. The visitor spends a day watching the traffic on the roads, turns to us and says, 'You earthlings have a very conformist view of driving. Everyone I have seen drives on the left hand side of the road. On Mars we would regard that as an infringement of freedom. For us it is a matter of principle that we are free to choose on which side of the road to drive.' 'But that would cause chaos,' we reply. 'Chaos', says the Martian, 'is the price we are prepared to pay for freedom.' 'Well, we are not prepared to pay that price,' we say. 'Better a world of conformity than chaos.'

Now apply the argument to abortion. 'Better a world in which everyone obeys the same law, No abortion, than one in which there is moral chaos,' says the traditionalist. 'How can you compare the two cases?' replies the liberal. 'It doesn't much matter which side of the road you drive on. To insist that everyone obeys the same rule does not involve any real sacrifice of liberty. But it matters very much indeed whether a woman is or is not allowed to have an abortion.' 'Quite so,' replies the traditionalist. 'All the more reason to avoid moral chaos. If you accept conformity in a minor matter, all the more should you do so on a major one.' Hence Bernard Williams' paradox. The very thing that seems to make tolerance necessary – significant, substantive moral disagreement – also seems to make it impossible.

In fact, a stranger to our world might find the keyword of liberalism – autonomy (self-legislation) – strange, even a contradiction in terms. For what is a law if not something that binds our behaviour regardless of what we choose? I may want to do X, I may have a moral conviction that requires me to do X, but I am deterred, and if necessary prevented, from doing X because there is a law against it. A situation in which everyone is their own legislator is a system without law at all. The very meaning of the word 'law' means that some legislative power has decided to take the matter out of our hands for the greater good of society. The Bible has an apt description of a society of autonomous individuals: 'In those days there was no king in Israel; everyone did what was right in their own eyes.' This is not the description of a free society but of anarchy. Law is of its very nature heteronomous, that is, legislated by someone other than me, the choosing self. So tolerance is indeed an elusive virtue.

The Birth of Toleration

We will, I think, only understand it if we remind ourselves how it arose. It made its appearance in the seventeenth century, most famously in the writings of John Locke, in the form of the concept (not of tolerance but) of toleration. The question to which it was an answer concerned religious practice. Should Jews and Muslims be free to practise their faith in a Christian country? Should Catholicism be allowed in a Protestant nation? These may seem absurd questions to us now, but in their time they led to civil war. Locke's *Letter Concerning Toleration* was addressed, he wrote, 'to the consciences of those that persecute, torment, destroy and kill other men on pretence of religion'.

Why should, say, a Christian country tolerate the practice of a religion they regard as false? Why should not the force of law be used to impose truth, and thus salvation, on all? The answer given by Locke is that the idea of changing someone's religious views by coercion is a contradiction in terms. You cannot force me to believe what I do not. I can *say* I believe, I can *pretend* to believe. But if the only reason I do so is because you are forcing me to by threat of punishment or death, then absent the force and there is no belief. Neither conviction nor conversion can be achieved through coercion.

Locke presents this as an obvious truth, which it is. But there were times when people believed otherwise. Between 1391 and 1492 the Spanish used discrimination and intimidation to attract Jews and Muslims to become Christians. Some did. Many did not. Eventually, in 1492, they were expelled from Spain. Some took refuge in Portugal, believing it to be a more tolerant country. This hope was disappointed. In 1497, Spain forcibly converted all its Jews to Christianity.

Many of those who had converted under duress in Spain, remained committed Jews who practised their faith in secret. They were known in Judaism as the *anusim* (victims of coercion). The Spanish called them *marranos*, 'pigs'. That was one reason for the Spanish Inquisition. Jews were tried for practising their faith in secret, and if found guilty were burned at the stake. The Inquisition continued until the mid-nineteenth century.

Nor was this all. The Spanish took objection to Jews. Evidently at one stage they believed that this could be cured by converting them to Christianity. Yet the hatred persisted even after their conversion. It could no longer be justified on religious grounds because the ex-Jews were now Christians. It was then that a fateful phenomenon made its first appearance in history: racial anti-Semitism. Laws were passed discriminating against ex-Jews, not on religious grounds, but because of *limpieza de sangre*, 'purity of blood'. It was this doctrine that reappeared in late nineteenth-century Germany and led to the Holocaust.

So it took Locke to remind us that this entire chapter in the history of religion, in which people were either forcibly converted to another faith, or burned at the stake for remaining faithful to their own, was based on a fallacy. You cannot coerce people to believe. *Truth is not established by power.* This idea (not toleration per se, but the logic behind it) had long been present in both Judaism and Islam. In Judaism it is set out in a Talmudic passage in which the sages argued that if God himself had forced the Israelites to accept the covenant at Mount Sinai, it would be invalid. Coerced consent is not consent. Islam has a similar principle in the Koran: 'There shall be no compulsion in religion.' Those who are forced to believe, simply do not believe.

There was, though, a second factor at work in seventeenth-century Europe, namely the shifting fortunes of different faiths. At times of political instability, each faith has a reason not to see its doctrines enforced by law because there is always a possibility that the situation may be reversed. It may suit me now to see my faith enshrined in law because it is currently in the ascendancy. But at some future date another faith may be in the ascendancy, and I would then face the danger of being persecuted, or at least disadvantaged, because of mine. This is the pragmatic version of the golden rule: do to others as you would wish them to do to you. Its negative corollary is: do not do to others what you would not like them to do to you.

Despite the fact that this principle is obvious and has been held by almost every civilization in history, surprisingly few cultures have acted on it. The reason is that it asks us to imagine a role reversal. What if today's majority is tomorrow's minority? Most people at most times have found it hard to imagine the world being different. On the contrary, we act on the assumption that it will continue to be more or less what it is. The very need for psychological security means that we edit out such possibilities.

But not always, especially if nations teeter between two competing powers, either of which may come to prevail today, only to be dislodged tomorrow. That is when role reversal becomes not an act of the moral imagination, but a fact of political possibility. It is no coincidence that Locke's doctrine of toleration appeared where and when it did, in the seventeenth century, after a century in which Catholics and Protestants had fought each other across Europe. That is when you seek to create an island of stability in an age of instability. The doctrine of toleration sets out, as it were, the rules of the game when you do not know which side will win.

Toleration arose in the seventeenth century not because people were any more tolerant in that age than others – they weren't – but because it solved a problem that had not been acute before: namely, how to ensure the peaceable coexistence of different groups within society. Why was this not always a reason for toleration? Because previously, societies had either been monocultural (until 1656 the practice of Judaism was illegal in Britain, or so it was believed), or they had been multi-national empires. The Ottoman Empire operated what was called the millet system by which each religious group essentially managed its own internal affairs. Jews and Christians were not equal citizens. They were *dhimmi*. They had to pay a poll tax. They could not build houses of worship without permission. They had to show subservience to members of the dominant faith. But they were at least allowed to live and practise their religion. The Ottoman Empire was not tolerant in the modern sense, but it did practise a form of benign coexistence.

We can now understand what toleration is, and why it seems paradoxical. It is not a *religious* but a *political* virtue. It is not an answer to the question: What is the way of life that brings salvation? It is an answer to the question: How shall people with different religious views live together? It aims not at truth but at peace. It is a political necessity, not a religious imperative, and it arises when people have lived through the alternative: the war of all against all.

Toleration, as opposed to tolerance, is specifically about the coexistence of different religions within the same society. The revolution it represents is *the formal or substantive separation of religion from politics.* Religion is about the exercise of conscience. Politics is about the exercise of power. When a nation seeks to accommodate more than one system of religion, it must separate faith from power. Nations and religious establishments learn this the hard way – only when they have lived through bitter civil wars. No religion, no ideology, voluntarily relinquishes power. It only does so when it sees the full, bitter, devastating cost of trying to force salvation on the unwilling. The demigods of power always demand human sacrifices, sometimes millions of them. That is when the wise remember what they should never have forgotten, that the voice of the prophet speaks truth to power. It does not use power to impose truth.

From Toleration to Tolerance

European toleration was born in the seventeenth century, but it did not happen all at once. The first stage was to allow people to practise their own faith when it was not the established faith of the nation. It did not, however, give them full civil rights. In Britain, until the nineteenth century, Catholics, Jews and Dissenters could not attend university, obtain a degree, enter the professions, hold public office, or be elected and take their seat in Parliament. The granting of these rights – Emancipation – was the second stage.

The third – the liberal revolution of the 1960s – did for morality what toleration and emancipation had done for religion. The legalization of homosexual behaviour and abortion were among its firstfruits. Having seen that people of different religions could live peaceably together, liberals went on to argue that the same applied to people of different moral beliefs. If governments had decided long ago not to dictate what religion people should practise, then neither should they tell people what lives to lead either, except where a clear, direct, physical harm might ensue to someone else. This was the move marked linguistically by the word 'tolerance', as opposed to the more narrowly religious term 'toleration'.

But this was when two confusions were born. The first was between two ideas that sound similar but are in fact not: *political liberalism* and *moral relativism.* Political liberalism is built on the idea of tolerance, meaning, we do not legislate for virtue. We separate morality from politics and the law. We may judge something wrong, but at the same time believe that it is wrong to make it illegal. Moral relativism is not tolerance. It is the quite different belief that morality is like aesthetics. There is no absolute right or wrong at all.

These are completely different views. Tolerance is about politics, not morality. Moral relativism is about morality, not politics. Yet it is easy to confuse them. All it takes is the move from 'John *has a right* to do X' to 'John *is right* to do X.' The two sentences sound almost the same, but they belong in fact to two different languages, two distinct systems of thought. The first is a political statement. The second is a moral one. The first is about law. The second is about ethics. To be sure, there are connections between morality and law, but they are many, and different, and change over time.

The liberal revolution of the 1960s was precisely the decision to *separate* morality from law. *That is what constitutes tolerance:* the ability to say 'John is wrong to do X, but he has a right to do X', meaning, there is no impediment in law to doing X. We decide not to enforce morals, just as Britain in the seventeenth century decided not to enforce Christianity. Liberalism is the separation of the moral from the political, just as earlier governments had decided, formally or substantively, to separate church and state.

When political liberalism is combined with moral relativism it reconnects morality and politics, the very thing liberalism was supposed to avoid. The

200

political statement, 'I have a right to do X', becomes the moral statement, 'I am right to do X'. If I then teach that one is wrong to do X, I can be accused of intolerance. That, as I showed in chapter 4, is why the Roman Catholic Rocco Buttiglioni was barred from taking office in the European Commission. It was this move, as I explained there, that turned Political Correctness from thoughtfulness to thought-control. In actual fact, the belief that X is wrong but there should not be a law against it, is tolerance. The belief that I am (morally) right to do anything I have a (legal) right to do is not tolerance but moral relativism. This, the first confusion, was not progress but regress into a new form of barbarism.

From Tolerance to Multiculturalism

The second development was the mutation, between the 1960s and the 1990s, of individual rights into group rights. If I have rights in law, why should the same not apply to the group to which I belong? There is an answer to that question, but it was not acted on at that time.

It lies in the distinction I have been making throughout: between state and society; between law and free association; between social contract and social covenant. The social contract, which creates the state, is between individuals and the body to which they delegate power, the king, the ruler, or the democratically elected government. That is the political domain. It has two players and two only: the individual and the state.

There is a different domain, variously known as civil society, the third sector, Tocqueville's associations, Burke's little platoons, friendly societies, neighbourhood groups and religious congregations. Here relationships are covenantal, not contractual. They have nothing to do with the market or the state, other than the fact that the state allows them to exist under the rules of freedom of association. They exist because we need the company of others, practically and psychologically. In the nation state, as opposed to the corporate state of the Middle Ages, they are voluntary associations. I can join, I can decide not to join, or I can leave. If they existed on any other than a voluntary basis, they would constitute a state-within-the-state and they would destroy the liberalism of liberal democracy.

So, to give the most basic example: marriage is a voluntary association. I can decide to marry or not to marry, and if I have married, I can seek a divorce. *Marriage is not a liberal institution.* It means giving up certain freedoms. It means agreeing to be bound in a bond of fidelity and mutual responsibility. What allows marriage, and every other non-liberal institution, to exist within a liberal society is that fact that I can choose not to enter, or at the very least I can choose to leave.

So, in a liberal democracy, there are two spheres that are kept rigidly apart: the *political*, the contract between the individual and the state; and the *social*, the covenants that bind us to one another in community or communion. The first exists in the form of laws, the second in the form of voluntary association. The first is paid for by taxes; the second by voluntary contributions. Confuse the two, and you endanger liberal democracy.

That is precisely what the demand for group rights does. It confuses covenant and contract, voluntary association and law, society and the state. If I demand rights not for me-as-citizen, but me-as-member-of-the-group to which I belong, then I am not campaigning for liberal democracy but for a return to the corporate state of the Middle Ages, or something like the Ottoman Empire, in which groups did indeed have, in many spheres, self-governing powers.

So the move from liberalism to multiculturalism, from individual to group rights, is not a new stage on the path of tolerance, but a move back to the state of affairs that existed before that path began. How does this play out in practice?

The Dutch Example

I have referred in earlier chapters to one of the most important books in recent years, Paul Sniderman and Louk Hagendoorn's study of contemporary Holland, *When Ways of Life Collide*. This is a scrupulously researched, carefully nuanced account of the condition of Dutch society, and its findings deserve to be widely known.

They discovered that most of the Dutch have a high regard for Muslims. They believe they have much to offer Dutch culture. They do not believe that there is a clash of civilizations. They think that Muslims respect non-Muslims, that Islam and the West are compatible, and that Muslims have the right in Holland to live according to their beliefs. The authors candidly admit that they did not expect to find such positive attitudes. They are, however, quite clear as to what they mean. They mean that *Dutch society is tolerant.* They do not mean that the Dutch favour multiculturalism. They don't. They oppose it. That is their key finding.

The whole thrust of multiculturalism, they conclude, is 'to accentuate, even exaggerate, differences between majority and minority'. They continue:

> Sharing a common identity builds support for inclusion; bringing differences of ethnic and religious identity to the fore evokes the very exclusionary reactions it is meant to avoid.[3]

Multiculturalists in Holland argued that it is necessary to go beyond 'mere' tolerance. Tolerance involves 'freedom for groups to develop and defend their identity and values "in private or through associations of their members"; public assistance targeted to minorities to help them make educational and economic advances; and what is more, an injunction on governments to respect the cultural identities of minorities.'[4] This, said the multiculturalists, is not enough. Tolerance is 'grudging and patronizing'. It can lead to minorities having a low self-image.

Yet, as Sniderman and Hagendoorn make clear, the Dutch *are* tolerant. They *do* think well of minorities. What they resist, even resent, is the extra step from tolerance to multiculturalism. It drives a wedge between majority and minorities. It emphasizes difference instead of minimizing it. It gives incentives to leaders of minority groups 'to emphasize the disjunction between themselves and the majority culture'. It also 'gives more reasons to the majority to believe that there is indeed a disjunction'. It poisons group relationships. It creates reciprocal intolerance. It undermines the sense of loyalty to the common good on which integration depends. The benefits of tolerance, they say, 'are large and the costs negligible'. The benefits of multiculturalism 'appear negligible and the costs high'.

I have tried to show why this is. At a certain point, tolerance mutated into its opposite. Political liberalism became moral relativism. Individual rights became group rights. The first means that morality becomes politicized: the very thing tolerance was intended to avoid. The second means that politics accentuates instead of minimizing difference. Liberal politics is race-, gender-, and religion-blind. It means that we can all relate to the state on equal terms as individuals regardless of our colour, creed or code. Multicultural politics is the opposite: a claim for attention on the basis of colour, creed or code. It brings divisive issues back into the political domain from where they had been banished in the name of toleration and tolerance.

Liberal democracy depends on the ability to make and honour distinctions: between politics on the one hand, religion and morality on the other; between state and society; the individual and the group; matters of law and those that belong to voluntary association. Those distinctions have not been honoured in recent decades. They have been blurred. The result is the return of the very religious conflicts liberalism was created to resolve.

Tolerance means ignoring differences. Multiculturalism means emphasizing them. You can have tolerance or multiculturalism, but not both. We must now decide which we prefer.

Chapter 18

Mending the Broken Family

In our own time the whole of Greece has been subject to a low
birth rate and a general decrease of the population, owing to
which cities have become deserted and the land has ceased to
yield fruit, although there have neither been continuous wars nor
epidemics ... For as men had fallen into such a state of pre-
tentiousness, avarice and indolence that they did not wish to
marry, or if they married to rear the children born to them, or at
most as a rule but one or two of them, so as to leave these in
affluence and bring them up to waste their substance, the evil
rapidly and insensibly grew.[1]

Polybius (circa 150 BCE)

Europe is slowly dying.[2] Its population is ageing and diminishing. More
die than are born. Children have become scarce.[3] To maintain the size
of a population – zero-population growth – the birthrate must be on
average 2.1 children per woman. In Greece the rate is now 1.28, in
Spain 1.34, in Italy 1.34, in Germany 1.34, in the Netherlands 1.73, in
Britain 1.80. In Europe as a whole the average is down to 1.52. In 1990,
three countries – Germany, Bulgaria and Hungary – were declining for
the first time. By 2002 this applied to 15 countries.[4] If present trends
continue, the proportion of those aged 65 and over to those of working
age, now one-to-four, is set to become one-to-two in 2050. Measured by
birthrates, Europe is losing the will to live.

Fewer people are getting married. A report issued by the Office of
National Statistics in February 2007 showed that the number of Britons
choosing to marry has fallen to the lowest levels in 111 years. The
number of marriages fell by 10 per cent in one year alone, between
2004 and 2005. Those who are marrying are doing so later: the average
for men is now 36.2 years, and for women 33.6, up by three years since
1995. Since the 1970s the number of couples getting married has fallen

by a third, and the marriage rate has fallen by two-thirds, from 71 to 26 per thousand unmarried adults per year.[5] Those who marry are not staying married. In Britain more than 40 per cent of marriages end in divorce: in 2005 there were 155,052 divorces, as against just over 244,000 marriages.

Virtually every society ever studied by anthropologists has some form of normative family structure, some agreed convention by which others – usually, though not always, a husband – support a mother and child. The West, Britain especially, has embarked on an unprecedented experiment of sexual and reproductive anomie: cohabitation, a succession of step-parents, same-sex partnerships, limited commitment marriages, children shuttling between households, and above all single-parent households. Nearly one in two children in Britain are born to unmarried parents, up from one in eight in 1980; 26 per cent of British children currently live in lone-parent households. Britain has the highest rate of teenage pregnancies in Europe as well as the highest percentage of children living in single-parent families. The results are devastating.

A UNICEF survey published in February 2007 reported that Britain's children are the unhappiest in the Western world.[6] They drink and smoke more, take more drugs, have more underage sex, rate their health as poorer and dislike school more than their peers in other countries. They are more prone to failure at school, more likely to experience violence and bullying, and suffer more unhappy relationships within and outside the home. They are the least satisfied with life.

Already in 1997 Oliver James in his *Britain on the Couch* was documenting the spectacular rise, especially among children, of depression, drug and alcohol abuse, eating disorders, stress-related syndromes, violence suffered and committed, suicides and suicide attempts.[7] Britain had become, he said, a low serotonin society, serotonin being the chemical associated with feelings of well-being.

One of the results of family breakdown is poverty, despite rising levels of affluence in society as a whole, and massive government expenditure on low-income families. In 1999 a research report concluded that a third of Britain's children, more than four million, were living in poverty, three times as many as in the 1970s.[8] In 2005, a UNICEF report noted the significant progress that had been made, but said Britain still had one of the highest rates of child poverty in the developed world, with more than 15 per cent of families with children living on less than half the UK average income.[9] In 2006, the charity Shelter reported that 1.6 million youngsters in Britain were living in housing judged to be temporary, overcrowded or unfit.[10] Lone parents are 2.5 times more likely to live in poverty than are couples, and their children suffer as a result.[11]

The breakdown of marriage has a significant impact on adult well-being. Research in seventeen countries has shown that married people are happier than unmarried ones; they have higher incomes, enjoy greater emotional support, are healthier and live longer.[12] The mortality risk for unmarried women is 50 per cent higher than for married women; 250 per cent higher for unmarried than married men.[13] Cohabitation is no substitute.[14] In America the average cohabitation lasts for no more than 1.3 years. In Sweden, women who have cohabited before marriage have a divorce rate 80 per cent higher than those who have not.[15]

The main victims, though, are the children. Massive research in recent years has exposed the systemic disadvantages suffered by those who do not grow up in stable, secure association with their biological parents. Children in single-parent homes are more likely to drop out of, or be expelled from, school, to become juvenile delinquents, to take drugs and to commit adult crimes, to have poor jobs or no jobs.[16] Stepfathers are far more likely than natural parents to harm children. In England, children living with cohabiting parents are twenty times more likely to suffer child abuse than those with married parents.[17]

Divorce too has long-lasting effects. Children whose parents divorce tend to have lower educational achievement, poorer socio-economic chances, and emotional problems. The effects can last decades, even a lifetime. Children of divorcees tend to be fearful of betrayal and abandonment. They are more likely to throw themselves into unsatisfactory relationships, to become teenage mothers or fathers, or to become divorced themselves. Barbara Dafoe Whitehead said about the 'divorce culture': 'Divorce abrogates children's rights to be reasonably free from adults' cares and woes, to enjoy the association of both parents on a daily basis, to remain innocent of social services and therapy and to spend family time in ways that are not dictated by the courts.'[18] She concludes: 'Divorce involves a radical redistribution of hardship from adults to children and therefore cannot be viewed as a morally neutral act.'

Behind the statistics lie human tragedies. One of the most powerful features of the Social Justice Policy Group's 'Fractured Families' (2006) is the testimony of children themselves. This is Katie, aged 10: ' I don't like living with my mum and her boyfriend. They don't love me. Since the divorce I never see my dad and I have to lie and say everything is OK to the social worker or my mum will get angry.' This is Paul, age 12: 'My dad cheated on my mum and now they are splitting up. Mum is always drinking alcohol and taking sleeping pills and I don't know what to do. I hate all the shouting and sometimes I feel like killing myself.' And this is Abby aged 13: 'My parents are going through a divorce at the moment and mum is taking it out on me, always shouting and hitting me for everything that goes wrong. I feel scared and do not know what to do now that dad has gone.'

Children who have not experienced normal nurturing and support survive. But they do so at a cost, often an extreme reluctance to commit themselves, to invest emotionally in a long-term relationship. Through their own experience, they have learned not to trust people. So they live within a narrow emotional register, making friends but not deep ones, not fully able to invest their emotions in long-term projects.

I discovered some of the emotional injuries of broken families when I spent a day filming young criminals at Sherbourne House, a centre for young offenders that gives them a six-week vocational training course in the hope that they will be able to get a job and stay out of prison. The young men I spoke to – they were all about eighteen years old – had spent the last ten years in petty crime. This was their last chance of a non-custodial sentence. I wanted to know about their own childhoods. On that subject they were defensive – for the best reason. They were loyal to their families. They didn't want to criticize mothers, fathers or stepfathers. So I tried putting the question a different way. I said: 'Soon you are likely to become parents yourselves. What kind of father would you like to be?'

This opened the floodgates of feeling. They started crying. They said things like: 'I'd be strict. But I'd be there for my children. I'd discipline them but I'd be there.' That is what they had missed: a stable father-figure in their childhood who was firm, consistent, capable of saying No, but at the same time available, dependable. That was when I saw the cost of the almost casual abandonment of the family in the past forty years. Fractured families create fractured lives.

None of this is meant to be judgemental. People in fractured families need our support not our condemnation, which can only make things worse for them. There are outstanding single parents. There are times when divorce is better for all concerned than the alternatives. Besides this, there are other interpretations of the research findings. Some blame poverty rather than the breakup of the family. Some accept the facts but regard them as a fair price to pay for the end of an institution they find objectionable. There are psychotherapists who see the family as emotionally repressive, feminists who regard it as an instrument of male dominance, and libertarians who see it as an unnecessary constraint on the open-ended possibilities of self-expression.

Let us accept these alternative voices. In any case, when dealing with so widespread a phenomenon, no individual, no group, no institution is to blame. Yet only by denial on a massive scale can we ignore the pathos of the situation. If children have the right to anything, it is the right to the responsible, caring presence of those who brought them into being. John Stuart Mill thought so and said so: 'The fact itself, of causing the existence of a human being, is one of the most responsible actions in the range of human life. To undertake this responsibility – to bestow a life which may be either a curse or a blessing – unless the being on whom it is to be bestowed will have at least the ordinary chances of a desirable existence, is a crime against that being.'[19]

In 1994, as part of a television documentary I was making about the family, I interviewed the sociologist and sage, A. H. Halsey. One remark he made has stayed with me across the years. The twentieth century, he said, has been called the century of the child. It should more accurately be called the century of child neglect.

*   *   *

If we care about the common good, the cohesion of society and the support it gives to individuals, the family must be at the very heart of our concern. The fact that something like a half of children grow up without knowing the security of a stable family means, by all the available evidence, that they will suffer lifelong disadvantage – not always, but often enough for our concern.

In Victorian England, Benjamin Disraeli warned of the division of Britain into 'two nations, between whom there is no intercourse and no sympathy; who are as ignorant of each other's habits, thoughts and feelings, as if they were dwellers in different zones, or inhabitants of different planets'. He was speaking of rich and poor. Today there is a similar disparity, not of wealth but of childhood experience. This is how James Q. Wilson puts it:

> In one nation, a child, raised by two parents, acquires an edu-cation, a job, a spouse, and a home kept separate from crime and disorder by distance, fences or guards. In the other nation, a child is raised by an unwed girl, lives in a neighborhood filled with many sexual men but few committed fathers, and finds gang life to be necessary for self-protection and valuable for self-advancement. In the first nation, children look to the future and believe that they control what place they will occupy in it; in the second, they live for the moment and think that fate, not plans, will shape their lives. In both nations harms occur, but in the second they proliferate – child abuse and drug abuse, gang vio-lence and personal criminality, economic dependency and con-tinued illegitimacy.[20]

How did it happen?

Sex, Philip Larkin famously said, 'began in 1963. . . between the end of the Chatterley ban / and the Beatles' first LP'. What he was

209

referring to was the sudden collapse of the codes and constraints that have surrounded physical intimacy, certainly since Victorian times, but actually for much of the history of civilization.

It happened almost simultaneously throughout the West. A generation challenged the standards of its parents and found that the world did not suddenly collapse. Since then sex has become, for the first time since the conversion to Christianity of the Roman Emperor Constantine, an almost value-free zone. Whatever happens between two consenting adults in private is, most people now believe, entirely a matter for them. The law may not intervene; neither may social sanction. It is simply not other people's business.

Together with a whole series of other changes, the result has been that what marriage brought together has now split apart. There has been a divorce between sex and love, love and marriage, marriage and reproduction, reproduction and education and nurture. Sex is for pleasure. Love is a feeling, not a commitment. Marriage is now deeply unfashionable. Nurture has been outsourced to specialized child-carers. Education is the responsibility of the state. And the consequences of failure are delegated to social workers.

The sexual revolution seemed costless. Forty years later, we are counting the costs, and they are high. There is, after all, an obvious question. Why should sexual codes and family conventions have had the prominence and power they have had through most of time? The answer according to sociobiologists is that we are genetically conditioned to care for the transmission of our genes to the next generation. Human beings are unique among life forms because of the length of time that children are dependent on their parents.

The sheer size of the human brain means that children cannot be born as fully developed as are most other animal species. Biology reached a compromise. Children would be born long before physical maturity. They would spend years dependent on adult members of the tribe. Hence, not biology but culture would have to evolve a way of ensuring that society protected its infants. The way most cultures did this was to ensure that the biological parents stayed together to nurture the child until it was able to fend for itself. Hence marriage and all the codes and constraints designed to protect and safeguard it.

It is not the only way. Plato would not, in his Republic, entrust a child to its parents. Children were the responsibility of the *polis* as a whole. Indeed, children in antiquity were not sacrosanct at all. Often they were regarded as property, not persons. There were cultures that practised child sacrifice. Others practised abortion on a wide scale. Others allowed handicapped children to be killed or left to die. The myth of Oedipus, which Freud saw as the key to the father-son relationship, begins with attempted infanticide and culminates in parricide. The complex cluster of relationships between men and women, sex and childbirth, parents and children is among the most fraught of all human phenomena, and the subject of warring drives.

Seen from this perspective, the bringing together of sex, reproduction, love, loyalty, compassion, nurture, education and primary socialization in the form of marriage is perhaps the most beautiful solution to the evolutionary endeavour since man first set foot on earth. It linked men and women together in a bond of mutual responsibility and love. It joined the generations in a chain of cultural transmission. It meant that at the very heart of society there was an institution that created and sustained human dignity without reference to the state.

As Ferdinand Mount has pointed out, the family is the greatest refuge of freedom,[21] which is why totalitarian states – from Plato's Republic to Soviet Communism – have been hostile to it. It brings together the most primal of human desires with the most elevated of human ideals. It is one of the greatest of moral institutions but also one of the most fragile. The mother-child bond is constant in most animal species; the father-child bond is not. Men, who invest less in childbirth, have an interest in distributing their genes more widely by serial relationships. Turning promiscuous males into responsible fathers is the hardest task in any culture, which may be why, in 1963, the family collapsed with so few dissenting voices.

The phrase Richard Dawkins coined and made famous – the selfish gene – is only a metaphor. Genes are neither selfish nor selfless; they have neither thought nor intention; they do what they do. But certainly there is in each of us an ongoing struggle between selfishness and selflessness. Freud saw this as the central dynamic of civilization. He called it the capacity to defer the gratification of instinct. Our age has witnessed one of the most fateful human experiments: the attempt to construct a civilization without deferring instinctual gratification. The collapse of the sexual ethic of the West happened more or less simultaneously with the appearance of the credit card, one of which was advertised with the slogan, 'It takes the waiting out of wanting.'

These two factors, sex and civilization, were the themes of Aldous Huxley's dystopian novel, *Brave New World*. This is how Mustapha Mond, one of the World Controllers, explains to his students their good fortune in living when they did:

'Consider your own lives,' said Mustapha Mond. 'Has any of you ever encountered an insurmountable obstacle?'

The question was answered by a negative silence.

'Has any of you been compelled to live through a long time-interval between the consciousness of a desire and its fulfillment?'

'Well,' began one of the boys, and hesitated.
'Speak up,' said the Director of Hatcheries and Conditioning . . .
'I once had to wait nearly four weeks before a girl I wanted would let me have her.'
'And you felt a strong emotion in consequence?'
'Horrible!'
'Horrible; precisely,' said the Controller.

On this, Theodore Dalrymple comments: 'Huxley surmised that life lived as the satisfaction of one desire after another would result in shallow and egotistical people . . . after gratifying their desires instantly throughout their lives, people would cease to carry the divine spark that distinguished man from the rest of creation.' [22]

*   *   *

So central are marriage and the family to Judaism, Christianity and Islam that it would not be surprising if this were one of the most compelling reasons for the inward turn of faith communities, the growth of faith schools, even the reaction against Western culture on the part of young extremists. Many parents do not want their children to be taught that marriage is no more than one lifestyle choice among many, or that premarital sex is fine as long as you take protective measures against pregnancy and disease. They do not want to expose their children to the risk of becoming sexually promiscuous, having teenage pregnancies, indulging in drug and alcohol abuse, and in general of being unfitted to a world in which instinctual deferral is necessary to survival.

No one should doubt the significance of this phenomenon. It is leading large numbers of parents to send their children to schools where they will be taught what are sometimes dismissed as 'traditional values', but which are in fact the values held by most cultures in most countries at most times. No society has opted for unconstrained sexual freedom and survived for long. The most famous counter-example, Margaret Mead's famous study of Samoa, was later shown to have been false. The Samoans were nowhere near as sexually open-minded as she thought.

Overwhelmingly the evidence points to the fact that the breakdown of marriage is slowly destroying Western civilization. It is leading to less-than-replacement birthrates, child poverty, depression and stress-related illness, social deprivation and personal unhappiness. Yet we have developed almost impregnable defences against reversing the trend. Politicians moralize at their peril. Parliament is not a pulpit. Legislation is not ethical education. To defend one way of life as more likely to lead to happiness than others is to risk accusations of being judgemental, Victorian, hypocritical, homophobic, a reactionary, a sentimentalist, a religious fanatic, a 'heterosexist', guilty of blaming the victim and seeking to turn back an unstoppable tide. As far as personal life is concerned, the merest suggestion that there is more to wisdom than personal choice is heresy. It can cost people their jobs. Libertarians can be fundamentalists too, and often are.

The fact that we have deconstructed the family – morally, psychologically, economically, politically – is the single most fateful cultural development of our times. But any attempt to reverse the trend collides with a culture racing in the opposite direction. Consumerism discourages loyalty. It continually encourages us to look elsewhere for the better deal, the higher return, the more attractive option. Those who wish to hand on to their children a sense of responsibility and restraint will find themselves trying to swim upstream against a river in full flood. To be sure, people still get married, and stay married. But this is now almost entirely dependent on the couple themselves. There is little if any support for the institution from the wider society. Each year I help launch National Marriage Week. The first time I did so, a reporter said to me, 'Marriage? Isn't that very politically incorrect?' To which I replied, 'Of course. If it weren't, we wouldn't need a special event to support it.' Today the cultural environment too often leaves couples to fight the temptations and blandishments of self-indulgence alone. No one should have to fight for one of the central values of a humane social order alone. Which brings us back to the place of religion in society.

*   *   *

Marriage is the most personal and intimate of all forms of human association, and the deepest matrix of faith. We can face any future without fear if we know we will not face it alone. There is no redemption of solitude deeper than to share a life with someone we love and trust, who we know will never desert us, who lifts us when we fall and believes in us even when we fail.

Yet at most times and places, couples could rely on the support of a culture. In Judaism, for example, many of the most important rituals, like the Sabbath and Passover, take place primarily in the home. The prophets saw marriage as the supreme metaphor of the relationship between God and his people. I once took a childcare expert, Dr Penelope Leach, to a Jewish primary school, to see the five-year-old children rehearse for the Sabbath dinner table. She asked one of the children what he most liked about the Sabbath. He replied, 'It's the only time of the week when daddy doesn't have to rush off.' As we were

213

leaving the school, she turned to me and said, 'That Sabbath of yours (Penelope isn't Jewish) is saving their parents' marriages.' Families need time, and the Sabbath is sacred, dedicated time.

Hillary Clinton used an African proverb as the title of one of her books: It takes a village to raise a child. It takes a culture to sustain a marriage. It is a peculiar blindness of our time that we fail to see this. At a certain point in European history, we lost that insight. 'All you need is love,' sang the Beatles, echoing our collective forgetfulness that for love to be all you need, you also need in the background a moral infra-structure that sustains the idea of marriage as a covenantal commit-ment between two free individuals to be loyal to one another come what may. When this idea becomes attenuated, it takes only the lightest of pushes for the entire superstructure to come crashing down. Mar-riage died in a single generation, and with it much of the rest of the Judaeo-Christian heritage.

It should therefore come as no surprise that the groups that have the highest birthrates are the most religious, and the most segregated from the norms of contemporary society: Catholics, Orthodox Jews, Muslims and others. Among Orthodox Jews, for example, there is a profound disquiet about the collapse of the family and all its related symptoms, from casual sex to immodesty in dress, the hypersexualization of cul-ture, teenage pregnancies, cohabitation without marriage, birth of children outside marriage, and the speed with which couples facing difficulties turn to divorce. They feel – I feel – that some profound desecration is taking place. Something holy is being made profane. 'The unexamined life is not worth living,' said Socrates.[23] Neither is a life of immediate, unconstrained gratification of desire.

In truth, the only cultures that will survive into the future are those capable of making sacrifices for the future – for the future of their children and for generations to come. That is why religions exist; why traditions exist; why there are moral restraints that are difficult to explain in terms of short-term consequences. Jean-Jacques Rousseau understood this perfectly.[24] It is difficult, he said, 'for the individual, who has no taste for any scheme of government but that which serves his private interest, to appreciate the advantages to be derived from the lasting austerities which good laws impose'. We think short-term. We do not naturally factor into our calculations effects beyond our life-times. 'It is this which has obliged the founders of nations throughout history to appeal to divine intervention and to attribute their own wisdom to the gods.' In our time, Jared Diamond has documented the ways in which human cultures have destroyed ecologies.[25] They destroy social ecologies too. One of the vital tasks performed by religion is to encode and preserve the wisdom of the past that would otherwise be forgotten, with disastrous results, in the present.

Almost the only surviving environments in which the virtues related to marriage are still alive are religious communities and their faith schools. They teach fidelity, duty, respect for authority, commitment, sacrifice, self-restraint and the need at times to say No to desire. Indeed 'No' has become the hardest word to hear in our postmodern culture. I once spent a day in a centre for young heroin addicts. What, I asked the director, does she give them that enables them to break the habit. She replied: 'We are the first people they have met who give them unconditional love, and the first to care enough about them to say No.'

To be sure, the current conflict between religion and culture is not one-sided. Those who live in both wrestle with deep questions. Does tradition give equal dignity to women? Does it give space for children to grow? Does it accord with current scientific knowledge? Does it respect those outside the faith? So disturbing can these questions be that people in traditions that have not faced them before can become defensive. They turn inward to a protected environment where their faith can thrive in safety. That is why and when self-segregation occurs: when the gap between religious and secular becomes a chasm. Each sees the other as a threat. Hostility grows. Society fractures and we lose the sense of being part of a single, embracing order.

That is why few things could do more to aid the reintegration of religious and ethnic communities than our willingness to listen, rather than contemptuously to dismiss. When the Catholic Church defends heterosexual marriage, when Muslim women speak of their embrace of the veil as a protest against overt sexual display, when Orthodox Jews speak of modesty as a value and parenthood as a sacred responsibility, they are saying things we need to hear. And we need to hear them respectfully. It is no use saying that morality is relative, and at the same time refusing to give an intelligent hearing to those whose moral standards are different from our own. Moral relativism has an imperialism of its own, and political correctness is one of its cruder weapons.

What these faith communities and their secular counterparts are telling us is that the way we structure our lives around sex, love, marriage, childbirth and the care of the young are not marginal to the responsible life. They are central to it. The first experiences of a young child are of extreme dependency and vulnerability. It makes all the difference if that child experiences stability, attention and love, and if he or she is taught the rules of self-restraint through a consistent pattern of rewards and rebukes. He or she will learn, through a developing relationship with a mother and father, something about the differences between the sexes as well as the unique contributions of both.

Societies that become sexually anomic, without rules and restraints, die. That is what happened to Ancient Greece and Rome. People lose an interest in having children. Their focus is on pleasure in the present, not happiness in the future. They lose a sense of being part of a narrative that began before they were born and will continue after they die. That is the paradox at the heart of sociobiology: selfish genes have an interest in producing selfless people. For selfish people will simply not reproduce themselves – at any rate not in an age in which there are effective birth control methods: today, the pill; in antiquity, abortion and infanticide.

So the discovery of sex in 1963 turned out not to be cost free at all. The cost may well be the demise of European civilization, for no more profound reason than that libertarian X cannot bring him- or herself to make a commitment to libertarian Y for long enough to produce libertarian Z. As T. S. Eliot said: 'This is the way the world ends, / Not with a bang but a whimper.' That is why faith schools and religious communities are important. They protect endangered values. They are seedbeds of unfashionable virtues. Tocqueville saw this in nineteenth-century America: 'In the United States, religion exercises but little influence upon the laws and upon the details of public opinion; but it directs the customs of the community, and by regulating domestic life, it regulates the state.'[26] It sanctified marriage. Therefore, it preserved society. If marriage is to be renewed in our society, it will be, not least, because of our religious counter-cultures.

Religions are agents of personal and social change, the only such agents in an age of consumerism, managerial politics and society-as-hotel. As such, they deserve support not for their sake alone but for the common good. They are vital, dissenting voices in the democratic conversation. They enlarge our intellectual horizons, enrich our moral vocabulary, and remind us of truths we are otherwise minded to forget. Cultural diversity is as important as biodiversity. It helps retain within society the antibodies and immunities we need to protect us against social ills. Faith in a transcendental order is a form of resistance against worship of the status quo. At some stage it will begin to dawn on thoughtful people that what we are doing to our children by the deconstruction of marriage is harmful, irresponsible and ultimately unconscionable. The sanctity of marriage, the need for sexual restraint, and the responsibilities of parenthood, especially fatherhood, will be recovered, because there are in our midst communities that have done their best to preserve them, at the very least as ideals. That is the power of tradition in an untraditional age and religion in a secular society.

Chapter 19

A Religious Defence of Liberal Democracy

In France I had almost always seen the spirit of religion and the spirit of freedom marching in opposite directions. But in America I found they were intimately united and that they reigned in common over the same country.[1]

Alexis de Tocqueville

How small, of all that human hearts endure
That part which laws or kings can cause or cure.[2]

Oliver Goldsmith

Words confuse as well as clarify. The existence of an abstract noun may lead us to think that all ideas called by the same name are the same, or at least broadly similar. So we assume, for example, that what we mean by freedom is what other people mean by freedom, that what we have in mind when we speak of justice is what others have in mind. This has led to some of the most tragic misunderstandings in history. Not lightly did Wittgenstein describe philosophy as a battle against the bewitchment of the intelligence by means of language.

That is eminently the case with one of the key terms of modern politics, namely *democracy*. It is easy to see how some people, on both sides of the religious-secular divide, claim that religion and democracy are incompatible. The word 'democracy' comes to us from Ancient Greece and means 'rule by the people'. Religion implies rule by God. It involves believing that the will of God is holy; the will of the people is not. It seems to follow that the two systems are destined to collide. Religion must reject democracy. That is its virtue, say the believers. That is its danger, say the disbelievers. Religion, they both argue, must favour something else. Philo, in the first century, gave the something-else a name. He called it 'theocracy'.

A slightly more subtle version of the thesis might make the following

217

distinction. There is a strand within Christianity that makes a sharp distinction between the spheres of religion and politics. They are the 'two swords', the 'two cities', the two authorities: civil and ecclesiastical. One is concerned with the welfare of the body, the other with the salvation of the soul. Hence they can coexist: 'Render unto Caesar the things that are Caesar's, and to God the things that are God's.' But that, it might be said, applies to Christianity, not to Judaism or Islam, two faiths that see religion as coextensive with the whole of the human situation, the public domain as well as private life. So, not every religion is incompatible with democracy, but it could be argued that Judaism and Islam are.

This argument is based on a widespread but dangerous confusion, and in this chapter I want to explain what it is. It arises because the word 'democracy', like 'freedom' and 'justice', lures us into thinking that all abstract ideals described by the same word are basically the same. Often they are not. Specifically, *Athenian* democracy, the democracy of the Greek city state in the fifth and fourth centuries BCE, is not the *liberal* democracy of the contemporary West. What they have in common is an involvement of the public in the political process, whether directly (participative democracy) or indirectly by elections (representative democracy). But that is a relatively minor matter, one of process rather than of substance. What separates them is something far more significant: their respective views of the *place* of politics within the human domain.

For the Greeks and Romans of antiquity, politics was the highest good.[3] Ethics was first and foremost civic. It meant devotion to your native city, doing all you could to extend its welfare and glory. At its highest, it was a willingness to sacrifice one's life for it: *Dulce et decorum est pro patria mori*: 'It is pleasant and proper to die for one's country'. *Paideia*, the education of the young, meant training them in the virtues necessary for them to take their place in the life of the city, and included the development of physical prowess through athletics, games and hunting, and artistic capabilities through music, poetry and drama. Rhetoric, the ability to persuade through speech, was particularly important as a political skill. Sexual ethics seems to have played no part at all. Politics was a male preserve, and relationships between the sexes was outside its purview.

For the Abrahamic monotheisms in general, far from being the highest good, politics is a necessary evil. Two statements from the early centuries CE express the rabbinic view. 'Pray for the welfare of the government,' said Rabbi Hanina, the deputy High Priest, 'for were it not for fear of it, men would eat one another alive.'[4] On the other hand, said Rabban Gamliel son of Rabbi Judah the Prince, 'Be wary in your dealings with the ruling power, for they only befriend a man when it serves their needs. When it is to their advantage, they appear as friends but they do not stand by a person in his hour of need'.[5]

The fundamental principle of biblical morality is love: 'You shall love the Lord your God with all your heart' (Deut. 6:5), 'You shall love your neighbour as yourself' (Lev. 19:18), and 'You shall love the stranger, for you were strangers in the land of Egypt' (Deut. 10:19). The three are connected: loving God goes hand in hand with an ethic of justice, equity, mercy, compassion and loving kindness to one's fellow human beings. As we saw in an earlier chapter, the Hebrew Bible is profoundly ambivalent about politics. The rule of one human being over another is inherently antithetical to human dignity. Only God has that right. As the military hero Gideon puts it when the people ask him to become their king: 'I will not rule over you, nor will my son rule over you. The Lord will rule over you' (Judg. 8:23).

One profound distinction between the two systems is that in civic ethics the mark of failure is *shame*. In biblical morality, it is *guilt*. Shame has to do with how one appears to one's fellow citizens. It is a way of internalizing the ethic of the group. Guilt has to do with the voice within, conscience, the judgement of God who knows one's innermost thoughts. The first instinct of shame is to hide; that of guilt, to confess. Shame cultures produce other-directed personalities, guilt cultures inner-directed ones. In civic ethics the highest authority is that of the state itself. In biblical morality it is the transcendent authority of God. That is why the Bible grants so prominent a place to the prophet, the social critic who speaks truth to power and has no fear of confronting and criticizing kings.

So, we are faced with two different cultures, and thus two different kinds of democracy. They may both have the same political structure: a party system, general elections, universal suffrage, constituencies and so on. To an observer they may look identical but they are not, because they allocate to politics different places in their hierarchy of values. The politics of Greece and Rome, classical republicanism, is maximalist; it represents the highest good, the noblest expression of life. Biblical politics is minimalist. It is that set of arrangements that ensures civic peace and allows people to get on with the other business of life.

The reason we are less familiar with this distinction than we should be is that the Western tradition generally has drawn inspiration from both traditions: Athens and Jerusalem, Solon and Moses, Plato and Isaiah. But they really are different, and that difference still counts.

*   *   *

Hence the difference between two strands of thought in the eighteenth century: one associated with Britain, specifically the Scottish

Enlightenment, the other with France.[6] The French tradition was concerned with *civic virtue*, the Scottish with *civil society*.

The civil-society tradition tended to emphasize the quality of everyday relationships between human beings. Adam Smith, for example, begins his *The Theory of Moral Sentiments* with this sentence: 'How selfish soever man may be supposed, there are evidently some principles in his nature, which interest him in the fortune of others, and render their happiness necessary to him, though he derives nothing from it except the pleasure of seeing it.'[7] Adam Ferguson in *An Essay on the History of Civil Society* writes: 'If it be true, that men are united by instinct, that they act in society from affections of kindness and friendship' then 'the sense of a right which we maintain for ourselves, is by a movement of humanity and candour extended to our fellow creatures.'[8] Society is, in other words, founded on the moral sense, which expresses itself in the first instance among family and friends, community and congregation.

The civic-virtue tradition, by contrast, has little time for these human, non-political encounters and institutions. What preoccupies it, even obsesses it, is the relationship between the individual and the state. So much is this the case that Rousseau writes:

> But if groups, sectional associations are formed at the expense of the larger association, the will of each of these groups will become general in relation to its own members, and private in relation to the state ... Thus if the general will is to be clearly expressed, it is imperative that there should be no sectional associations in the state ... [9]

In this tradition, nothing, not family, not community, above all not religion, should stand between the individual and the state. Children should not be influenced by the 'understanding and prejudices' of parents. Education should lie entirely in the hands of the state, 'which must give souls the national form, and so direct their opinions and their tastes that they are patriots by inclination, by passion, by necessity. A child, on opening his eyes, should see his country, and until he dies he should see nothing but his country.' That is a formula for what J. L. Talmon called totalitarian democracy.[10]

Regardless, then, of particular influences on specific thinkers, the French republican tradition is recognizably in the mould of Ancient Greece. The British tradition, emerging at it did from a basically Protestant culture, is far closer to the Bible. For civic virtue, what matters is the relationship between the individual and the state. Families, friends and communities are distractions from the serious business of politics. Worse than that, they represent potentially competing loyalties. For the civil-society tradition, the opposite is true. Personal relationships and loyalties in contexts that have nothing to do with the state, are the bedrock of society and the matrix of the moral sense. Is there life outside politics? The civic-virtue tradition says No, the civil-society tradition says Yes. Britain and America belong firmly to the civil-society tradition. That is what makes their forms of liberal democracy uniquely congenial to the monotheistic imagination.

The virtue of liberal democratic politics, from the perspective of religion, is *modesty*. This sounds odd to those who see politicians as self-important. Yet no more modest view of politics has ever been formulated than liberal democracy. It is a system in which politics makes no claim to embody the true, the beautiful and the good. Political involvement promises neither salvation nor redemption. It claims merely to keep the peace between contending parties, to administer justice in such a way as to maximize the likelihood that justice will be seen to be done, and to provide the infrastructure – police, healthcare, education, defence – through which most people can lead lives of security and dignity. Liberal democracy is the form of politics that best understands the limitations of politics. It leaves the big questions to us.

*   *   *

Understanding this is essential. There is no more fraught issue than the relationship of religion and power. Wars and civil wars have been fought over it. They are still being fought over it. This makes it seem as if a clash is inevitable. Religion claims to represent the truth. Therefore, surely, it must seek to enforce the truth. To do so it must aspire to power. How could it be otherwise? Yet it is otherwise.

To show why it is otherwise, consider the biblical book of Ruth. It's a moving story of how Ruth, a woman from Moab, refuses to leave her mother-in-law, Naomi, after their husbands have died. They return to Israel, to Bethlehem, Naomi's home. There they meet Boaz, one of Naomi's kinsmen, who helps the two women and eventually marries Ruth. It's a tale of kindness to strangers. What, though, is it doing in the Bible?

The answer is straightforward. It is a prelude to the books of Samuel that tell the story of Israel's first kings. The connection is that one of Ruth's descendants is David, Israel's second and greatest king. Yet considered as a prelude it is surpassingly strange. David had many antecedents. One of them was Judah, son of the patriarch Jacob. If you wanted to construct a lineage for David, the simplest and most obvious would be to trace his descent from Judah. That is how the Bible does things.

Not only is it odd to emphasize his descent from a woman, a widow, Ruth. It is even odder when we recall that Ruth was a Moabite.

Politically, the Moabites were Israel's enemies. Religiously, the Israelites considered them pagans. They worshipped a 'strange god' called Chemosh. One would have expected the Bible to pass over this embarrassing fact in silence. Why does it go out of its way to emphasize it?

The answer, and it is a striking one, is that the book of Ruth is about *chessed,* usually translated as loving kindness. Perhaps a more accurate translation would be 'covenant love', the love on which a covenantal society is based. It is a strong form of the 'affections of kindness and friendship' that Adam Ferguson, Adam Smith and others saw as the basis of civil society. The book is about kindness, loyalty, compassion, steadfastness: Ruth's to Naomi, Boaz's to Ruth.

What the Bible is doing by making Ruth the prelude to the history of Israel's kings, is stating, as a fundamental principle, the *primacy of the personal over the political.* Yes, David's political achievements were immense. He united Israel's tribes, fought Israel's wars, made Jerusalem the capital of the kingdom and planned the building of the Temple. But the one story the Bible wanted its readers to know about his ancestry is that it had nothing to do with noble birth and everything to do with a story of *chessed,* kindness, several generations before.

That too is the function of the Bible's first book, Genesis. It tells the story of the patriarchs and matriarchs: Abraham, Isaac and Jacob, Sarah, Rebecca, Rachel and Leah. It too is strange. One of Judaism's early sages asked why we needed the book of Genesis at all. The Bible is the story of the Israelites as a nation. They did not become a nation until the beginning of the book of Exodus. Until then they were only a family. The answer is that Genesis stands to Exodus as Ruth does to the books of Samuel. It too is a prelude. Genesis is the pre-history of Israel's birth as a nation, as Ruth is to Israel's birth as a kingdom. Like Ruth, Genesis is about human relationships: husbands and wives, parents and children, and brothers. It too is about the primacy of the personal over the political. It is about *chessed*: loyalty, love, marriage, the family, and kindness to strangers. Stephen Carter, the Yale law professor who has written books about the 'prepolitical' virtues, translates *chessed* as 'civility'.

We begin to sense an idea we have lost sight of in modern politics. In covenant-based nations – England and Scotland in the seventeenth centuries, the United States to this day – society matters as much as the state. Society is created by the covenantal virtues, chief of which is, for the Bible, *chessed,* and for its Western heirs, civility. Civility is *not* loyalty to the state in the Greek or Roman sense. It is kindness and loyalty to other people, ordinary people: family, friends, neighbours, strangers. That is expressed in homes, neighbourhoods, communities, congregations; in other words, in civil society. In the republican tradition nothing stands between the individual and the state. In the covenant tradition, almost everything does. Governments are necessary. Otherwise there would be no rule of law, and no defence of the realm. But they are not the highest expression of human life. Love is. Not love in the romantic sense, but in the social sense of kindness to strangers.

That is why liberal democracy is the closest we have yet come to a secular equivalent of biblical politics, precisely because in it the state is *not* the embodiment of virtue. It makes no claim other than to keep the peace, internally and externally. It administers justice, ensures that everyone has access to the preconditions of human dignity, from education to health to welfare, and remains neutral on the big issues of human life: faith, morality, community, love. In liberal democracy these things belong to civil society, not the state. The state merely ensures that we can pursue the things that matter in peace, freedom and a basic equality of dignity.

From a biblical perspective, the desire on the part of religion to control the state is a confusion. Worse: it comes close to idolatry. Religion in the biblical sense is not about power but influence, not about secular law but love, not about the state but about families and communities. The Bible is first and foremost about freedom: how we construct relationships of trust without the use of power. That is why the Koran is right when it says that there must be no compulsion on matters of religion. When religion seeks power, the result is disastrous, if not immediately then ultimately. The result is tragic for the people, catastrophic for the state, and disastrous for religion. When religion, any religion, seizes power, it forfeits the respect of ordinary, decent, righteous people, who once respected it and now fear and resent it. The result is the defeat of religion, the birth of a new secularism, and a desecration of the holy.

*   *   *

It was Alexis de Tocqueville who, in the course of his visits to America in the early 1830s, noticed something remarkable. America was a religious society. But religion took no part in government. It had no political power. It operated in a different domain and concerned itself with other things. Yet this was not a state of affairs imposed by secularists. It was self-imposed by religious leaders themselves. They had made a conscious decision not to involve themselves in political debate. The absence of religion from the corridors of power had become a matter of religious principle. Hence the phenomenon that amazed and fascinated him: 'In France I had almost always seen the spirit of religion and the spirit of freedom marching in opposite directions. But in America I found they were intimately united and that they reigned in common over the same country.'[11]

The explanation, he found, lay in the separation of church and state. Talking to clerical leaders he found 'that most of its members seemed to retire of their own accord from the exercise of power, and that they made it the pride of their profession to abstain from politics'. The result was that although religion took no part in government, it was 'the first of their political institutions', providing the moral base of civic society – what he called its 'habits of the heart'.

It created communities, strengthened families, and motivated philanthropic endeavours. It lifted people beyond what he saw as the great danger of democracy – individualism, the retreat of people from public life into private satisfaction. Religion strengthened the 'art of association', the underlying strength of American society. Relinquishing power, religion was able to avoid the inescapable danger of those who wear the mantle of politics:

> The church cannot share the temporal power of the state without being the object of a portion of that animosity which the latter excites. In proportion as a nation assumes a democratic condition of society and those communities display democratic propensities, it becomes more and more dangerous to connect religion with political institutions … The American clergy were the first to perceive this truth and to act in conformity with it. They saw that they must renounce their religious influence if they were to strive for political power, and they chose to give up the support of the state rather than share in its vicissitudes.[12]

In America, religion sought a voice, not a vote. It was involved in society rather than the state. It opted for influence rather than power.

The Pilgrim Fathers of America were deeply religious. They came to America to practise their religion without persecution. When they decided as a matter of principle not to get involved in politics, that was a religious decision. They knew that the great religious leaders – the sages, the saints, the prophets, the philosophers, the mystics – had no power at all. They chose not to have. They looked at the political domain, its intrigues, its conflicts, its compromises, and sought something higher, purer, nobler. They chose words not weapons, visions not accommodations. They opted for what Vaclav Havel called 'the art of the impossible'. They spoke to people's consciences and aspirations. They bodied forth new landscapes of the mind. Or they worked by personal example, healing the sick, giving their food to the hungry, heeding the unheard, valuing the unvalued. That is how they achieved immortality.

Who today remembers the kings of ancient Israel or Judah? Yet the words of Amos and Isaiah, almost three thousand years ago, continue to inspire. When a king dies, his power ends. When a prophet dies, his influence begins. Power rearranges the deckchairs. Influence changes lives.

* * *

So it is neither incidental nor accidental that the founders of the United States of America, themselves deeply religious, came to embrace the separation of church and state. They were refugees from oppression. They had seen how, when one religion holds power, it can persecute others, robbing them of their freedom, and in many cases of their lives. They sought freedom to practise their own faith but not to impose it by means of force on others. For they knew others might one day come to power and force their faith on them.

The only way of securing religious freedom is to create a 'wall of separation' between religion and power. For what is truly religious is the concept of the *moral limits of power*. Might does not confer right. Justice is not, as Plato's Glaucon argued, the interests of the stronger party. Earthly authority is subject to overarching ethical imperatives. No earthly power is ultimate. That is the greatest religious contribution to liberty. A prophet is one who is unafraid of power, who challenges its holders in the name of justice, equality and human dignity. That is what Nathan did to David, Elijah to Ahab, Amos, Hosea and Jeremiah to their contemporaries. Prophets have immense *authority* but no *power*. They never sought it.

The concept of the moral limits of power is more important to freedom than is democracy. For democracy contains within it a fatal danger. Tocqueville gave it a name: the 'tyranny of the majority'. A majority can oppress a minority. The only defence against this is to establish the moral limits of power. That is the basis of human rights.

Religion understands the truth in Oliver Goldsmith's remark: 'How small, of all that human hearts endure / That part which laws or kings can cause or cure.' What creates families, communities, relationships, the microsystems of virtue, lie outside the realm of power. Virtue cannot be coerced. Righteousness cannot be legislated. Compassion is beyond the reach of governmental fiat.

The conflict between human dignity and freedom on the one hand, and law-governed liberty on the other, has a resolution. There must be some central power: Hobbes' Leviathan. But it must be circumscribed by the overarching authority of morality. It must be exercised only with the consent of the governed. And it must be limited to the minimum needed to yield the common good. Biblical politics is limited politics – the politics of liberal democracies, not of the Greek city state.

What the great religions understand is that society is larger than the state. Politics depends on pre-political virtues, nurtured in non-political environments: the family, the community, the congregation. These are where we first discover the give and take of reciprocity and the healing power of love and forgiveness. They are where we learn to negotiate the tensions between independence and inter-dependence. They are the matrix of the larger 'We' that makes possible the 'I'. They are where we acquire moral intelligence. Without families, communities and friends, society becomes a mere aggregation of individuals, 'the lonely crowd', without trust or grace or meaning: without hope.

Yet families and communities alone are not enough to sustain a society. As soon as we step outside the doors of what is local, we encounter not friends but strangers. There will be conflicts for scarce goods. If all we have is loyalty to the family or the group, then that larger world will be torn by internecine strife: Montagus against Capulets, Christians against Muslims, Hutus against Tutsis. If all we have is the tribe, violence will beget counterviolence in a circle that has a beginning but no end.

When we realize this, a particular kind of politics is born – the politics that does not see human beings as servants of the state, but the state as the servant of human beings. That is modest politics, politics as non-violent conflict resolution, and as the provider, not of the good life, but of basic preconditions – safety, order, education, health – without which no good life is possible. That is why there is a religious case for liberal democracy, for a politics that does not seek to embody the good but merely keep the peace between different groups with conflicting views of the good.

Keeping the Peace

As I write, people are murdering one another in Iraq, Afghanistan, Algeria and Lebanon. Racial and religious disputes are simmering in many parts of the world. Others are ruled by tyrannical or totalitarian regimes without freedom of speech, freedom of worship, the rule of law, a free press or an independent judiciary. From a global perspective we are back in the war of every man against every man. Never have the virtues of liberal democracy been more needed. A new dark age seems frighteningly close.

Liberal democracy is the single best solution yet devised for a problem as old as mankind: how different groups with different beliefs may live graciously together within an overarching political framework that respects the integrity of each and ensures the equal rights of all under the impartial rule of law. The virtue of liberal, as opposed to Athenian democracy, is that it does not regard loyalty to the state as the highest virtue, or political life as the highest calling. On the contrary, it values the virtues that belong to substate institutions: the family, the school, the congregation, the community. It sees loyalty to the state as no more and no less than the basic precondition of civil coexistence.

I have proposed a religious defence of liberal democracy. A free society is a moral achievement and rests on moral foundations. What it needs is a division: not between things earthly and heavenly, the world and the soul, nor even between private and public, the self and the citizen. The key distinction is between the personal and the political, society and the state. One is woven out of the filaments of influence; the other is built on the lineaments of power. Power and influence, the political and the spiritual, are different spheres, have different logics, operate by different rules, and call for different virtues.

Religion creates communities. Politics mediates between communities. Religion lives in justice and compassion, righteousness and mercy, loyalty and loving kindness. Politics requires compromise, tolerance, a willingness to live and let live: the 'liberal virtues'. The liberal virtues are not religious ones. On the contrary, in the religious realm compromise is not a virtue but a vice. From a religious perspective liberalism looks like laxity. The two types of virtue – those of commitment on the one hand, conciliation on the other – are not incompatible, even though they are opposed. That is because they have different tasks to perform. It is one thing to create a community of faith, quite another to keep the peace between communities of faith.

Liberal democratic politics is the politics of peace. It is not dramatic, heroic, the stuff of Homer or Virgil. But it does stop us killing one another in the name of faith. And it does honour the greatest of all religious truths: that God speaks not in the whirlwind, the earthquake or the fire but in the still, small voice that echoes in the silence of the soul and helps us, in Robert Kennedy's fine phrase, 'to tame the savageness of man and make gentle the life of this world'.

Chapter 20

A Time to Build

The time for the healing of the wounds has come. The moment to bridge the chasms that divide us has come. The time to build is upon us.[1]

Nelson Mandela

In 1968 a young American in his late twenties faced a personal crisis.[2] Trained as a lawyer, he had become a successful businessman. Married with a young family, he was a millionaire, with a large house, an expensive car, a two-thousand acre farm, two speedboats and a holiday home by a lake. He was making plans to achieve his next target, ten million dollars, when his wife came to him in the office and told him she was about to leave. He reminded her of all he had given her. 'What you haven't given me', she said, 'is yourself.' She never saw him. He was devoting all his time to the business, and none to the family. She no longer wanted to live like that.

The name of the young man was Millard Fuller. Shocked by this totally unexpected blow, he decided that if making money was destroying his marriage and family, he didn't want to do it any more. He cancelled his plans and took his wife and their children on a holiday. They agreed that he would sell his share in the business and find another way to live. Visiting a friend in a Christian community in the American South, he heard that they were planning to build houses for poor rural families. He decided to join them and for five years he built homes. Then he went to Zaire, and built houses there. So was born one of the most successful voluntary projects of recent times: Habitat for Humanity. Up to the present it has built 150,000 houses throughout the world, including Britain. It has transformed lives in the most effective and practical way, by giving people in poverty a 'simple, decent place to live'.

I first encountered Millard Fuller at a conference I was attending in

New York. He was giving a talk on his work. As I listened, I quickly realized what a powerful idea this was. A scene from a film came into my mind: the barn-raising scene in *Witness*, the film about a young Amish child who is the sole witness to a murder. Harrison Ford plays the detective who goes to live among the Amish. While he is there a couple get married and the entire community leaves everything aside for a day to build them a barn. Evocatively filmed, it was a vivid meta- phor for the kind of community we feel we have lost in the pace of contemporary life.

A sentence came into my head: A community is a group of people who build something together. I remembered a passage from the Jewish prayer book based on a verse from Isaiah: 'All your children shall be taught of the Lord and great will be the peace of your chil- dren.'[3] To this the rabbis added a comment, based on a Hebrew wordplay: 'Call them not your children (*banayich*) but your builders (*bonayich*).' How do you lay the groundwork for peace? asked the rabbis. By turning children into builders: people who will create and construct together.

So, when the opportunity arose, I went to see one of Habitat for Humanity's projects in London. I spent a day working there together with a group of volunteers from a large city bank. I began to under- stand the principles. The homes are built by volunteers together with the recipients themselves and their friends. They are not built *for* the poor families but *with* them. They contribute 'sweat equity', their work and time. They pay for the house through no-profit, no-interest, long- term loans.

I met the family who were going to move into the house we were building: a single mother with three teenage children who had been living in a one-bedroom flat for seventeen years. I will never forget her excitement as she showed me around the half-built interior and told me what it meant to her that for the first time she and her children would have their own rooms. Months later, when the house was fin- ished, the entire neighbourhood organized a street party to celebrate. Millard Fuller came over from America to be there. On the way home I realized that I had witnessed something significant. I had seen all the ideas I had written about – family, community, volunteering, charity, social justice – come to life. This was it, I thought; it really works.

Identity, community, society – these abstractions become real in the doing. We are what we make, and when we make something together we become something together. That was when I understood why the construction of the Tabernacle takes up so much space at the end of the book of Exodus, the story of the journey from slavery to freedom. Nothing else, not the miracles, the division of the Red Sea, even the revelation at Mount Sinai, turned the Israelites into a nation. The simplest of projects, the making of a Tabernacle did. Set in the centre of the camp, it was the symbol of the public square and the common good, the good we share because it only exists by the act of making it together. None of the miracles succeeded in uniting the Israelites into a nation. It is *what we do*, not *what is done for us*, even by God himself, that transforms us.

I began to understand the connection between *giving* and *belonging*. I saw how group identity might be created without an 'us' and 'them', by setting a team a practical task rather than defining it in opposition to, or competition with, others. I also saw how barriers between faiths might be broken down. Habitat for Humanity is a Christian charity, but Jews helped in the building, as did others from other non-Christian faiths. That was because it was a side-by-side, not a face-to-face project. It needed no delicate negotiation of beliefs and sensibilities. You don't need theology to understand why you should help someone build a house. Habitat for Humanity is a metaphor for our common life. Metaphors are easier to understand than theories. That is why I have chosen a metaphor to summarize the themes of this book: society is the home we build together.

*   *   *

I have argued that Britain, and not only Britain – the same applies to many European states – faces challenges of a scope and scale it has rarely faced before. It has fought and won wars, but it is easier to fight wars than to sustain peace. Britain has faced external enemies. But what happens when the challenge lies within, in the fissuring and fracturing of society itself?

For much of British history the identity of its citizens could be taken for granted. There were conflicts between classes and religions: in the seventeenth century between Catholics and the Church of England, in the nineteenth century between Disraeli's 'two nations' of rich and poor. There were immigrant groups: the Huguenots, the Irish, Jews. Weaving different groups together took time, but the assumption was that eventually it would happen. It did.

Why? Because, in effect, there was no other choice. Britishness, or Englishness, was in the air you breathed, the books you read, the conversations you had, the news you heard about, the history and destiny you shared. There was a national culture, and by participating in it, you integrated. You came to feel you belonged. Yes, there were residual prejudices: anti-Catholicism, anti-Semitism, racism, a general mistrust of foreigners, a little-Englander mentality that has not, even now, entirely disappeared. So newcomers were conscious of being outsiders. But they also internalized an identity. They became British.

Judging by my parents' generation, they were proud to be British. Integration, often to the point of assimilation, was a natural process.

Today, massive forces are threatening the viability of the nation state: political, economic, but above all cultural. The nation state came into existence because of one form of communications technology: printing. It is being threatened by another: instantaneous global communication via satellite television, email and the internet. The nation state was predicated on the conjunction of cultural identity and political organization. Culture created society; politics created the state; and they ruled together over the same territory.

The internet fragments and de-territorializes culture. The global economy – transnational corporations, the outsourcing of production and services – weakens the power and authority of the state. We can be in closer touch with our fellow enthusiasts or co-religionists throughout the world than we are to the people living next door. Space has been replaced by cyberspace. Physical communities have given way to virtual ones. Our bodies and minds no longer inhabit the same domain. Physically we are here; mentally we could be anywhere. The idea that we are linked together with those with whom we live in physical proximity is weaker today than at any time since the corporate state of the Middle Ages. What is society? Does it exist any more?

I have argued that the liberal democratic society is too precious to lose. It achieves what no organized religion or secular political ideology has ever done. It has allowed people of deeply conflicting views, habits and practices to live together in peace. It has done so precisely because liberal democracy is not an ideology. It is held together by simple human needs – for shelter, safety, security, medical care, welfare support, an economic infrastructure and an educational system. Whatever our religion, culture or creed we need such things. That is why we come together. A modest politics perhaps, but its modesty is its salvation.

The liberal democratic state is not the *polis* as it was in Athens. It does not claim to embody the highest ethical ideals. It does not demand a monopoly of our loyalties. In liberal democracy the state serves the people; the people do not serve the state. It is thus an environment in which many different kinds of lives can flourish, some pursuing individualist projects, others bound together in communities of commitment. It leaves space for life outside politics.

Epic literature was written in Greece and Rome about the glory of the state. No such literature will ever be written about liberal democracy. But sometimes the most modest social projects can achieve more than utopian ideals. The prophets saw ecstatic visions of peace, the lion and the lamb together, and a little child leading. Their successors, the sages, had no such poetic aspirations. They saw peace prosaically as good neighbourly relations: helping the needy, visiting the sick, feeding the hungry, across the boundary lines separating faith from faith, community from community. The prophetic dream remains a dream. The programme of the sages is 'doable'. In Habitat for Humanity and countless other community projects, it is being done.

The need for the liberal democratic state has never been greater than now, when elsewhere in the new international disorder, people are being split into ever more sectarian forms of identity, ever more intractable ethnic and religious conflicts. At apocalyptic times, when people are murdering one another in the name of high ideals, we need a politics of peace: not utopian peace, but the modest, live-and-let-live peace of good community relations, active citizenship, volunteering, community service and civic engagement.

These are not things we can continue to take for granted. Already as a result of the disturbances in the summer of 2001, the Cantle Report revealed deep segregation along ethnic and religious lines in several Midlands towns, and things have got worse since. The new communications globalize conflict. Today, when Sunni and Shia clash in Iraq, or Muslims and Hindus in Kashmir, or Buddhists and Hindus in Sri Lanka, or Muslims and Jews on Israel's borders, we feel the tremors in Europe. Conflicts, once containable, have become contagious. They can be carried, transmitted and spread until they become epidemics.

Conflict anywhere can be broadcast everywhere. Battles fought thousands of miles away are broadcast throughout the world, creating tensions in university campuses, charities and churches, polarizing opinion, straining friendships and dividing societies. Minorities today are more like diasporas than subcommunities: physically here, but mentally elsewhere. The bonds of belonging need to be strengthened if nations are to remain nations, not just places where people happen to be.

The previous models no longer work. The country-house, assimilationist model is neither morally acceptable nor practically viable. Members of minorities are not guests. They are citizens. We have seen in the twentieth century what happens when entire minority populations are branded as alien presences. Never may we go down that road again.

The hotel, multicultural model was intended precisely to counter that danger. In a multicultural society no one is a guest, because everyone is. We each have our own rooms, our own religion, our own culture, our own protected space. But this too has failed. The country in which it was implemented most thoroughly, Holland, has been the place in which it has been seen, by the Dutch themselves, to have failed most acutely.

Multiculturalism was undertaken with the most generous of motives. It has suffered, as all social policies eventually do, from the law of unintended consequences. But it is now counterproductive. It has encouraged segregation rather than integration. Instead of reducing differences, it has highlighted them. Undertaken in the name of tolerance, it has created new forms of intolerance.

Difference matters to me as a Jew, as it does to all those who care about their identities. We benefit immensely from the rich variety of cultures to be found in Britain and every other European country today. Each has its own style, grace, customs, cuisine, music and manners. Each has a contribution to make to national life, as did the Huguenots, the Irish and the Jews. As James Surowiecki showed in his *The Wisdom of Crowds*, the more open a group is, the more likely it is to make sound decisions. All-of-us is smarter than any-of-us. We need multiple perspectives, a plurality of world views. The idea that we should melt and merge and become some new amorphous hybrid is neither likely nor desirable.

The problem is not difference but what we do with it. Does it lead us to segregate or integrate? Does it encourage us to turn inward or outward? I have argued for *integration without assimilation*. That means seeing our differences as gifts we bring to the common good. But that requires a concept of the common good, which in turn means that there must be a strong sense of national identity, a felt reality of collective belonging. Lacking this, charities, churches and other third-sector institutions become pressure groups, representing sectional interests, not the common good.

*   *   *

Integration means a conscious decision to undertake the work of society building. I have tried to show how this is best done. We need to think in terms of covenant, not just contract. Contract is about what the individual gets from the state in return for laws and taxes. Covenant is about the values we share and the identity we construct together. Freedom needs a society as well as a state. That is why we must find a way of renewing British identity. We need a national narrative; we need collective memories; we need some articulate answer to the question: who are we?

Covenant complements the two great contractual institutions: the state and the market. We enter the state and the market as self-interested individuals. We enter a covenant as altruistic individuals seeking the common good. The state and the market are essentially competitive. In the state we compete for power; in the market we compete for wealth. Covenantal institutions are essentially co-operative. When they become competitive, they die.

Covenants do not displace contracts; they merely address different aspects of our lives. A society that is all competition and no co-operation is not a society at all. But a society that is all co-operation and no competition is equally not a society. It is a sect. On a larger scale it is a totalitarianism. Throughout history, utopian thinkers have dreamed of a perfect world in which all competitive striving is abolished, its place taken by harmony. That dream has led to some of the worst bloodshed in history. Utopias have no room for difference, and difference is what makes us human.

What then would a covenantal politics look like? First and foremost it would recognize the limits of politics and the importance of strengthening non-political institutions. Of these, the first is the family. Nothing more profoundly undermines the future of liberal democracy than the weakening of marriage and the responsibilities of parenthood – of fathers as well as mothers. Marriage, once a covenant, has become a contract, a temporary partnership for as long as the mood lasts.

How do you rebuild the family? Not the only, but perhaps the strongest force is religion. Judaism, Christianity and Islam all emphasize the family, in different ways and to different degrees. So do most other faith communities in Britain, as do many non-religious groups. They preserve a truth almost extinct in the wider secular culture: that our deepest happiness comes from the intimate grammar of love-as-loyalty, and that means placing a limit on the pursuit of desire. Religions change people. Politics and economics serve them. When a problem is technical – I have a need that you can supply – politics and economics suffice. When a problem is transformational – when it is not the world but we who must change – then religion or its functional equivalent enters the picture.

Governments cannot do much to strengthen the family, but what they can do, they should. Above all, they should set themselves to do no harm. Married couples should not be penalized by the tax system. The government should look at ways of making housing affordable for young couples with children. Today perhaps only faith schools are able to teach the importance of marriage, but all schools should teach the importance of long-term relationships of mutuality, fidelity and trust.

We must protect social space, by which I mean not only parks, public gardens, beaches and forests but also universities, professional associations, NGOs, charities and churches. These are neutral spaces where we leave politics and prejudice outside the door, like shoes when we enter sacred ground. Because they are neutral spaces, they heal. They bridge difference. They bring people together who would not otherwise meet except in competition. A society without neutral spaces would be like a city without trees, efficient perhaps, but ugly and ultimately unbearable.

I have watched with dismay as one social space after another has become politicized, enlisted in campaigns to boycott this, ban that, protest something else. Quite apart from the fact that gesture politics usually harms those it claims to help, it also destroys the fragile bonds on which civil society depends: it harms the would-be helper as well. We must take a stand against this. It is frightening to see how easy it is to gain control of an institution and subvert it for political ends. Heads of charities, universities and the like must say candidly: politics has a place, but not here. Here we are engaged in something that unites, not divides.

Covenant is about the diffusion, not the delegation, of responsibility. Schools cannot educate children without help from parents and the local community. They cannot counter the effect of a ruthlessly consumer culture. If what children worry about is what advertisers want them to worry about – clothes, mobile phones, iPods – they will not be builders of a free and gracious social order. If public-service broadcasting becomes mere entertainment with a smattering of modish opinions, we will not have an educated, principled public at all.

Modern culture slices responsibility too thinly and distributes it too narrowly. If schools fail, it must be the fault of the teachers. If crime rises, it must be the fault of the police. If cynicism reigns, it must be the fault of the media. If there is no one else to blame it must be the government, or at least the prime minister. This is absurd. Environmental damage is caused by billions of acts daily; so too is moral damage. Covenant puts responsibility back where it belongs, with each of us individually and all of us collectively.

Covenant is ultimately about social solidarity – a particular kind of social solidarity that does not sacrifice the individual to the collective as in Plato's Republic, the French Revolution, the Prussian state, Fascist Germany or Soviet Communism. Covenants are made between free individuals who cherish their differences while bringing them as gifts to the common good.

Social solidarity used to be produced in the natural course of events. It is no accident, for example, that great leaps in social provision like the welfare state occur in the aftermath of war, for war unites a nation more powerfully than anything else. In peace I can ignore my neighbour; in war I need him to fight alongside me. Thereafter, we acknowledge the debt we owe each other. But that sensibility fades. You can't hand it on to your children who never experienced what brought it about. Peace brings self-preoccupation, and the longer the peace, the more social solidarity is at risk.

I have argued that social solidarity cannot exist without rituals and narratives, celebrations and commemorations, moments when we affirm our shared commitment to the values that make our society what it is. There must be moments when we set politics and economics aside

236

and celebrate our shared belonging. That is when history becomes memory, and anticipation, hope. A Britain Day, community weeks and citizenship ceremonies all have their part to play. National celebrations are important, but they will only be effective if they filter down into local events that bring people in neighbourhoods together across ethnicities and faiths. Local government, civic associations, schools and religious congregations should all be brought into this process.

*   *   *

Solidarity has to do with society, not the state, but it would be absurd to pretend that the state has no effect on society. There are things that damage it that only governments can address: deep poverty in the midst of affluence, for example, or areas of high and persistent unemployment. These tear at the fabric of society because they mean that not everyone has access to the minimum conditions of human dignity. Not by accident were these the very things that the prophets saw as signs of social corruption: selling 'the righteous for silver and the poor for a pair of shoes'.

The same applies to the environment. Global warming, threatened species, air pollution, the over-exploitation of natural resources: these are paradigm cases of the common good at risk. But exhortation alone will never be enough to counter the perennial temptation to be a free rider. Legislative and financial measures are necessary and they will have to become progressively stronger over the years.

This only serves to show how deeply state and society are intertwined. Without the state, society could not function. But without society, the state will lack the public consensus needed to enact the necessary measures, especially those that have a long time-frame. Maintaining the balance between what government does and what we must do, is difficult but necessary.

Governments must leave space for the arenas in which social capital is produced. That means empowering charities, voluntary and faith-based groups. Some of these may need government funding: faith schools do. So do other institutions run by religious groups, from old-age homes to adoption agencies. This raises an intensely delicate issue: to what extent should a liberal state fund non-liberal institutions?

This is a political question, not a moral one, but the following principles suggest themselves: (a) governments may fund non-liberal institutions so long as they are purely voluntary – people have a free choice as to whether to enter or leave; (b) there is equal provision available elsewhere (state schools, non-religious adoption agencies and so on); (c) the institutions are based on values compatible with political (not moral) liberalism. These principles would, for example, have allowed the government to continue funding Catholic adoption agencies despite the fact that they do not cater for same-sex couples. I do not pretend there is an easy answer to this problem. Governments need voluntary associations; voluntary associations need governments. Yet they operate by different rules and have different priorities. It is all too easy for governments to have the Midas touch, killing those they turn to gold. Grown-up politics means accepting the tensions and complexities of our lives together without pretending there are easy solutions, universal rules. We must fight against political simple-mindedness.

That means relearning the habits of complexity against the siren calls of a soundbite, quick-fix culture. We have multiple identities and sometimes conflicting loyalties. We have to learn to distinguish between tolerance and multiculturalism; between the rights of individuals and those of groups; between liberalism in politics and in morality. These are not the same kinds of thing. They are conflicting things. Multiculturalism is not tolerance. Group rights endanger individual rights. Liberal politics need to be undergirded by non-liberal institutions such as the family.

I have argued the case for covenantal institutions: families, communities and civil society. But these too need a counter-balance. Families can be oppressive and abusive. Communities can be narrow and exclusive. Charities can sometimes be less good service-providers than the state. Yet without strong families, communities and charities, society cannot survive and we must defend them against the intrusions of politics and the market. We need to understand the ecological balance between different domains.

Perhaps we need to revisit the challenging imperative set out by Moses: 'You shall teach these things repeatedly to your children, speaking of them when you sit at home and when you travel on the way, when you lie down and when you rise.' Perhaps we need to become a nation of educators. Freedom needs an ongoing conversation of all-with-all if it is to avoid the war of all-against-all.

Certainly our national conversation is under-institutionalized. We have no place where academics and politicians, religious leaders and heads of charities, people in the professions and the media, come together in shared deliberation about our collective future. We have islands of conversation – campuses, think tanks, newspaper columns, pulpits – but no mainland where they connect and forge a common vocabulary. It may be that the new communications media – blogs, chatrooms, YouTube, MySpace, Facebook and the like – will generate new ways of creating communities of interest and ideas.

In general, the new technologies, even as they threaten the nation state, can also be used to build it. Emails help build communities.

Church and synagogue newsletters, for example, tell people who in the community is ill and needs visiting, bereaved and needs comforting, has had a celebration and needs congratulating. In an age of hyper-mobility familes scattered across the globe can stay in touch by Skype or videophones. The internet is an extraordinarily powerful educational tool. I used to give a class on the weekly Bible portion to a hundred people in a synagogue study room. Now I can give it to people across the world and anyone can access it.

Community service should be a normative part of school activities. It should be part of the citizenship curriculum, which should be taught in terms of responsibilities, not just rights. Each school will have its own way of doing this – in some it will be compulsory, in others voluntary – but there should be a national community service award which will become a significant part of a pupil's CV. Active citizenship is learned more by doing than by teaching, and emphasis should be placed on pupils encountering people outside their normal range, across barriers of age or ethnicity or faith.

Schools are already doing a fine job in integrating students from diverse backgrounds, and should be seen as a primary resource in creating social cohesion. They bring parents together, not just pupils. They should be seen as neighbourhood community centres, not just educational establishments.

Side-by-side relationships should be encouraged in all religious congregations. Faith leaders should urge their communities to reach out to others in the neighbourhood. We are about to begin a training programme within the Jewish community. Religious representatives should take a lead in creating a covenant around the values we share and our collective commitment to the common good. Faith divides; citizenship unites. That is why it is important for faith leaders to spell out the need for shared space where we celebrate our common humanity, not just our theological particularities.

*   *   *

Jews spoke Yiddish for a thousand years. They lost it in a single generation – because one generation did not teach it to their children. Freedom can be lost in the same space of time, if we do not teach our children why we are here, in this country, with these traditions, and how it came to be what it is.

There is no way back to before multiculturalism, but there is a way beyond. The story of the future tells of how Britain, where wars were once fought between Protestants and Catholics, became a pioneer of tolerance in the twenty-first century by finding ways of bringing to-gether the diverse histories of its inhabitants while maintaining its strongly individual character. It became a place where minorities who elsewhere fought one another, became friends. Without ceasing to be a Christian country it embraced Hindus and Sikhs and Muslims, as it had embraced Catholics and Dissenters and Jews. It respected others; it learned from them; it incorporated their distinctive gifts into national life. It established informal ground rules – there are certain things you do and don't do if you want to be part of a society that values diversity. Civility matters. So does service to others. So do neutral spaces where people of all kinds meet.

Belonging means giving. It involves a responsibility-based culture of respect, not a rights-based culture of complaint. The majority culture must exercise restraint against needlessly provocative acts and utterances. Minorities have a responsibility to show that they respect Britain and its traditions. We each have a part to play in the national endeavour. That means orchestrated diversity, integration without assimilation. It cannot be done by governments alone; it cannot be done by us alone. We need to work out a new relationship between civil society and the state, and that will take time.

Not just time: it will take vision, determination and long-term thinking. The nation state has rarely faced challenges on this scale before. The best defence of liberal democracy is not personal autonomy and moral relativism. Instead, it is the fact that all of us, whatever our class, colour or creed, are in God's image – or in secular terms, we are ends, not means. We enter the political domain with non-negotiable dignity. We should all have a voice in the conversations that will shape the nation's future. We must each commit ourselves to the proposition that reason and persuasion are the only acceptable ways of conflict resolution. Liberal democracy needs its own habits of the heart. If we seek space to be ourselves, we must respect the space others need to be themselves, even if they use it in ways we find objectionable. That requires humility and generosity.

What then is society? It is where we set aside all considerations of wealth and power and value people for what they are and what they give. It is where Jew and Christian, Muslim and Hindu, Buddhist and Sikh, can come together, bound by their commonalities, enlarged by their differences. It is where we join in civil conversation about the kind of society we wish to create for the sake of our grandchildren not yet born. It is where we share an overarching identity, a first language of citizenship, despite our different second languages of ethnicity or faith. It is where strangers can become friends. It is not a vehicle of salvation, but it is the most effective form yet devised for respectful coexistence. Society is the home we build together when we bring our several gifts to the common good.

240

Notes

Chapter 1. Introduction

1 Walter Lippman, *The Good Society* (London: George Allen and Unwin, 1937), 370–71.
2 Pym Fortuyn, *Daily Telegraph*, 4 May 2002.
3 Paul Sniderman and Louk Hagendoorn, *When Ways of Life Collide*: Multiculturalism and its Discontents in the Netherlands (Princeton, NJ: Princeton University Press, 2007), 5.
4 Aristotle, *The Politics*, Book II, 2.
5 *The Times*, 24 January 2007.
6 John Naisbitt and Patricia Aburdene, *Megatrends 2000: Ten New Directions for the 1990s* (New York: Morrow), 990.
7 'World Without Walls', BBC, The Dimbleby Lecture 2001. http://www.australianpolitics.com/news/2001/01-12-14.shtml.
8 *Democracy in America*, abridged with an Introduction by Thomas Bender (New York: The Modern Library, 1981), 403.
9 J. L. Talmon, *The Origins of Totalitarian Democracy* (London: Secker & Warburg, 1952), 1–13.

Chapter 2. Society as Country House, Hotel or Home

1 Quoted in Michael Sandel, *Democracy's Discontent* (Cambridge, Mass: Harvard University Press, 1996), 302–303.
2 In P. N. Furbank and W. R. Owens (eds), *The True-Born Ernglishman and other writings* (Harmondsworth: Penguin Classics, 1997), 28–30.
3 Ford Madox Ford, *The Spirit of the People: An Analysis of the English Mind.* (London: Alston Rivers, 1907), 44.
4 Quoted in Ian Buruma, *Anglomania: A European Love Affair* (New York: Vintage, 2000), 29.
5 Quoted in A. O. Hirschman, *The Passions and the Interests* (Princeton, NJ: Princeton University Press, 1996), 80.

241

6 Quoted in Robert Winder, *Bloody Foreigners: The Story of Immigration to Britain* (London: Little, Brown, 2004), 113.

7 *Truth* magazine, vol. 34, No. 879, quoted in Lucio Sponza, *Italian Immigrants in Nineteenth-century Britain: Realities and Images* (Leicester: Leicester University Press, 1988), 120.

8 See Robert Winder, *Bloody Foreigners, op. cit.*

9 See Theodore Dalrymple, *Our Culture, What's Left of it: The Mandarins and the Masses* (Chicago: Ivan R. Dee, 2005), 273–82.

10 Daniel Bell, *The End of Ideology* (Cambridge, Mass: Harvard University Press, 1988).

11 Following Michael Sandel's phrase, 'procedural republic', in *Democracy's Discontent, op. cit.*

12 Report available at http//image.guardian.co.uk/sys-files/Guardian/documents/2001/12/11/communitycohesionreport.pdf -.

13 See Anne J. Kershen, *Strangers, Aliens and Asians: Huguenots, Jews and Bangladeshis in Spitalfields, 1660–2000* (London: Routledge, 2005).

14 David Goodhart: 'The Discomfort of Strangers', *Prospect*, February 2004, reprinted in *The Guardian*, 24 February, 2004.

15 See http://www.cre.gov.uk/Default.aspx.LocID-0hgnew07s.RefLocID-0hg 00900c002.Lang-EN.htm.

16 See http://news.bbc.co.uk/1/hi/england/north_yorkshire/4459252.stm

17 See http://www.number-10.gov.uk/output/Page10563.asp.

18 *The Clash of Civilizations and the Remaking of World Order* (New York: Simon & Schuster, 1996), 310.

19 *Who Are We? The Challenges to America's National Identity* (New York: Simon & Schuster, 2004), 363.

Chapter 3. A Brief History of Multiculturalism

1 William Morris, *A Dream of John Ball* (London: Longmans, Green, 1938), 39–40, cited in Adam Seligman, *The Idea of Civil Society*, 206.

2 See Milton M. Gordon, *Assimilation in American Life* (New York: Oxford University Press, 1964), 120–21.

3 See Ibid., 116.

4 Anne J. Kershen, *Strangers, Aliens and Asians*, 201.

5 Ibid.

6 Ibid., 202.

7 Ibid., 205.

8 Winder, *Bloody Foreigners*, 178–79.

9 This quotation, like those in the following paragraph, is from Gerry Black, *JFS: The History of the Jews' Free School, London since 1732* (London: Tymsder, 1998), 123–33.

10 Reprinted in Sonia and V. D. Lipman (eds), *The Century of Moses Montefiore* (Oxford: Littman Library of Jewish Civilization and Oxford University Press, 1985), 362–68.

11 Gerry Black, *JFS*, 127.

12 *The Shooting Party* (Harmondsworth: Penguin, 1980), 9.

13 In *The Zionist Idea: A Historical Analysis and Reader*, edited and with an introduction, an afterword and biographical notes by Arthur Hertzberg (Philadelphia: Jewish Publication Society, c. 1997).

14 Articles reprinted in Horace Kallen, *Culture and Democracy in the United States* (New York: Boni and Liveright, 1924). See also Milton R. Konvitz (ed.), *The Legacy of Horace M. Kallen* (Rutherford, NJ: Fairleigh Dickinson University Press), 1987.

15 John Dewey, 'Nationalizing Education', National Education Association of the United States, *Addresses and Proceedings of the Fifty-Fourth Annual Meeting*, 1916, 185–86.

16 Quoted in Arthur M. Schlesinger, Jr., *The Disuniting of America* (New York: Norton, 1992), 37.

17 Paul Sniderman and Louk Hagendoorn, *When Ways of Life Collide*, 1.

18 See 'My intellectual path' in Isaiah Berlin, *The Power of Ideas*, ed. Henry Hardy (London: Pimlico, 2001), 1–23; John Gray, *Isaiah Berlin* (London: HarperCollins, 1995), 38–75.

19 See T. W. Adorno, *The Authoritarian Personality* (New York: Harper, 1950); Erich H. Fromm, *Escape from freedom* (New York: H. Holt, 1994); Abraham H. Maslow, *Toward a Psychology of Being* (New York: J. Wiley & Sons), 1999.

20 *Speculations*, ed. Herbert Read (London: Kegan Paul, 1924), 116.

Chapter 4. The Defeat of Freedom in the Name of Freedom

1 Friedrich Hayek, *The Constitution of Liberty* (London: Routledge and Kegan Paul, 1976), 62.

2 Emile Durkheim, *Professional Ethics* (London: Routledge, 1991), 7.

3 George Orwell, *The Lion and the Unicorn* (London: Penguin, 1941), 17.

4 George Mikes, 'How to be an alien', in George Mikes, *How to be a Brit* (London: Penguin, 1986), 54.

5 Patrick Devlin, *The Enforcement of Morals* (Oxford, Oxford Univerity Press, 1965), 10.

6 H. L. A. Hart, *Law, Liberty and Morality* (Oxford: Oxford Univerity Press, 1963).

7 In *Utilitarianism, On Liberty, and Considerations on Representative Government* (London: Dent, Everyman's Library, 1984), 78.

8 Hart, *op. cit.*, Introduction.

9 Nietzsche, *The Gay Science*, trans. with commentary by Walter Kaufmann (New York: Vintage Books, 1974), para. 125, 181–82.

10 Alasdair MacIntyre, *After Virtue* (London: Duckworth, 1981).

11 Ibid., 236.

12 See Richard Bernstein, *Dictatorship of Virtue: Multiculturalism, and the Battle for America's Future* (New York: Knopf, 1994); Anthony Browne, *The Retreat of Reason: Political Correctness and the Corruption of Public Debate in Modern Britain*

(London: Civitas, 2006); David G. Green, *We're (Nearly) All Victims Now: How Political Correctness Is Undermining Our Liberal Culture* (London: Civitas, 2006).

13 *Babylonian Talmud, Berakhot* 58a.

14 Alan Ryan, *John Stuart Mill* (New York: Pantheon, 1970), 233–55.

15 Mill, *On Liberty*, 122.

16 Ed Husain, *The Islamist* (London: Penguin, 2007).

17 Shakespeare, *Troilus and Cressida*, I. iii.

18 Karlheinz Stockhhausen: The following gives the text of the article that appeared in *Die Zeit*, September 2001: http://www.andante.com/article/article.cfm?id=14377.

19 Jean Baudrillard, *The Spirit of Terrorism*, trans. Chris Turner (London: Verso, 2003), 4–5.

20 Julien Benda, *The Treason of the Intellectuals*, trans. Richard Aldington (New Brunswick, NJ: Transaction Publishers, 2006), 27.

21 John Stuart Mill, 'Coleridge' in *Collected Works of John Stuart Mill*, vol. 10 (Indianapolis: Liberty Fund, 2006), 133.

Chapter 5. Victims

1 Michael Walzer, 'Multiculturalism and the politics of interest', in David Biale, Michael Galchinsky, and Susannah Heschel (eds), *Insider/outsider: American Jews and Multiculturalism* (Berkeley: University of California Press, 1998), 89.

2 Roy F. Baumeister, *Evil: Inside Human Cruelty and Violence* (New York: W. H. Freeman, 1997), 26–27.

3 Christopher Lasch, *The Culture of Narcissism: American Life in an Age of Diminishing Expectations* (New York: Warner Books, 1979), 87–88.

4 *Washington Post*, Thursday, 19 April 2007.

5 Roy F. Baumeister, *Evil*, 1–59.

6 Stuart Kaufman, *Modern Hatreds: the Symbolic Politics of Ethnic War* (New York: Cornell University Press, 2001).

7 Ibid., 3.

8 Ibid., 205.

9 Genesis 3:12–13.

10 Leviticus 19:16.

11 Isaiah 1:17.

12 Philip Rieff, *The Triumph of the Therapeutic: Uses of Faith after Freud* (New York: Harper & Row, 1966).

13 Abraham Lincoln: The Gettysburg Address. http://www.loc.gov/exhibits/gadd/gadrft.html.

14 Michael Walzer, *Politics and Passion: Toward a More Egalitarian Liberalism* (New Haven: Yale University Press, 2004), 37.

15 Genesis 4:7.

16 Jack Miles, *God, a Biography* (New York: Simon and Schuster, 1995), 397–408.

17 Quoted in J. A. Cuddon, *The Penguin Dictionary of Literary Terms and Literary Theory* (London: Penguin, 1992), 985.

18 Exodus 3:14.

19 Viktor Frankl, *Man's Search for Meaning: An Introduction to Logotherapy*, trans. Ilse Lasch (New York: Simon & Schuster, 1984).

20 See Charles J. Sykes, *A Nation of Victims: The Decay of the American Character* (New York: St. Martin's Press, 1992).

21 See http://www.newsday.com/news/nationworld/world/ny-wojeru185175 987apr18,0,3012504.story?coll=ny-worldnews-print.

Chapter 6. Technology and the Fragmentation of Culture

1 John Donne, 'An Anatomy Of The World', line 213, in *John Donne – The Major Works*, ed. John Carey (Oxford: Oxford World Classics, 1990), 212.

2 Achille Luchaire, *La Société Française au Temps de Philippe-Auguste*, 278; quoted in Norbert Elias, *The History of Manners*, trans. Edmund Jephcott (Oxford: Blackwell, 1978), 201.

3 Benedict Anderson, *Imagined Communities: Reflections on the Origin and Spread of Nationalism* (London: Verso, 1991).

4 Ernst Gellner, *Nations and nationalism* (Oxford: Blackwell, 1983).

5 Ibid., 36.

6 See Walter J. Ong, *Orality and Literacy* (London: Methuen, 1982).

7 Leonard Shlain, *The Alphabet Versus the Goddess: The Conflict Between Word and Image* (New York: Viking, 1998).

8 See Samuel Huntington, *Who Are We?*, 276–291.

Chapter 7. The Inward Turn

1 Alexis de Tocqueville, *Democracy in America*, 135.

2 Winston Churchill, 'The Spirit of England', speech at The Honourable Artillery Company, St George's Day, Dinner, 23 April 1953, in Gerry Hanson, *England my England* (London: Robson Books, 2005), 64.

3 Roger Scruton, *England: An Elegy* (London: Chatto and Windus, 2000);Peter Hitchens, *The Abolition of Britain* (London: Quartet, 2000); Peter Vansittart, *In Memory of England* (London: John Murray, 1999).

4 Alan Bennett, 'An Englishman abroad' in Alan Bennett, *Plays* (London: Faber, 1998).

5 *Areopagitica and Other Political Writings of* John Milton (Indianapolis: Liberty Fund, 1999), 40.

6 Kate Fox, *Watching the English* (London: Hodder and Stoughton, 2004), 135.

7 George Orwell, 'Notes on Nationalism', in *The Penguin Essays of George Orwell* (Harmondsworth: Penguin, 1984), 318–319.

8   Lionel Trilling, *Beyond Culture: Essays on Literature and Learning* (New York: Harcourt Brace Jovanovich, 1979); Daniel Bell, *The Cultural Contradictions of Capitalism* (New York: Basic Books, 1996).
9   *The Penguin Essays of George Orwell*, 30–67.
10 Amartya Sen, *Identity and Violence: The Illusion of Destiny* (New York: W. W. Norton, 2006). Kwame Anthony Appiah, *The Ethics of Identity* (Princeton, NJ: Princeton University Press, 2005); *Cosmopolitanism: Ethics in a World of Strangers* (London: Allen Lane, 2006). See also Carol A. Breckenridge (ed.), *Cosmopolitanism* (Durham NC: Duke University Press, 2002).
11 Zygmunt Bauman, 'From Pilgrim to Tourist - or a Short History of Identity', in Stuart Hall and Paul de Gay (eds), *Question of Cultural Identity* (Sage Publications, 1996).
12 Walt Whitman, 'Song of Myself', Lines 1321–24.
13 Milton Gordon, *Assimilation in American Life*, 234.
14 Gerhard Lenski, *The Religious Factor: A Sociological Study of Religion's Impact on Politics, Economics, and Family Life* (Garden City, NY: Doubleday, 1961), 329–30.
15 Harold R. Isaacs, *Idols of the Tribe: Group Identity and Political Change* (New York: Harper & Row, 1975), 24.
16 Charles Liebman, 'Orthodoxy in American Jewish Life', *American Jewish Year Book*, 1965, 21–92.
17 Ed Husain: *The Islamist*, 73.
18 Jonathan Sacks, *Will we have Jewish grandchildren?* (Ilford: Vallentine Mitchell, 1994).
19 Teacher Support Network report, February 2007.
20 Michael Walzer, *Spheres of Justice: A Defence of Pluralism and Equality* (Oxford: Martin Robertson, 1983), 38–39.
21 Alasdair MacIntyre, *After Virtue*, 244.

Chapter 8. A Forgotten Political Classic

1   Richard M. Weaver, *Ideas Have Consequences* (Chicago: University of Chicago Press, 1984), 176.
2   Joseph S. Nye, *Soft Power: The Means to Success in World Politics* (PublicAffairs, 2005); *The Paradox of American Power* (New York: Oxford University Press, 2003).
3   'Two Concepts of Liberty', in Isaiah Berlin, *Four Essays on Liberty* (Oxford: Oxford University Press, 1969), 172.
4   Michael J. Sandel (ed.), *Liberalism and its Critics* (Oxford: Blackwell, 1984), 8.
5   John Stuart Mill, *On Liberty*, op. cit.; Sir Karl Popper, *The Open Society and its Enemies* (London: Routledge & Kegan Paul, 1962).
6   Christopher Hill, *The English Bible and the Seventeenth Century Revolution* (London: Penguin, 1994), 20.
7   Martin Luther King, Jr., *I Have a Dream: Writings and Speeches that Changed the*

World, ed. James Melvin (Washington, San Francisco: HarperSanFrancisco, 1992), 203.

8   See Exod. 12:38, Numbers 11:4, Nehemiah 13:3, Jeremiah 25:20, 50:37.

9   Jean-Jacques Rousseau unpublished papers. They are to be found in the public library at Neuchâtel (*Cahiers de brouillons, notes et extraits*, no. 7843).

Chapter 9. Social Contract, Social Covenant

1   Joseph Allen, *Love and Conflict: A Covenantal Model of Christian Ethics* (Lanham, Md: University Press of America, 1995), 17.

2   I Samuel 8.

3   I Samuel 8:11–18.

4   Rabbi Zvi Hirsch Chajes, *Torat nevi'im*, ch. 7, in *Kol Kitvei Maharatz Chajes* (Jerusalem, 1958), vol. 1, 43–49.

5   See Delbert R. Hillers, *Covenant: The History of a Biblical Idea* (Baltimore: Johns Hopkins Press, 1969), Daniel J. Elazar, *Covenant & Polity in Biblical Israel: Biblical Foundations & Jewish Expressions* (New Brunswick, NJ: Transaction Publishers, 1995).

6   *Babylonian Talmud Shabbat* 10a, 119b.

7   *Thomas Paine: Political Writings*, ed. Bruce Kuklick (Cambridge: Cambridge University Press, 1997), 3.

8   Daniel J. Elazar, *Covenant & Polity in Biblical Israel*, 35–51.

9   Shakespeare, *Troilus and Cressida*, Act I, Scene 3.

10 John Milton, *Tenure of Kings and Magistrates* (Cambridge University Press, 1991), cited in Daniel J. Elazar, *Covenant & Commonwealth: From Christian Separation Through the Protestant Reformation* (New Brunswick, NJ: Transaction Publishers, 1996), 244.

11 Daniel J. Elazar, *Covenant & Commonwealth*, 269–309.

12 Daniel J. Elazar , *Covenant & Constitutionalism: The Great Frontier and the Matrix of Federal Democracy* (New Brunswick, NJ: Transaction Publishers, 1998), 17–46.

13 Richard Niebuhr, 'The Idea of Covenant and American Democracy', *Church History* 23 (June 1954), 133.

Chapter 10. Telling the Story

1   Alasdair MacIntyre, *After Virtue*, 201.

2   Jean Paul Sartre, cited in Dan P. McAdams, *The Stories We Live By: Personal Myths and the Making of the Self* (New York & London: Guilford Press, 1993), 17.

3   John F. Kennedy's Inaugural Address can be found at: http://www.bartleby.com/124/pres56.html.

4   See http://www.bartleby.com/124/pres57.html.

5 Isaiah Berlin, *Against the Current: Essays in the History of Ideas*, ed. Henry Hardy (London: Pimlico, 1997), 252.

6 See Yosef Hayim Yerushalmi, *Zakhor: Jewish History and Jewish Memory* (Seattle, London: University of Washington Press, 1996).

7 *Mishnah Pesachim* 10:5.

8 Jerome Bruner, *Actual Minds, Possible Worlds* (Cambridge, Mass: Harvard University Press), 1986.

9 Ibid., 13. The notion of the Joycean epiphany was first outlined in *Stephen Hero*, Joyce's early version of *A Portrait of the Artist as a Young Man*.

10 Paul Ricoeur, *Time and Narrative*, trans. Kathleen McLaughlin and David Pellauer (Chicago, Ill: University of Chicago Press), 1984.

11 Anthony Smith, *Chosen Peoples: Sacred Sources of National Identity* (Oxford: Oxford University Press, 2003), 260.

12 John H. Schaar, *Legitimacy in the Modern State* (New Brunswick, NJ: Transaction Publishers, 1981), 291.

13 Jean-Francois Lyotard, *The Postmodern Condition* (Manchester: Manchester University Press), 1984.

Chapter 11. The Responsible Society

1 Hillel, *Ethics of the Fathers*, 1:14.

2 Jonathan Freedland, *Bring Home the Revolution* (London: Fourth Estate, 1998), 221.

3 Philip Selznick, *The Moral Commonwealth: Social Theory and the Promise of Community* (Berkeley: University of California Press, 1992), 477–81.

4 Robert F. Kennedy: speech on the Assassination of Martin Luther King Jr., Indianapolis, Indiana, April 4 1968.

5 Maimonides, Mishneh Torah, Laws of Festival Rest, 6:18.

6 Matthew 25:34–40.

7 Frank Prochaska, *Christianity and Social Service in Modern Britain: The Disinherited Spirit* (Oxford: Oxford University Press, 2006). See also Prochaska's *Schools of Citizenship: Charity and Civic Virtue* (London: Civitas, 2002); and his *Royal Bounty: The Making of a Welfare Monarchy* (New Haven: Yale University Press, 1995).

8 A. J. P. Taylor, *English History, 1914–1945* (Oxford: Clarendon Press, 1965), 175.

9 John Stuart Mill, *Principles of Political Economy*, Book V, ch. 11, para. 6.

10 Alexis de Tocqueville, *Democracy in America*, 584.

11 See Robert D. Putnam, *Bowling Alone: The Collapse and Revival of American Community* (London: Simon & Schuster, 2000); Robert D. Putnam and Lewis M. Feldstein, *Better Together: Restoring the American Community* (London: Simon & Schuster, 2004); Francis Fukuyama, *Trust: The Social Virtues and the Creation of Prosperity* (London: H. Hamilton, 1995).

Notes

Chapter 12. The Home We Build Together

1 *Leviticus Rabbah* 4:6.
2 *Babylonian Talmud Berakhot* 64a.
3 Milton, *Areopagitica*, 41–42.
4 John Donne, *Meditation* XVII.

Chapter 13. The Uses of Covenant

1 Michael Novak, *Free Persons and the Common Good* (Lanham: Madison, 1989), 80.
2 Survey by the Commission for Architecture and the Built Environment, June 2004. http://news.bbc.co.uk/1/hi/england/3812699.stm.
3 On loyalty see Josiah Royce, *The Philosophy of Loyalty* (New York, 1909).
4 Full text at: http://www.constitution.org/eng/conpur058.htm. See also Daniel J. Elazar, *Covenant and Commonwealth*, 254–58, 280–83.
5 Bertrand Russell, Introduction, *History of Western Philosophy*, 18–19.

Chapter 14. Who Am I?

1 Roger Scruton, *England: An Elegy*, 16.
2 Michael Sandel, *Democracy's Discontent*, 350–51.
3 Shelley, *Prometheus Unbound*, III, iv. 194–5.
4 Michel Foucault, *The Order of Things: An Archaeology of the Human Sciences* (London: Tavistock, 1970).
5 John Murray Cuddihy, *The Ordeal of Civility: Freud, Marx, Lévi-Strauss, and the Jewish Struggle with Modernity* (New York: Basic Books, 1974).
6 Sir Stanley Baldwin, speech to the Annual Dinner of the Royal Society of St George, 6 May 1924, in Gerry Hanson, *England, my England*, 60–62.
7 George Orwell, *England, Your England and Other Essays* (London: Secker & Warburg, 1953), 194.
8 John Major, speech to the Conservative Group for Europe, 22 April 1993.
9 Jeremy Paxman, *The English: A Portrait of a People* (London: Michael Joseph, 1998), 142. Peter Mandler, *The English National Character*, 234, likewise comments, 'This farrago of half-remembered Englishnesses ... triggered only a volley of sniggers, not the feelings of warm familiarity Major sought to evoke.'
10 Jonathan Freedland, *Bring Home the Revolution*, 228.
11 Gertrude Himmelfarb, *The Roads to Modernity: The British, French, and American Enlightenments* (New York: Knopf, 2004), 234.
12 Jack Straw, 'Identity and Democracy: The Way We Are', in *The World Today*, Chatham House, May 2007.
13 Wordsworth, *The Prelude*, Book XIV, 1, 446–47.

Chapter 15. Face-to-Face, Side-by-Side

1 Jacques Maritain, *Man and the State* (Washington, DC: Catholic University of America Press, 1998), 111.
2 Muzafer Sherif, O. J. Harvey, B. Jack White, William R. Hood, Carolyn W. Sherif, *Intergroup Conflict and Cooperation: The Robbers Cave Experiment* (1954/ 1961). Full text available at: http://psychclassics.yorku.ca/Sherif/.
3 For a theological account of the difference, through an exegesis of Gen. 1–3, see Joseph Soloveitchik, *The Lonely Man of Faith* (New York: Doubleday, 1992).
4 *Mishnah Shevi'it*, 4:3, 5:9, *Gittin* 5:9, *Tosefta, Gittin* 3:13–14, *Avodah Zarah* 1:3; *Babylonian Talmud, Gittin* 59a–61a.
5 See Robert Putnam, *Bowling Alone*, 22–24, 357–363; Robert Putnam and Lewis Feldstein, *Better Together*, 2–3.

Chapter 16. Civility

1 Edward Shils, *The Virtue of Civility: Selected Essays on Liberalism, Tradition, and Civil Society*, ed. Steven Grosby (Indianapolis: Liberty Fund, 1997), 4.
2 Stephen L. Carter, *Civility: Manners, Morals, and the Etiquette of Democracy* (New York: Basic Books, 1998), 11.
3 Norbert Elias, *The Civilizing Process: The History of Manners* (Oxford: Blackwell, 1978).
4 David Riesman in collaboration with Reuel Denney and Nathan Glazer, *The Lonely Crowd: A Study of the Changing American Character* (New Haven: Yale University Press, 1952).
5 Adam Ferguson, *Essay on the History of Civil Society*, ed. Fania Oz-Salzberger (Cambridge: Cambridge University Press, 1996), 179.
6 Alexis de Tocqueville, *Democracy in America*, 403–4.
7 Ibid., 407.
8 George Orwell, 'The English People', in *The Collected Essays, Journalism and Letters of George Orwell*, ed. Sonia Orwell & Ian Angus, vol. 3. *As I Please: 1943–1945* (London: Secker & Warburg, 1968), 2–3.
9 Geoffrey Gorer, *Exploring English Character* (London: Cresset Press, 1955), 13.
10 I am indebted, in much of what follows, to Christie Davis, *The Strange Death of Moral Britain* (New Brunswick, NJ: Transaction Publishers, 2006).
11 Edward Shils, *The Virtue of Civility*, 4.
12 Michael Walzer, *Interpretation and Social Criticism* (Cambridge, Mass: Harvard University Press, 1987); *The Company of Critics: Social Criticism and Political Commitment in the Twentieth Century* (New York: Basic Books, 1988); *Thick and Thin: Moral Argument at Home and Abroad* (Notre Dame: University of Notre Dame Press, 1994).
13 Edward Shils, *The Virtue of Civility*, 14.

14 Richard John Neuhaus, *The Naked Public Square: Religion and Democracy in America* (Grand Rapids, Mich: Eerdmans, 1986).

Chapter 17. Multiculturalism or Tolerance?

1 'An Essay Concerning Toleration' in John Locke, *Political Writings* (London: Penguin, 1993), 202.
2 On toleration and tolerance, see: John Horton & Susan Mendus (eds), *Aspects of Toleration* (London: Methuen, 1985); Susan Mendus (ed.), *Justifying Toleration: Conceptual and Historical Perspectives* (Cambridge: Cambridge University Press, 1988); Susan Mendus and David Edwards (eds), *On Toleration* (Oxford: Clarendon, 1987); Susan Mendus, *Toleration and the Limits of Liberalism* (Basingstoke: Macmillan, 1989). David Heyd (ed.), *Toleration: An Elusive Virtue* (Princeton, NJ: Princeton University Press, 1996).
3 Paul Sniderman and Louk Hagendoorn, *When Ways of Life Collide*, 135.
4 David Miller, *Principles of Social Justice*, Cambridge, MA: Harvard University Press, 1999, 63.

Chapter 18. Mending the Broken Family

1 Polybius, *The Histories*, Book XXXVI.
2 See Mark Steyn, *America Alone: The End of the World as We Know it* (Washington, DC: Regnery Pub., 2006).
3 Children have become scarce: Eurostat, 2005 figures.
4 *Demographic Year Book*, 2004, Council of Europe.
5 *Breakdown Britain: Fractured Families* (London: Social Justice Policy Group, December 2006), 28.
6 *An Overview of Child Well-being in Rich Countries*, UNICEF Innocenti Research Centre, Report Card 7, 2007.
7 Oliver James, *Britain on the Couch* (London: Century, 1997).
8 See http://news.bbc.co.uk/1/hi/uk/398666.stm.
9 See http://news.bbc.co.uk/1/hi/uk/4307419.stm.
10 See http://news.bbc.co.uk/1/hi/uk/6194116.stm.
11 *Breakdown Britain*, 34.
12 Linda Waite and Maggie Gallagher, *The Case for Marriage* (New York: Doubleday, 2000); Steven Stack and J. Ross Eshelman, 'Marital Status and Happiness: A Seventeen Nation Study', *Journal of Marriage and the Family* 60, (1998), 527–36.
13 C. E. Ross, J. Mirowski and K. Goldsteen, 'The Impact of the Family on Health: a Decade in Review', *Journal of Marriage and the Family*, vol. 52: 4, 1990, 1059–78.
14 Larry L. Bumpass and James A. Sweet, 'National Estimates of Cohabitation', *Demography* 26 (1989), 620–21.

15 Neil Bennett, Anne Kilmas Blanc and David E. Bloom, 'Commitment and the Modern Union: Assessing the Link Between Premarital Cohabitation and Subsequent Marital Stability', *American Sociological Review* 53 (1988), 127–38.

16 Wade Horn, *Father Facts*, third edn (Gaithersburg, Md: National Fatherhood Initiative, 1998), 54–73.

17 Robert Whelan, *Broken Homes and Battered Children* (London: Family Education Trust, 1993).

18 Barbara Dafoe Whitehead, *The Divorce Culture* (New York: Random House, 1997).

19 John Stuart Mill, *On Liberty*, ch. 5.

20 James Q. Wilson, *The Marriage Problem: How Our Culture Has Weakened Families* (New York, NY: HarperCollins, 2002), 2.

21 Ferdinand Mount, *The Subversive Family: An Alternative History of Love and Marriage* (London: Cape, 1982).

22 Theodore Dalrymple, *Our Culture: What's Left of It* (Chicago: Ivan R. Dee, 2005), 103–15.

23 Plato, *Apology* 38a.

24 Rousseau, *Social Contract*, 86–87.

25 Jared Diamond, *The Rise and Fall of the Third Chimpanzee* (London: Radius, 1991); *Guns, Germs and Steel* (London: Vintage, 1998).

26 Alexis de Tocqueville, *Democracy in America*, 183.

Chapter 19. A Religious Defence of Liberal Democracy

1 Alexis de Tocqueville, *Democracy in America*, 185.

2 Oliver Goldsmith, *The Traveller*, l. 427.

3 For the Greeks and Romans: on civic ethics, see Harry Redner, *Ethical Life: The Past and Present of Ethical Cultures* (Lanham, Md: Rowman & Littlefield, 2001), 68–84.

4 Ethics of the Fathers, 3: 2.

5 Ethics of the Fathers, 2:3.

6 See Adam B. Seligman, *The Problem of Trust* (Princeton, NJ: Princeton University Press, 1997), especially 103–23, and more generally Gertrude Himmelfarb, *The Roads to Modernity*.

7 Adam Smith, *The Theory of Moral Sentiments* (Indianapolis: Liberty Classics, 1982), 9.

8 Adam Ferguson, *An Essay on the History of Civil Society*, 38.

9 Rousseau, *The Social Contract*, trans Maurice Cranston (London: Penguin, 1968), 73.

10 J. L. Talmon, *The Origins of Totalitarian Democracy* (London: Secker & Warburg, 1952).

11 *Democracy in America*, 185.

12 Ibid., 187.

Chapter 20. A Time to Build

1 Nelson Mandela, 'Let freedom reign', inaugural address as President of South Africa, 10 May 1994, in Brian MacArthur (ed.), *The Penguin Book of Historic Speeches*, 499.

2 Millard Fuller, *A Simple, Decent Place to Live: The Building Realization of Habitat for Humanity* (Dallas, TX: World Publishing, 1995).

3 Isaiah 54:13; *Babylonian Talmud Berakhot* 64a.

Suggestions For Further Reading

On Multiculturalism

Appiah, Anthony, *The Ethics of Identity* (Princeton, NJ: Princeton University Press, 2005).

—*Cosmopolitanism* (London: W. W. Norton, 2006).

Berger, Peter L. (ed.), *The Limits of Social Cohesion* (Oxford, Westview Press, 1998).

Bernstein, Richard, *Dictatorship of Virtue* (New York: A. A. Knopf, 1994).

Cantle, Ted, *Community Cohesion* (Basingstoke: Palgrave Macmillan, 2005).

Gilman, Sander L., *Multiculturalism and the Jews* (London: Routledge, 2006).

Gordon, Milton, *Assimilation in American Life* (New York: Oxford University Press, 1964). Huntington, Samuel P., *Who Are We?* (New York: Simon & Schuster, 2004).

Isaacs, Harold, *Idols of the Tribe* (Cambridge, Mass: Harvard University Press, 1975).

Kymlicka, Will, *Multicultural Citizenship* (Oxford: Clarendon Press, 1995).

—(ed.), *The Rights of Minority Cultures* (Oxford: Oxford University Press, 1995).

—and Wayne, Norman, *Citizenship in Diverse Societies* (Oxford: Oxford University Press, 2000).

Levy, Jacob T., *The Multiculturalism of Fear* (Oxford: Oxford University Press, 2000).

Modood, Tariq, *Multiculturalism, Muslims and Citizenship* (London: Routledge, 2006).

Parekh, Bhikhu, *Rethinking Multiculturalism* (Basingstoke: Palgrave Macmillan, 2006).

—*The Future of Multi-Ethnic Britain: Report of the Commission on the Future of Multi-Ethnic Britain* (London: Profile Books, 2000).

Sacks, Jonathan, *The Persistence of Faith* (London: Continuum, 2005).

Schlesinger, Arthur, *The Disuniting of America* (New York: Norton, 1992).

Sniderman Paul M. and Hagendoorn, Louk, *When Ways of Life Collide:*

Multiculturalism and Its Discontents in the Netherlands (Princeton, NJ: Princeton University, 2007).

Taylor, Charles, *The Ethics of Authenticity* (Cambridge, Mass: Harvard University Press, 1992).

—*Multiculturalism and the Politics of Recognition* (Princeton, NJ: Princeton University Press, 1994).

Walzer, Michael, *Politics and Passion* (New Haven: Yale University Press, 2004).

West, Patrick, *The Poverty of Multiculturalism* (London: Civitas, 2005).

Wood, Peter, *Diversity: The Invention of a Concept* (San Francisco: Encounter Books, 2003).

On English/British Identity

Alibhai-Brown, Yasmin, *Who Do We Think We Are?* (London: Penguin, 2001).

Buruma, Ian, *Anglomania* (London: Vintage, 2000).

Colley, Linda, *Britons* (London: Pimlico, 2003).

Dalrymple, Theodore, *Our Culture, What's Left of It* (Chicago; [Great Britain]: Ivan R. Dee, 2005).

Davies, Christie, *The Strange Death of Moral Britain* (New Brunswick, NJ: Transaction Publishers, 2006).

Fox, Kate, *Watching the English* (London: Hodder, 2005).

Hanson, Gerry (ed.), *England, my England* (London: Robson Books, 2005).

Kershen, Anne, *Strangers, Aliens and Asians* (London: Routledge, 2005).

Mandler, Peter, *The English National Character* (London: Yale University Press, 2006). Orwell, George, *The Penguin Essays of George Orwell* (Harmondsworth: Penguin, 1984). Paxman, Jeremy, *The English: A Portrait of a People* (London: Penguin,1999).

Scruton, Roger, *England: An Elegy* (London: Chatto & Windus, 2000).

Winder, Robert, *Bloody Foreigners: The Story of Immigration to Britain* (London: Little, Brown, 2004).

On the Politics of Covenant

Allen, Joseph L., *Love and Conflict: A Covenantal Model of Christian Ethics* (Lanham, Md: University Press of America, 1995).

Bellah, Robert N., *Broken Covenant: American Civil Religion in Time of Trial* (New York: Seabury Press, 1975).

—*Beyond Belief: Essays on Religion in a Post-Traditional World* (Berkeley: University of California Press, 1991).

Elazar, Daniel, *People and Polity* (Detroit: Wayne State University Press, 1989).

—*Covenant and Polity in Biblical Israel* (New Brunswick, NJ: Transaction Publishers, 1995).

—*Covenant and Commonwealth* (New Brunswick, NJ: Transaction Publishers, 1996).

—*Covenant and Constitutionalism* (New Brunswick, NJ: Transaction Publishers, 1998).

—*Covenant and Civil Society* (New Brunswick, NJ: Transaction Publishers, 1998).

—(ed.), *Kinship and Consent* (Brunswick, NJ: Transaction Publishers, 1997).

—and Cohen, Stuart A., *The Jewish Polity: Jewish Political Organization from Biblical Times to the Present* (Bloomington: Indiana University Press, 1985).

Hillers, Delbert, *Covenant: The History of a Biblical Idea* (Baltimore: Johns Hopkins University Press, 1969).

Miller, Perry, *The New England Mind: The Seventeenth Century* (Cambridge, Mass: 1954).

Selznick, Philip, *The Moral Commonwealth* (Berkeley CA: University of California Press, 1994).

Smith, Anthony D., *Chosen Peoples* (Oxford: Oxford University Press, 2003).

Index

259

Germany
anti-semitism 29–30
birthrate 205
ethnic identity 16
Fascist Germany 236
Gladstone, William Ewart 70
global economy 7, 11, 232
globalization 7, 8, 70–3
global communication *see*
communications technology
global cultures 9, 73
Gnosticism 71
Goldsmith, Oliver 225
Goodhart, David 17
Gordon Evans, William 27
Gorer, Geoffrey 188
Greece 205
Ancient 56–7, 98, 215
Greek philosophy 97–8
see also individual philosophers
Greek politics 97–8, 219
Athenian democracy 218, 219
Greek tragedy 57, 59
guilt
confession and 219
forgiveness and 57
retribution and 59
victims and 51, 53
Gulf War (1991) 7, 68
Gustincic, Andrej 52

Ha-am, Achad 68
Habitat for Humanity 229, 230, 231
Halevi, Judah 8
Halsey, A. H. 209
Hanina, Rabbi 218
Hart, H. L. A. 38, 39, 40
hate 52
literature of 168
self-hatred 78
Havel, Vaclav 224
Hayek, Friedrich 33, 174
Hegel, Georg Wilhelm Friedrich 66,
108, 135
Heidegger, Martin 168
Hellenistic politics *see* Greek politics
Herder, Johann Gottfried 16
Herzl, Theodore 30

heteronomy 93
Hill, Octavia 167
Himmelfarb, Gertrude 167
Hindus 18, 76, 131
Hindu leaders in Britain 9
history
as memory 115–16, 119
of multiculturalism 25–35
as narrative 115–22
racism in British history 16–17
as a weapon 51–2
Hitler, Adolf 34, 78, 150
Hobbes, Thomas 10, 60, 96, 104, 135,
189
Holland *see* Netherlands
Holocaust 34, 50, 76
concentration camps 30, 34, 46
Holocaust survivors 61–2
homosexuality 38–9, 40, 42–3, 44–5
legalization of 200
politicization of gays' victimhood
54
same-sex partnerships 206
see also gays; lesbians
Honeyford, Ray 18
hope 57–8
Hosea 109
Huguenots 16, 17, 20, 231, 234
Hulme, T. E. 35
Hume, David 40, 52
Hungarian refugees 18
Hungary 205
Huntington, Samuel 21–2, 86–7
Husain, Ed 45, 82
Hussein (ibn Talal), king of Jordan
173
Hutus 53
Huxley, Aldous: *Brave New World*
211–12

identity
belongingness and 54 *see also*
belonging
British 76–8, 163–9
complex identities 155–6
covenantal shared identity 109,
121–2, 136, 158, 160–1
ethnic 9, 31